New Designs for Teaching
and Learning

Dennis Adams
Mary Hamm

New Designs for Teaching and Learning

Promoting Active Learning in Tomorrow's Schools

Jossey-Bass Publishers • San Francisco

The poem "Abandoned Farmhouse" in Exhibit 6.4 in Chapter Six is reprinted from *Sure Signs: New and Selected Poems* by Ted Kooser. By permission of the University of Pittsburgh Press. Copyright 1980 by Ted Kooser.

The poem "Mother to Son" in Chapter Three is from *Selected Poems* by Langston Hughes. Copyright 1926 by Alfred A. Knopf, Inc., and renewed 1954 by Langston Hughes. Reprinted by permission of the publisher.

The Langston Hughes poem in Chapter Nine is from *The Dream Keeper and Other Poems* by Langston Hughes. Copyright 1932 and renewed 1960 by Langston Hughes. Reprinted by permission of Alfred A. Knopf, Inc.

The poem "Fireworks" by James Reeves in Chapter Nine is from *Once Upon a Rhyme: 101 Poems for Young Children*. S. Corrin and S. Corrin (eds.). London: Faber & Faber (1982). Reprinted with permission.

In Chapter Nine the poem "Eel-Grass" is by Edna St. Vincent Millay. From *Collected Poems*, HarperCollins. Copyright 1921, 1948 by Edna St. Vincent Millay. Reprinted by permission of Elizabeth Barnett, literary executor.

Substantial discounts on bulk quantities of Jossey-Bass books are available to corporations, professional associations, and other organizations. For details and discount information, contact the special sales department at Jossey-Bass Inc., Publishers.
(415) 433–1740; Fax (415) 433–0499.
For international orders, please contact your local Paramount Publishing International Office.

Manufactured in the United States of America. Nearly all Jossey-Bass books and jackets are printed on recycled paper containing at least 10 percent postconsumer waste, and many are printed with either soy- or vegetable-based ink, which emits fewer volatile organic compounds during the printing process than petroleum-based ink.

Library of Congress Cataloging-in-Publication Data

Adams, Dennis M.
  New designs for teaching and learning: promoting active learning in tomorrow's schools/Dennis Adams. Mary Hamm. — 1st ed.
      p.   cm. — (The Jossey-Bass education series)
  Includes biographical references and index.
  ISBN 0-7879-0020-6
  1. Education, Elementary—United States—Curricula. 2. Education, Secondary—United States—Curricula. 3. Crtitical thinking—Study and teaching—United States. 4. Active learning—United States.
5. Educational change—United States. I. Hamm, Mary. II. Title.
III. Series.
LB1570.A26 1994
371.1'09'0973—dc20   94-13231
                                                                              CIP

first edition
HB Printing   10 9 8 7 6 5 4 3 2 1   Code 94102

Contents

Preface

How do the social and educational problems we currently face in the United States challenge our old assumptions about education and invite new dreams? What can teachers do to help our nation achieve the goals set for U.S. education? What are the important trends in schooling today and how can the best of these innovations be translated into practice? How can successful instructional models become part of the educational mainstream? *New Designs for Teaching and Learning* addresses these and other questions in order to help educators design classroom programs that will achieve our nation's educational goals and build a responsible society. It both delves into what the K–12 curriculum can and should accomplish and describes practical teaching methods and activities for teachers.

Changing How We Think About
Teaching and Learning

The United States is reaching a state of readiness for new approaches to schooling. We now view our national habit of being comfortable with just being average as inadequate for meeting the extraordinary economic and social challenges of today and tomorrow. The workplace is demanding workers who are knowledgeable, flexible, and able to work in groups. The polity is demanding informed citizens with moral character. And our possibilities for a satisfying life are increasingly connected to a high-quality public education that includes tools for critical thinking.

But offering universal, high-quality teaching for understanding that helps students develop collaborative learning skills, critical thinking skills, and moral character means reinventing our schools and changing how we think about instruction. It also means changing the traditional school culture and those who can influence it. It is the authors' belief that, to play their part, the educational theorists who influence school culture will have to both *act* differently and *think* differently. Teachers, too, will have to act and think differently if they wish to explore the promising directions educational reformers are mapping today, since it is the authors' contention that teachers can make many of the necessary changes themselves, without the burden of numerous bureaucratic strictures, and that teachers should be the ones leading education reform. This book is meant to provide them with many of the tools they will need and ideas and attitudes that will help them invent further tools.

Change flows in waves across any structure that is being built. The days of stationary educational goals are over; we must all learn to define and then to hit moving targets. Rallying teachers, parents, and students around new curriculum beliefs and new missions is a shared responsibility for principals and staff, and the process is more an adventure than a search for certainties. When students do learn to do a good job of critical thinking and of solving problems in cooperative groups, it is usually because they have had good teachers who have given them plenty of opportunities to practice these skills as they also learned specific content areas. However, even the best teaching and intention can harden into orthodoxy. If we are to continuously reinvent our schools, getting better and better at meeting the world's challenges to us, we will also have to put continuous effort into staff development. The goal must be to energize teachers and their students, to make them open to positive change, so that they will continue to emphasize professional development and lifelong learning. At the heart of teaching for understanding and continuous learning must be the creation of a learning community built on a complex internal scaffolding of information and insight. Both students and teachers must feel that they are members of this community, working to become skilled and well informed.

Reflecting, discussing, and cultivating their own dispositions for critical thinking can inform and enrich teachers' teaching (Sternberg & Wagner, 1986). So can assessment structures, such as portfolios, that are more authentic than traditional assessment devices. Even teaching "to the test" does not have to be a learning disaster if there is also opportunity for meaning-centered performance assessment. Whether they take the form of a teacher's professional reflections or a student's work samples over time, performance assessment processes are a step toward making the fundamental changes in our methods of school assessment that can support changes in instruction, school culture, and the professional development of teachers.

Our aspirations for educational change must be bold, broad, and generous enough to connect with needed social change. The future of everyone in this country depends on our activating the possibilities for a better-educated, freer, and more efficient and stable nation. The most powerful way to strengthen our society and culture is to strengthen our schools. The question at the center of the debate and the one this book addresses is, How can we translate our aspirations and goals into classroom practice?

Audience

This book is written to be accessible to classroom teachers first but also to others active in K–12 education. Although the concepts in the book are applicable across all grades, the activities are directed to the elementary and middle school levels. Teachers of early childhood and secondary education can adapt the concepts and modify the activities as appropriate. The instructional ideas and techniques will have high utility for classroom teachers, curriculum directors, those responsible for staff development, and administrators interested in keeping up with the latest research, theory, and techniques.

The book may also be used in graduate and undergraduate methods courses.

Overview of the Contents

The overarching idea behind *New Designs for Teaching and Learning* is that good schools in the twenty-first century will teach for understanding, help children take an active role in their own learning, and value and build instruction around students' diverse cultures. The enhancement of reasoning ability, cooperation, and active communication are primary educational concerns in this book, and the ideas and techniques provided are intended to help educators design effective classroom programs that require teamwork and critical thinking and that involve children actively and physically in learning. Building on these themes of collaboration, thoughtfulness, and a meaning-centered curriculum, the authors suggest possibilities for transforming traditional teaching, learning, and assessment.

The book is divided into two main sections. Chapters One through Five address new instructional developments in the areas of critical thinking, collaborative inquiry, electronic learning, and assessment. Chapter One is a frame of reference, describing the world in which teachers teach today; the nature of the education provided; the relationship between society, culture, and education; and the desirable role of schools in the future. Chapter Two focuses on critical and creative thinking and shows how learning experiences can contribute to the developments and refinement of children's thinking skills. Successful teaching goes beyond the transmission of knowledge and involves students in the construction of new understandings. This chapter suggests some general methods for fostering critical thinking within learning communities. Chapter Three emphasizes practical ideas for providing instruction in cooperative learning so that children can experience effective collaborative inquiry. Many of the suggestions build on children's natural sociability and tap their natural enthusiasm for learning. Also included are helpful strategies for organizing small-group collaborations that foster group harmony as children help each other.

Chapter Four takes the reader on a journey through the educational potential of computers, television, and multimedia (a new technology linking television, computers, videodiscs, and telecommunication). The authors offer ideas and activities to make sense of television, describe what teachers and students should look for when reviewing computer software, illustrate how multimedia programs expand electronic learning, and discuss the ways the new information highways and digital interactions place students in charge of their own learning. Some of the authors' current favorite computer, videodisc, and multimedia programs are presented, along with ideas and activities that apply many of the new instructional developments discussed in Part One. Chapter Five overviews alternative assessment strategies, including portfolios, and argues that good teachers need continuing opportunities to learn and grow and time to plan cooperatively, revise the curriculum, experiment with new practices, and reflect on their own teaching.

Part Two discusses how critical thinking and constructing meaning, cooperative learning, electronic learning, and new forms of assessment and teacher development can be effectively practiced in the content areas of the traditional basics (language arts and mathematics) and the new basics (the sciences, technology, and the arts). An element of social studies was included because of our belief that it is part of the foundation of a democratic society that respects diversity and the uniqueness of each citizen. Each chapter includes specific classroom activities and a discussion of the role of the content area in preparing students for today's world.

Chapter Six addresses a literature-based approach to language arts study, including ideas for using stories, poetry, and newspapers to develop children's thinking ability; creative drama techniques; suggestions for reading and writing activities in small collaborative groups; a description of the uses of hypertext, hyperfiction, and multimedia in reading and writing activities; and a discussion of holistic grading. Chapter Seven deals with the new curriculum standards of the National Council of Teachers of Mathematics and ways to give children mathematical power. In addition to suggestions for relating mathematical studies to the world outside the classroom and to the ways children learn, and activities that foster critical and connected thinking and collaborative inquiry, this chapter discusses both electronic and interdisciplinary teaching methods. In addition to looking at ways to foster teaching for understanding and cooperative activity in the discipline of science, Chapter Eight analyzes the misconceptions about science that can inhibit effective teaching and suggests activities and a constructivist view of science that can enhance scientific literacy.

Chapter Nine examines the arts and the vital role they play in inviting thoughtfulness, creativity, and vision. While performance is still considered important, other aspects of the arts are brought forward, and the authors suggest activities that teach for understanding through conversation, experience, criticism, engagement, and examination of purpose. Chapter Ten addresses the issue of social responsibility and citizenship education, tying together many of the activity-based collaborative themes presented in this book. This chapter argues that social studies can be used to encourage the well-rounded development of each student as a citizen who will be essential to our nation's future economic, political, and cultural progress in an increasingly complex world.

We cannot predict our individual or collective futures, but we can learn the current educational and social terrain we must operate on. And we can devise the basic principles that can guide us through the uncharted territory that lies ahead. This book is both a map of routes to be taken today and a set of principles to help us choose even better routes tomorrow.

August 1994

Dennis Adams
West Chester, Pennsylvania

Mary Hamm
San Francisco

The Authors

Dennis Adams is a professor at West Chester University of Pennsylvania, Department of Education, where he teaches a wide range of subjects, including communication, reading, language arts, social studies, educational technology, cooperative learning, and in-service training. His areas of specialization also include educational computing and television production. He holds a Ph.D. degree in curriculum from the University of Wisconsin, and he is the author or coauthor of more than half a dozen books on such topics as language arts, electronic learning, media literacy, critical thinking, and cooperative learning. He has published over one hundred articles, in such journals as *Reading Horizons, Schools Arts, Teaching K–8, The Writing Teacher, The School Administrator, Educational Technology, British Journal of Educational Technology, Educational Research Quarterly, Social Education, Think,* and *Technological Horizons in Education.*

Mary Hamm is a professor of education at San Francisco State University, where she teaches math and science education. She has an M.A. degree in environmental studies from the University of Wisconsin and an E.Ed. degree in elementary education from the University of Northern Colorado. She has authored or coauthored eight books, and she has published articles in such journals as the *Journal of Creative Thinking, Experimental Education, Journal of Research in Science Teaching, Epsilon Pi Tau, School Science and Mathematics, Journal of Children and Youth,* and *Science, Technology, and Human*

Values. She has also been a consultant for the Macmillan/McGraw-Hill School Division for science grade levels K–8.

The books Dennis Adams and Mary Hamm have coauthored include *Cooperative Learning and Critical Thinking Across the Curriculum* (1990), *Cooperative Learning and Educational Media* (1990), *Media and Literacy* (1989), and *Electronic Learning* (1987). Both authors have taught extensively at the elementary and middle school levels.

Chapter One

Introduction:
Revitalizing Teaching

The educational improvement of its people may well be the toughest and most momentous challenge facing the United States on the eve of the twenty-first century. As today's educational reform movement attempts to bring successful instructional models into the majority of our schools nothing less than the shape of our collective future is at stake. The successful curriculum of the future will be one that helps students collaboratively perceive, analyze, interpret, and discover a whole new range of meanings. It will be at home in the new world we see around us, a world crying out for new definitions and people who can redefine themselves to succeed in a rapidly changing environment marked by successive economic dislocations as whole classes of jobs become obsolete and new jobs demand batteries of new skills and highly trained professionals. The result of ever faster global change and fewer economic and social certainties is a demand for ever higher levels of education and competency. Therefore, one of the most important features of a modern educational system will be its *capacity for self-renewal and continuous change*. This change must encompass what is taught, how it is taught, the relationship of our schools and classrooms to society beyond the school, and the ways we regard teachers and they regard themselves and strive to develop their abilities.

The new curriculum envisions educators and students learning to ask insightful questions together, engage in self-monitoring, and debate the major controversies of our time. Why try to conceal our disagreements? Instead of allowing groups defined by ethnicity, culture, or gender to turn inward upon themselves, we will do better

1

as a nation if, together, we study the interrelationships among cultures. Contentment and self-satisfaction are the enemies of change. As part of reestablishing our national commitment to the future, we can look forward to an interactive, meaning-centered curriculum that does not avoid controversial issues. A teacher-mediated clash of ideas, frameworks, cultures, languages, and methodologies can lead to insightful, unexpected, and formative classroom conversations.

New Social Realities and Educational Needs

Some recent social changes have been for the good, but many have been for the worse. Schools are finding it more difficult than ever to provide a safe sanctuary for children and young adults (Werner & Smith, 1992). In a number of areas, school reform will require broad special initiatives to change educational outcomes in the face of the deadly gumbo of crime, gangs, AIDS, easy availability of guns and drugs, broken families, parents who lack both competencies in child rearing and the social support networks that can bring generations together, and huge inequities between rich and poor school districts. Reality intrudes into the classroom as never before. Guns and sex are realities for many U.S. children before they reach junior high school. To give these children an education sufficient for healthy and productive lives, to deal with these real-world problems and stay relevant, teachers must incorporate current social problems into reading, writing, and mathematics lessons. They must explore relevant material in a manner that sparks curiosity and allows students to learn by doing and to demonstrate knowledge through presentations, exhibitions, or portfolios, not just tests of current facts.

In the present social milieu, there is an ever more compelling need for schools to be socially and intellectually stimulating *communities of learners*. These communities spring up when schools create a caring atmosphere, attend to student interests, promote meaningful learning, encourage acceptance, and respect creative potential—when they draw on new principles of learning and take into account the multiple cultures, languages, and backgrounds of students. Personal connectedness occurs when students feel accepted by teachers and peers.

At the heart of schooling is the personal relationship between student and teacher that develops over matters of content. Studies show that when students and teachers cooperate to reach a common goal they learn to appreciate and respect one another more fully (Babad, 1990). Even when the curriculum emphasizes the critical thinking, cooperation, and meaning-centered learning that make education relevant, it is how teachers adapt and use that curriculum that determines what really happens for the students. When the school culture values both academic achievement and personal commitment, it breaks down barriers to learning and moves students toward academic success.

The devastating social conditions disadvantaged children face must be attended to. Children in the underclass face a wider array of difficulties than others and their educational problems may require a different set of solutions (Hamburg, 1992). But these social issues should not divert attention from how poorly some schools are prepared to serve *all* children (Brophy & Good, 1986). Students can be placed at a disadvantage by their schools as well as their environments, making it more difficult than ever for some students to have equal life opportunities. To reach all of today's students—and ensure that they become productive citizens—both the schools *and* those they serve will have to change dramatically. Schools *and* children must be better prepared.

Characteristics of Today's Successful Teachers

While not many of the radical education proposals of the 1980s took hold, one that did was the professionalization of teaching. We are moving away from the old in-service training models to broader

forms of professional development in which teachers take responsibility for such new areas as action research (to assess performance)
and on-site management. Staff development that contributes to
teachers' ability to improve their own work will be a central feature
of schools in the near future, and although the precise direction of
teacher professionalization remains uncertain, the concept of the
teacher as an autonomous professional is now a given (Finn, 1992).
Teachers should not have to strive to function creatively under
overly restrictive rules and demands.

Many efforts, including the research that follows, have been
undertaken to identify what characterizes a successful teacher. This
research is a result of an ongoing collaboration among a consortium
of experienced educators currently working in schools across the
country. It strongly suggests that schools and school leaders need
to take every opportunity to recognize the impact and positive
influence that teachers can have on children's outcomes, since
teachers' daily interactions with students are, collectively, the most
powerful influences on those students.

Successful teachers provide a supportive environment. This
means that they organize and manage the classroom as an effective
learning environment. Meaningful learning objectives are in place.
Activities teach things that are worth learning at an appropriate
level of difficulty. Successful teachers are flexible. They master and
use a variety of motivational strategies (Good & Brophy, 1994).

One vital trait of successful teachers is that they bring a positive attitude to their teaching. Experienced educators characterize
successful teachers as those who are loving, caring, and humane;
who treat children fairly; and who interact with children in non-
judgmental ways (Natriello, McDill, & Pallas, 1990). Successful
teachers' commitment is reinforced in schools that adopt partic-
ipatory decision-making and collaborative problem-solving strategies to address school issues (Kagan & Tippins, 1993). Teachers also
believe that school districts can make teaching more successful by

doing more to promote cooperation and democratic governance at all levels (Abi-Nader, 1993). Staff development and in-service programs should take this research into account as they help teachers address the challenges of teaching. These programs should also recognize the dedication and commitment that many experienced teachers bring to their work, and they should make sustaining teachers' commitment a major goal.

Educational reform requires that pre-service teachers acquire foundational skills and, in particular, strategic learning and pedagogical methods upon which they can build the teaching repertoire they will need to address students' different learning needs. They also need to experience and reflect upon the nature of learning communities. A critical training factor for future teachers is extensive early field-work experiences in urban communities and school settings (Natriello, McDill, & Pallas, 1990). After their pre-service training, teachers must continue to grow in knowledge and understanding through active participation in staff development programs. For example, collaborative relations with other teachers, administrators, and human service professionals allow teachers to promote those policies and procedures that will positively support at-risk students and be effective in dropout prevention.

In addition, successful teachers understand that teaching is a complex undertaking that requires time. They know that conditions may be difficult, but they accept and enjoy the challenges of teaching—even as they wait for increased support for their efforts. They also believe in their ability to provide an effective learning environment that will make a difference in students' lives (Hayden, 1992).

Teachers' understanding of context, inside and outside the classroom, is the single most critical factor influencing success in teaching (Forsyth & Tallerico, 1993). Teachers describe success in personal terms and view it as related to their personal durability and capability. Content knowledge is not seen to be as important as possessing teaching skills and knowledge about the students being taught. That is, successful teachers understand the outside context of community, personal abilities, and feelings, while they establish an inside context or environment conducive to learning.

Knowing the child and understanding the community is at the heart of success, but attractive school conditions in which teachers feel in control of the classroom environment are also important factors in quality teaching. Schools that retain teachers benefit because most teachers who elect to remain in the same school for more than three years feel more in control of their environment and have a stronger belief that teaching is a rich and rewarding experience than do teachers of lesser tenure (Glickman, 1993).

Martin Haberman (1993, p. 88) suggests that these general principles guide the day-to-day teaching of effective teachers:

- Children can always learn more. The teacher's effort and energy is instrumental in students' learning.
- Children who are given the opportunity for fresh, novel, stimulating experiences have a powerful incentive for learning.
- Students will involve themselves wholeheartedly in projects when they have truly participated in, selected, and planned the activity.
- Children try hardest when they are fairly certain of success but not absolutely positive.
- Threats, punishment, repeated failure, and constant teacher direction lead children to demonstrate apathy, defiance, hostility toward others, and self-depreciation.
- Children learn most from teachers who believe that effort rather than ability predicts achievement.
- Children learn most when their honest questions are connected with great ideas (key concepts).

The following activities are also preconditions for quality instruction:

- Students actively interpret knowledge in light of current experience.
- Students learn stories and concepts that matter and develop attitudes of curiosity and wonder.

Education Inevitably Relates to Culture

The revitalization of teaching and of our public schools must remain central to our social and educational aspirations. Public schools are where the majority of U.S. children will continue to be educated, make major life choices, and connect to youngsters from different backgrounds. Public schools are also where images can be formed of what it means to be a good person, have a good life, and live in a good society.

Any large-scale educational change must involve a widespread cadre of public school educators who are willing to implement further reforms. Small-scale private sector experiments are fine, but to reach the majority of students, innovations must be transferred successfully to the public sector. Our ultimate goal should be nothing less than transforming all our nation's schools into the world-class system Americans deserve. Ideally, new curriculum designs will build on U.S. traditions, values, and culture—helping the schools carry out rigorous self-examinations, vigorous innovations, and a commitment to ever greater effectiveness.

Students learn lessons about life from both formal instruction and what they see around them. Schools must model the world they want to create through education, yet a recent survey by the Civil Rights Office of the Department of Education shows that enrollment of minority students—primarily African Americans and Hispanics—has grown to about 40 percent of the school population (Children's Defense Fund, 1991), while the American Council on Education (1992) reports that the number of minority and male elementary school teachers has dropped precipitously. The result is the loss of male (now only 12 percent of teachers) and minority (now only 6 percent of teachers) models for students.

Obviously, school revitalization must reverse this trend, or we will drift towards a racial, sexual, and cultural apartheid in the schools that will then negatively affect the national culture as these students become adults.

Change will not come easily. Transforming our schools for the twenty-first century will occasionally require fighting state and district systems that are hostile to change. In some schools today, students are made to feel unwelcome, intellectually inadequate, uncomfortable, and bored. At the earliest opportunity, they drop out. Over one million students a year leave high school without graduating. Even for those who stay, the schools may offer little encouragement if their talents fall outside the ability to manipulate words and numbers. Grim social hardships and fears weigh heavily on the shoulders of some children. But difficult circumstances in early childhood or early adolescence do not have to doom these students, and the right kind of support can make a permanent difference (Hamburg, 1992). The schools can make the inevitable relationship between education and culture a positive relationship.

Culture can be viewed as a coherent system of attitudes, values, and institutions that influence both individual and group behavior. Abundant natural resources, a temperate climate, fortuitous geography, democratic traditions, and good levels of formal education among citizens all play a role in a modern nation's successful development. However, more subtle factors also come into play. Cultures that nurture the human creative capacity across age groups usually do better than those that do not. And when a nation views education as a continuum running from prenatal care through adult life, that view seems to have a more powerful effect. The United States may be caught in an economic, civic, and moral drought, but it is still seen by many as the very embodiment of freedom and progress. In addition to work, frugality, excellence, and community, education was one of the traditional American values that contributed to our unparalleled mid twentieth-century successes, and education can contribute positively once again to our culture. Yet a great deal of professional educators' work is done with minimal cultural understanding and limited social perspective. A cultural, political, or moral crisis is ipso facto an educational crisis, and our attack on U.S. social and educational problems must fight uphill against the profound social trends that are causing the crisis. If we accept the basic proposition that the United States must make drastic changes to forestall social disaster and facilitate growth, then clearly educational institutions must be part of that process. Teaching children to balance respect for divergent cultures with unifying ideas of democracy, human rights tolerance, and personal and social responsibility is a desirable educational goal. Whether appreciating the perspective that can be gained from different cultures or fighting against debilitating social trends of moral numbness, individualism degenerating into greed, spiritual alienation, social injustice, and diminishing prospects for our children's healthy future, the schools *influence* community conditions while they also *reflect* those conditions.

For our schools to make a major impact on the childhood difficulties that translate into adult failures, parallel changes in our basic cultural beliefs and social incentives related to schooling and the status of teachers must occur. Fundamental change in schools requires fundamental change in society. Hard questions must be asked and fundamental issues dealt with. Limiting our focus to the issues of national testing and school choice may be more comfortable, but the debilitating trends will not go away simply because we are not confronting them.

For too long, we have not worried enough about future generations or met our obligations to each other. When hard social realities are connected to an inadequate educational system, it becomes clear that the United States is not now the swiftest in the race to compete. Moreover, to deal with many of the issues most important to our children's future, teachers will have to educate in ways we have not fully conceived of yet.

It may not be possible to change yesterday's mistakes, but it *is* possible to change the future. The show is not over. And although much of the current public debate over education concerns funding, the key issue is not money. Even though without public spending everything in a school suffers, from building safety to staff development to new curriculum materials, and even though without public spending, little can be done about changing children's home environments or providing a good early-childhood program (one of the most effective tools we have to nourish the roots of the tree of progress), the issue that is even more important is a willingness to define values, to find the best ways to teach thinking and collaborative skills, and to look at children and young adults in their individual totalities. Today, unifying ideals of human rights, tolerance of differences, and shared community resources seem temporary victims of individual desires. Our economic growth and political freedom will require a new ethos of caring and individual responsibility. It is a real struggle to come up with ideas to handle new problem structures, to commit when problems are hard to quantify. Yet our challenge is to do just that, and despite uncertainties, mysteries, and doubts, core learning principles and practices can help us all engage productively in a democratic society.

Teaching for understanding and building on learning activities that emphasize reasoning, collaboration, and communication is important. The most powerful way to achieve this kind of teaching is to integrate curriculum reform with the professional development of teachers. There are scattered examples of this positive change around the country: Robert Slavin's Success for All program, Theodore Sizer's Coalition of Essential Schools, Henry Levin's Accelerated Schools, to name just a few. Central to the efforts of these educators is the creation of learning communities and of classrooms where students actively participate in constructing meaning. Our schools can develop teachers' abilities to create similar classrooms that promote critical thinking and learning communities and that result in people's linking arms and reaching past today's obstacles. The following chapters are intended to give teachers the instructional tools that will help them establish learning communities equipped with the skills for our new world.

Part One

New Instructional Developments

Chapter Two

Critical Thinking

Higher order thinking is the hallmark of successful
learning at all levels—not only the more advanced.

—*Lauren Resnick (1987)*

Developing methods that extend students' critical thinking across
the classroom curriculum is an educational reform strategy that is
widely supported—and is working. It has shown staying power.
Both the strategy and the concept of critical thinking have quietly
become part of the new curriculum, and expertise in teaching critical thinking is becoming widely dispersed. Here we examine the
characteristics of critical thinking and its relevance, and some general principles for teaching and assessing thinking skills.

Teaching thinking skills and the construction of meaning
requires developing students' abilities to assess information and
make creative and critical judgments. Although some of the methods that guide critical thinking and its teaching date back to the
methods of Socrates, today's efforts to place critical, creative, or
self-connected thinking in the curriculum started in the 1980s in
university philosophy departments, where it was felt that philosophy had something to contribute to the school reform movement.
Next, cognitive psychologists and educators began to build on the
philosophers' views about critical thinking to advance their own
research into the operation of the human intellect. Then teachers
saw that critical thinking was a generalizable method of learning
as well as an explanation of how learning happens, and they
quickly picked up on the concept as a way to improve the teaching of traditional subjects. The strategy of teaching critical thinking

to improve students' ability to learn any discipline is continuing to grow in popularity as a new awareness takes hold that critical thinking is an academic competency as crucial to a child's future as literacy and numeracy.

Of course, this progression of ideas from philosophers to researchers to teachers must not be a one-time occurrence. Philosophers must continue to study critical thinking as a dimension of knowledge, educational researchers and social scientists must continue to think critically about the study of critical thinking in order to tell us how people learn to think and organize knowledge, and teachers must continue to find ways to apply critical thinking in the classroom. The wave of U.S. educational reform that began in the mid 1980s resulted in some incremental changes in teaching; however, the basic patterns, structures and methods of teaching were left in place. The current wave is after something more fundamental, a strategic change that will restructure the way schools are organized, the way subjects are taught, and the way elements like thinking skills are embedded in the curriculum. For this change to occur, we all must dislodge our thinking about teaching and learning from the places where it gets stuck and imagine a better state of things. We must put our best minds and our accumulated national wisdom and expertise to work.

What Critical Thinking Is

Critical thinking occurs when students *construct meaning* by interpreting, analyzing, and manipulating information in response to a problem or question that requires more than a direct, one-right-answer application of previously learned knowledge. Critical, creative, or self-connected thinking is a natural human process that can be amplified by awareness and practice. And it is characterized by specific core thinking skills, which can be developed in the classroom through instruction and guided practice (Marzano et al., 1988, p. 146).

- *Focusing skills*: attending to selected chunks of information. These skills include defining, identifying key concepts, recognizing a problem, and setting goals.

- *Information gathering skills*: becoming aware of substance or content needed. These skills include observing, obtaining information, forming questions, and clarifying through inquiry.

- *Remembering skills*: storing and retrieving information. Encoding and recalling are thinking skills that have been found to improve retention. Remembering skills involve such strategies as rehearsal, mnemonics, and visualization.

- *Organizing skills*: arranging information so that it can be understood or presented more effectively. Some organizing skills are comparing, classifying (categorizing), ordering, and representing information.

- *Analyzing skills*: classifying and examining information of components and relationships. Analysis is at the heart of critical thinking. Recognizing and articulating attributes and component parts, focusing on details and structure, identifying relationships and patterns, grasping a central idea, and finding errors are elements of analysis.

- *Generating skills*: using prior knowledge to add information beyond what is known or given. Connecting new ideas, inferring, identifying similarities and differences, predicting, and elaborating add new meaning to information. Generating skills also involve such higher-order thinking as making comparisons, constructing metaphors, producing analogies, providing explanations, and forming mental models.

- *Integrating skills*: putting things together, solving, understanding, forming principles, and creating compositions. These thinking strategies involve summarizing, combining information, deleting unnecessary material, graphically organizing, outlining, and restructuring to incorporate new information.

- *Evaluating skills*: assessing the reasonableness and quality of ideas. These skills include establishing criteria and proving or verifying data.

There are multiple possibilities for both *process* and *content* in any individual's critical or creative thinking. The human brain has a multiplicity of functions and voices that speak independently and quite differently for different individuals (Bandura, 1986). Howard Gardner is one of those who has attempted to broadly define the different kinds of thought processes and abilities (Gardner, 1991). He suggests viewing the mathematical and verbal abilities on which teachers have traditionally focused as but two of seven crucial abilities or "intelligences." The other five are spatial intelligence (art and navigation are two examples), kinesthetic intelligence (movement and dance), musical intelligence, intrapersonal intelligence (self-reflection), and interpersonal intelligence (the result of work in groups). There is nothing sacred about these particular categories. The point is the range of abilities: no one is great at everything, and it is best not to restrict educational avenues to a single path of representing, knowing, or learning (Sternberg & Frensch, 1992). The research evidence suggests that giving students multiple perspectives and entry points into subject matter increases both thinking and learning (Sears & Marshall, 1990). Thus, teachers should pluralize their ideas about how students learn a subject. They should approach important concepts from multiple directions, emphasizing understanding and making meaningful connections across subjects, while making the school a home for inquiry.

When teachers respect students' multiple ways of making meaning, they make learning more accessible. A teacher who settles on a single representation of either subject matter or pedagogical reality shelves many possibilities for learning and, in the process, shelves critical thinking. Under these circumstances, students whose thinking or learning styles happen to be different from the style of the teacher (or the textbook) frequently experience more difficulty than their peers (Shulman, 1986). When teachers recognize that critical thinking comes in many forms and can reach varying conclusions, when they then identify their own thinking styles and help students find *their* own styles from multiple possibilities provided by the teacher, there is a greater likelihood of student success (Bamberger, 1991). Reflective teachers who are aware of multiple paths to understanding can make suggestions for thinking that broaden students' intellectual and cultural bases without destroying initiative.

Teaching that ignores the powerful ideas of students will miss many opportunities for students to illuminate the human condition for themselves, each other, and indeed, the teacher. The critical thinking process is one in which the student connects a variety of points of knowledge about a subject and ends up mentally transforming those separate points into a form that has special coherence for him or her. To teach content without regard for self-connected thinking prevents that transformation. Thus, if teaching is to enhance *being* and the ability to have self-connected thought, rather than merely impart knowledge and skills, then the teaching of reasoned decision making must be part of the classroom process (Berman et al., 1991).

Information and Thinking

Information and thinking are not antithetical. Nor is information a substitute for thinking. Thinking transforms information, and information invites thinking. But, traditional schooling has tended to leave students content paralyzed. In today's classrooms, time must be taken to be sure that student thinking can transform knowledge in a way that makes the knowledge transferable to the outside world (Siegler, 1985). There will never be enough time to teach all the information that we feel is useful, but when teachers take time from lecturing about knowledge in order to instill habits of inquiry and reflection, students will actually learn more even though less knowledge is covered. As the old lecture-for-recall methods of instruction are abandoned, new collaborative work structures will allow the thoughtful engagement that untangles the mysteries of learning and leads to deeper understanding.

It was Hannah Arendt who said that evil was not demonic but *the absence of thinking*—a kind of emptiness or blankness that leads to bad deeds. She also suggested that "thinking unfreezes what language has frozen into consciousness" (Arendt, 1958). For example, bringing conflicts to the surface, where they can be transformed by thought, turns them into opportunities for new understanding. It is the movement from subject matter to thought to action that contributes to human progress.

Moreover, since it is so difficult to figure out what information will be crucial to students in the future, it makes sense to pay more attention to the *intellectual tools* that will be required in any future. It makes sense to focus on how models of critical thought can be used differently at different times and in different situations. It makes sense to put more focus on concepts with high generalizability, such as civic responsibility, problem solving, reflection, perceptive thinking, self-direction, and the motivation needed for lifelong learning.

Dealing with the changing realities and new information of the late twentieth century is a shared responsibility. The need for educated public engagement is growing, and our nation faces decisions on political, aesthetic, and moral issues that require a broadly informed citizenry. This means that we have to educate *everyone* to think critically, creatively, and deeply.

Cultivating Thoughtfulness

It is helpful to consider what thoughtfulness looks like before we turn to specific means for teaching it. *Thoughtfulness* is used here to describe the tendency to support a position with carefully examined reasons. Student dispositions that constitute thoughtfulness include tendencies to be reflective, to think problems through, and to have the flexibility to consider original solutions and the curiosity to pose new questions.

A child's critical thinking ability evolves in relation to the dynamics of personal abilities, social values, and institutional values. All children, for example, bring their own models of how the world works to school with them, and they have a rich body of knowledge about that world (Gardner, 1991). From birth, they have been busy making sense of their environment. By grappling with the curious and the confusing, they have learned ways of understanding, developed schemes for thinking, and found meaning. They sing songs, tell stories, and read the tiniest gesture accurately in a wide variety of contexts. Children's natural abilities to construct meaning can be extended in school when the teacher cultivates a broad disposition to critical thinking throughout the school year. Such learning-centered instruction in thinking will advance children's abilities to work through misunderstandings and will develop mature thinkers.

The idea that thinking should assume a central place in the curriculum does not, of course, come as a surprise to most teachers. Psychologist Jean Piaget and his followers have insisted for over fifty years that memorization and factual knowledge are not true learning. Piaget viewed learning as constructing knowledge, not memorizing information (Resnick & Klopfer, 1989). Today's cognitive educators share with Piagetians a constructivist view of learning that teaches us to begin with real materials, respect knowledge, invite interactive learning, and model the various dimensions of thoughtfulness. Cognitive educators connect academic goals with practical problem solving and students' life experiences. Elements of thinking encouraged are inquiry, self-regulated learning, collaboration, experimentation, metacognition, and the relationship between various subjects and the child's life. The best of the new approaches also suggest simultaneously teaching content and the skills of thinking (Damon, 1988), because critical thinking is at its best when it is woven into other subject matter rather than treated as a separate subject. The embedding of thinking skills in the curriculum involves students intensely in reasoning, elaboration, hypothesis-forming, and problem-solving activities. Thoughtfulness is also cultivated when students have the ability to raise powerful questions about what they read, view or hear. "Better learning will not come from finding better ways for the teacher to instruct but from *giving the learner better opportunities to construct,*" says Papert (1990). Teachers who want to develop mature thinkers able both to acquire and to use knowledge must educate minds rather than train memories. Developing the motivation to think, engaging in solid decision making, elaborating one's ideas, and finally, constructing insights that suggest possibilities for action form the core structure of effective thinking and learning (Schoenfeld, 1982). New curriculum designs recognize the need to train minds and include teaching strategies that develop this core structure.

Moreover, thinking skills are learned in many ways—through interaction with the environment, mass media, peers, and subject matter. Students may acquire enhanced thinking skills through a well-structured and planned curriculum or through chance encounters formed by crazy collisions of elements. Opportunities for all these interactions must not be neglected.

Such innovative educational approaches pose a challenge. A few teachers even worry that neither they nor society can handle too many critical thinkers. They are wrong; without the magic of thoughtfulness and critical inquiry, schoolwork lacks much useful meaning. In addition, the elements of thinking *are* teachable. Although proficient learners seem to automatically integrate elements of critical thinking into their repertoire of techniques for making meaning, research has shown that learners who do not find critical thinking quite so automatic can have their skills enhanced by effective instruction. There is also strong evidence that many students—especially the youngest and the lower achievers—need explicit and sustained instruction to become skilled in thinking and in monitoring their own thinking processes (White & Gunstone, 1992). However, it is clear that the following thinking skills can be taught directly: generating multiple ideas about a topic, summarizing, figuring out meaning from context, understanding analogy, and detecting reasoning fallacies (Segal, Chipman, & Glaser, 1985). Teachers *can* learn to give this instruction well. To put thinking skills into classroom practice, teachers need to consciously question how they can best be taught, asking, How can I get students to focus their thinking, become aware of new information, ask questions, retrieve and organize information, analyze and generate new ideas, summarize, and evaluate? Each of these elements will require some reflection, elaboration, and action.

Finally, thoughtfulness is found not only in relation to academic material. It must be practiced in both the child's home and the school environment. For each individual's thinking process to reach its full potential, we need to teach in ways that encourage good intellectual habits and arouse passion both in and out of school.

Applying Knowledge and Creating New Knowledge

Although knowledge acquisition is needed to form a base, a new landscape, upon which thinking can be focused, that knowledge is useful only to the degree it can be seen with new eyes and thoughtfully applied or used to create new knowledge (Marzano et al., 1988, p. 33). Thus, students need opportunities to use their knowledge—to compose, make decisions, solve problems, and conduct research to discover new knowledge. As teachers facilitate critical thinking activities, they help students open their worlds and tap into a spectrum of intelligences, thus encouraging multiple readings of the world, the media, and written texts.

As we will see in more detail in Chapter Three, group discussion is a particularly powerful way to infuse thinking skill concepts into the curriculum. In group debates on content areas, students can see a number of thinking processes and learn to merge them into their personal repertoires. As the students become aware of the characteristics of critical thinking and experience its application, working together to extend and refine knowledge can be very satisfying to them. Moreover, such shared thoughtfulness and searches for meaning can connect to the social struggles of our times, maintaining a vital link between the school and students' daily realities outside the school.

Good teachers support diverse thinking styles and collaboration, helping students step outside the boundaries of their own experiences to construct meaning. This means that both teachers and students open themselves up to suggestions, styles of thinking, connections, and ambiguities previously unexamined. The potential for imaginative action grows out of this process. How thoughtful and strong-willed we become today will determine the pathways we all travel tomorrow.

Newmann (1990, 1992) has identified six key indicators of thoughtfulness in the classroom, which teachers can use to determine whether their students are learning to create and apply new knowledge.

- Students are given sufficient time to think before being required to answer questions.
- Interaction focuses on sustained examination of a few topics rather than superficial coverage of many.
- The teacher presses students to clarify or justify their opinions rather than accepting and reinforcing them indiscriminately.
- Interactions are characterized by substantive coherence and continuity.
- The teacher models the characteristics of a thoughtful person (showing interest in students' ideas and their suggestions for

solving problems, modeling problem-solving processes rather than just giving answers, and acknowledging the difficulties involved in gaining a clear understanding of problematic topics).

• Students generate original and unconventional ideas in the course of the interaction.

Clearing Pathways for Thought

The broad misconceptions, naïve theories, oversimplified explanations, and stereotyped views that any of us may have in certain areas are typically deeply ingrained. When such misconceptions are held by students, how can we bring this poor thinking to the surface and supplant it with critical thinking? We know that subject matters make more sense to students when the knowledge to be acquired is connected by a variety of paths to real situations. No concept is too difficult for students when the ideas at its heart have meaning for their lives.

As part of the search for meaning, teachers and peers can help a student understand the nature of a subject while they simultaneously leave room for that student to reshape his or her concepts as new information becomes available. Students' personal search to understand thinking (metacognitive awareness) is shaped by their own attitudes, subject matter, self-knowledge, and ability to work with others. They must learn that subjects can be approached in different ways—through descriptive accounts; logical, analytical, quantitative methods; and aesthetic expression (art, dance, or music). Thinking and its expression can take many forms; meaning is not limited to what can be expressed in print or numbers. Painting, music, and dance can resonate with meaning and are just one set of neglected imaginative abilities that can be brought to the fore. The idea is to have students work with various media and subject areas so that they go beyond literal and linear thought to probe areas that are ambiguous in meaning and rich in illusion.

Creative thinking is not limited to print.

In learning how to think, children need something concrete to think about. Thinking skills should connect subjects to the student's interests and environment. For example, while watching a newscast about whales trapped in ice, one fifth-grade class the authors worked with decided to find out more about the characteristics of whales and their migratory patterns. This led to an exploration of their status as an endangered species. In the process of conducting research, the children did mathematical calculations and explored geographical, environmental, and social issues, generating their own ideas and potential solutions to the trapped-in-the-ice problem. Information from books was augmented by newspapers, video clips, and experts in the field who visited the class. Editing a videotape and writing about the issues raised in these activities helped students think new ideas and develop a habit of academic discourse.

Many other lessons can follow a similar pattern of:

- Forming a topic area
- Exploring prior knowledge
- Sharing interesting new questions
- Researching a specific knowledge base
- Comparing, reporting, and reflective thinking
- Expressing the results to an audience

Goals and Activities for Teachers

Developing mature thinkers who can work with others has always been a major goal of elite educational institutions. Today's task is to teach these skills within all schools. Whether we choose to value thinking—or even follow the path towards a quality educational system—is as much a societal issue as it is a pedagogical one (Baron, 1988). If we make the wrong choice and diminish educational possibilities, we lose something of incalculable value.

Thinking is more than acquiring knowledge, it is a quest for meaning. In this quest, learning is an adventurous joint effort that connects invention, insightful reflection, and sound decision making and that depends on a combination of inquiring mental habits, good interpersonal ability, subject matter expertise, general strategic knowledge, and tenacity.

Although the activities and instructional methods described for specific disciplines in the later chapters foster critical thinking, here are some generally applicable ideas that all teachers should consider as they prepare to help students construct meaning.

Apply a Constructivist Approach in Teaching

The way children learn anything is by integrating observations and experiences into their personal framework (their model of the world composed of memories, associations, feelings, sounds, rules, and so forth). The richer this learning framework, the more likely it is that the student will have the ability to explain, predict, provide analogies, make connections, and possibly provide new perspectives. The goals of education should be to help students learn how to actively apply knowledge, solve problems, and promote conceptual understanding. In the process, students should be able to change their poorly examined theories and beliefs to more rigorously examined concepts that are personally meaningful. That is, they should develop conceptual understanding and a means for integrating knowledge into their personal experience.

Develop Critical Thinking Skills

Students who are exposed to a variety of viewpoints through various media and authentic materials must learn to contemplate these viewpoints critically. Students take their first step toward this goal when they learn to recognize the implicit argument in each presentation and to compare the similarities as well as the differences among various points of view. It is active learning that nurtures these thinking skills of recognition and analysis and not passive listening. Eventually active learning will enable students to develop self-reliance in their analysis of both literature and the media. One means of encouraging active learning rather than passive listening is to shift the classroom focus from a teacher-centered to a student-centered approach, from the teacher as authority figure who transmits knowledge to the teacher as facilitator of thinking. Instead of the traditional lecture and question sessions, students are assigned specific tasks (the interpretation of a literary passage or discussion of a news article, for example) to be accomplished cooperatively.

Students should develop the ability to question the presentation of information: the order in which facts are presented, the emphasis of certain facts over others, and the implicit slant of any "story" whether it be in literature, history books, or the news. Students also can learn to look for discrepancies between facts and the conclusions drawn from them or inconsistencies among the various versions of a particular news story. When reading literature, all students can discuss the characters' varying perspectives, and older students can analyze the different points of view held by narrators as opposed to the other characters. All these exercises should enable students to distinguish between fact and opinion and to question the possibility of any totally objective presentation of information.

Students can also learn elements of creative thinking from interpersonal communication behaviors: listening, speaking, arguing, problem solving, clarifying, and creating (Dissanayake, 1992).

In addition to instruction in the form of specific thinking skills, students also need guidance in how to use these skills. Such thinking processes as forming mental drawings, describing relationships applicable to many examples, problem solving, participating in oral discourse, and carrying out scientific inquiry require relatively complex mental sequences.

Shift the Learning Emphasis

In the student-centered class, the emphasis shifts from product to process, from a goal-oriented approach to learning to an approach in which the learning process itself is the central focus. Learning must involve not merely the acquisition of information but also the development of skills for evaluating and interpreting facts. When students share their various interpretations of a text, an extra dimension is added as they not only learn how others perceive a certain issue but also come to appreciate the reasoning processes and life experiences that support varied interpretations.

Analyze Stereotypes

As students learn about the perspectives of other cultures, including varying interpretations of such historical events as wars and political transitions, and as they critically view their own culture's interpretation of such events, they can explore the sources of stereotypes. In this learning process, each student's cultural background is viewed as a valuable tool for learning, a bridge to another worldview rather than a barrier. Of course the study of stereotypes on the one hand and of the diversity of voices on the other does not have to stand in the way of supplying students with the common and universal roots of present conditions and of helping them to understand universal truths that speak to everyone.

Use Moral Dilemma and Debate Activities

Argument (debate) may make some people uncomfortable, but it does result in an understanding of the issues. Bringing important controversial issues out into the open in the classroom is central to the health and vitality of U.S. education. Encouraging students to argue together can also help them reason together (just make sure that each side has an equal chance to be heard). The goal is an understanding of human community and an appreciation of overlapping cultural experiences.

For example:

- Provide opportunities for students to explore different viewpoints and domains of information that arouse frustration or outrage.

- Conduct debates and discussions on controversial issues. Ask students to work in small groups or pairs to develop an argument on a topic and then present their view to another group. Sides can then be switched, the opposite view defended, and different routes to a better social order explored. In this way, students learn to work creatively with conflicts, and some of this creativity may carry over and help students learn to resolve other disputes.

- Role-play historical events or current news happenings from conflicting viewpoints. Examine questionable television news images whose power is palpable but whose connection to reality is tenuous.

- Watch television broadcasts that present different viewpoints: for example, those that interview individuals with differing perspectives on a problem.

- Have students write letters to the editors of newspapers or popular journals, or letters to television producers, expressing the students' stance on an issue of importance.

These activities allow students to develop argumentative thinking skills. The basic goal is to stimulate and encourage a wide range of collaboration, divergent thinking, and discussion. By arguing important moral dilemmas in history, politics, literature, art, music, or sports, students can learn content, develop reasoning capabilities, and extend their ethical concepts. To have power over the history that dominates one's life means having the power to retell it, deconstruct it, joke about it, and change it as times change. Without this power, students find it difficult to think new thoughts and to act on them.

The fundamental search for meaning is made especially powerful when team efforts are connected to individuals' self-perception, attitudes, and accountability. In small-group contexts, metacognitive awareness can be amplified as the groups work to construct their own understandings and this self-reflection process can play a large role in the development of reasoning and interpersonal skills. Toward this end, students can work together to actively integrate new information with existing knowledge, select ideas that are important, deal with the unexpected, and learn to make inferences beyond the information given.

Assessing Critical Thinking

Assessment activities must focus both on students' improvement and on teachers' effectiveness and needs for further development.

Assessing Students

"Relationships to others, like thinking, are as incoherent and difficult to measure as truth. . . . But when previously unassociated ideas strike together the result is a little stunning," Herman Melville (1963 [1856], p. 52) once wrote. Melville's words give us some insight into assessing our teaching of critical thinking skills and habits. It is hard to measure attitudes, thinking, and interpersonal skills on a paper-and-pencil test, but we can observe the results of the development of critical thinking as changes in behavior, and that is a good first step toward assessment. For example, we can observe humor, anecdotes, parental reactions, and teacher-student interactions that indicate that ideas are being shared. We can also observe the ability of both students and teachers to pull together as a team, since this ability influences how well students reflect on their own thinking, pose powerful questions, and connect diverse ideas. Failure to cultivate these aspects of thinking may be a major source of difficulty when it comes to learning content (Anderson & Burns, 1989).

Other behaviors to look for in assessing the development of critical thinking (in addition to the six indicators of thoughtfulness listed earlier) include:

- Asking fewer how-do-I-do-it questions. (Students ask group members before asking the teacher.)
- Using trial-and-error discovery without frustration.
- Asking powerful *why* questions of peers and teachers.
- Using metaphor, simile, and allegory in speaking, writing, and thinking.
- Developing interpersonal discussion skills for shared inquiry.
- Working collaboratively in cooperative groups.
- Showing willingness to begin a task.
- Initiating inquiry.
- Showing comfort with ambiguity and open-ended assignments.
- Synthesizing and combining diverse ideas.

When the assessment focuses specifically on the creative aspect of critical thinking, educators should look for the following behaviors:

- Acquiring fluency and producing and considering many alternatives.
- Showing originality by producing ideas that go beyond the obvious and are unique and valued. (Students need to process information actively, relate it to their existing knowledge, put it in their own words, and make sure they understand it.)
- Highlighting the essence by finding and expressing the main idea.

- Elaborating; filling out an idea or set of ideas by adding details.

- Keeping an open mind and delaying closure, seeing many ideas, considering a range of information, making mental leaps.

- Developing and expressing emotional awareness, perseverance, involvement, and commitment.

- Combining and synthesizing; seeing relationships and joining parts and elements to form a whole.

- Visualizing richly and colorfully; perceiving and creating images that are vivid, strong, and alive.

- Visualizing the inside by seeing and presenting ideas and objects from an internal vantage point.

- Enjoying and using fantasy and using imagination in a playful way.

- Using movement and learning, thinking, and communicating kinesthetically.

- Interpreting and communicating ideas, concepts, and feelings through sound and music.

- Breaking through and extending boundaries; overcoming limitations and conventions and creating new solutions.

- Using humor and combining incongruous situations with wit, surprise, and amusement.

- Imagining the future by envisioning alternatives, predicting consequences, and planning ahead.

Assessing Teachers and Planning Teacher Development

Teachers, acting collectively, can break out of established patterns. They can jointly develop their own reflection and inquiry skills so that they can become students of their own teaching. Teachers who decide to participate with students in learning to think on a daily basis nourish human possibilities. Once connected with innovative methods and materials, they can build learning environments sensitive to students' growing abilities to think for themselves. By promoting thoughtful learning across the full spectrum of personalities and ways of knowing, teachers can make a tremendous difference and perform a unique service for our nation's future. But the professional development activities that supply the new methods and materials may have to go hand-in-hand with supplying ways of *organizing* instruction to accommodate new modes of representing knowledge and inviting reflective thinking. It is important for schools to provide diverse staff development activities to expand teachers' knowledge, horizons, and organizational possibilities. If given half a chance, many teachers will take what is now known about critical thinking and use it to support innovative practice.

Beyond specific teaching strategies, the climate of the classroom and the behavior of the teacher are very important. Teachers should be modeling critical thinking behaviors, setting the tone and atmosphere for learning. When the ideal and the actual behaviors are linked, the result can produce a dynamic, productive, and resilient form of learning. What we know about teaching thinking is increasingly being put into practice in model classrooms and schools (Boomer, 1992). These exemplary programs recognize that powerful inquiry can help students make personal discoveries that change their thinking and that critical thinking skills can turn an unexamined belief into a reasoned one. Thus, the control students exercise over their own lives now and in the future can be enhanced by a teacher's support of inquiry and caring.

Improving Schools Is Only Part of Improving Outcomes

Technology and communication have created a world economy where working smarter is just as important as working harder. Today's jobs require workers who are mentally fit and prepared to absorb new ideas, adapt to change, cope with ambiguity, and solve unconventional problems. Citizenship adds more requirements, including civic consciousness. Getting students ready to be productive workers and citizens requires rigorous academic training, moral development, and lessons and practice in thinking critically. Our schools are highly influential here, affecting a whole range of issues that reach across society, from attitudes about learning to productive mental habits. This influence is especially powerful when the generative power of higher education is added to the mix.

Quality instruction involves spending time on process (thoughtful discussions, reasoned discourse, criticism, reflection, and insightful questions) as well as content. Traditionally in our schools, logistics such as taking roll have gotten in the way of both process and content (Goodlad, 1983). In some schools, students are seldom asked for their opinions, nor are they encouraged to question each other, the teacher, or the textbook. This has to change. Higher-level questions must be valued and students must be helped to go beyond unsupported personal opinions and to supply good arguments and evidence to support their viewpoints. Argument, based on good information, can help form productive habits of the mind (White & Gunstone, 1992), and schools can play a major role in the development of critical and creative thinking (Wiggins, 1989).

Nevertheless, as schools continue to grope for valid solutions, it is important to recognize that improving the schools is only part of improving educational outcomes. Parents are the first teachers, and many of them need training in this vital duty—especially when one young parent is asked to do the work of two under extreme conditions. As a child grows, his or her community can also play a major educational role. Communities can assist their schools to organize cognitive apprenticeships that allow older students to participate in work environments (Resnick & Klopfer, 1989) and become involved in such real tasks as running a small business or using equipment in a biotechnology lab, for example. In these environments, students can also learn the value of being able to explain physical phenomena that are hard to understand and of writing messages of explanation for interested audiences. People's success in life outside of school is often dependent on their ability to use cognitive tools (like computers or calculators) and to work with others in ferreting out the right information when it is needed. Communities can help schools give students the experience in combining specialized skills, applying general knowledge and interpersonal skills, and using thinking ability that is crucial to learning to confront uncertainty and solve real problems. Without help from their schools *and* families *and* communities, instead of success, students may experience the frustration Emily Dickinson (1924) once imaginatively pictured.

> *The thought behind I strove to join*
> *Unto the thought before,*
> *But sequence ravelled out of reach*
> *Like balls upon the floor.*

Dealing with exploration, experimentation, exceptions, mistakes, and ambiguity should be part of the job description in our schools as well as the workplaces of tomorrow, along with dealing with failure in a way that makes it a stepping-stone to future accomplishment. Educational, parental, and social safety nets are necessary, but should not be employed to encourage dysfunctional dependency. The best teamwork, thinking, and problem solving is no guarantee of success—it just improves the odds. Students need nourishing support to get over the rough spots, but they do need to experience the rough spots. A willingness to *take risks* and *persevere* is the most important attribute for eventual success. Even the most experienced critical and creative thinkers make mistakes. The goal should be to learn from them.

Building Bridges to an Ambiguous Future

We are far from having all the answers needed to design a curriculum that invites thoughtfulness. But we do know enough to begin the intellectual adventure. And we know enough to institute educational practices that promote true understanding. A skilled teacher, open to new ideas, can open a number of doors to adventures in imaginativeness and creative perception that will help students understand and affect today's realities.

Tomorrow's realities will place an even higher tax on our social and educational traditions. Students need mental flexibility to survive in such a rapidly changing world with an uncertain future. No subject or approach should be treated as a religious icon. Deep understanding involves more questioning than reverencing. It also involves engaging students in discovering how to analyze, synthesize, make judgments, create new knowledge, and to apply these skills to such important activities as standing up for their rights without resorting to violence.

Students have to go beyond knowing to understanding how to do something—perhaps to engage in cognitive self-observation and take part in language-rich classroom interaction, perhaps to share inquiry as a method of preparation, discussion, and problem solving that develops knowledge. In the words of one sixth-grader, "Friends don't let friends write bad poetry. . . . They figure better ways to do things together."

Of course, the same collaboration that provokes thought can also conflict with people's traditional and deeply entrenched ways of making sense of the world and, thus, with teachers' traditional ways of teaching about the world. Yet these traditional methods of teaching and learning—primarily lecturing, listening, and working alone—were never effective for everyone, nor were the strategies expressed in such instructions as "read it again" or "remember what I showed you." Even those who *can* sit still for these traditional methods do not learn much about thinking, articulating questions, or solving problems along a variety of paths; there simply cannot be much practice with higher levels of thinking when someone else does most of the important work for you.

Contentment and self-satisfaction are the enemies of change. Real change most frequently comes during times when major players in a situation are simultaneously ill at ease and focused on an issue. After years of dwelling in a state of sleepy social and educational self-contentment, nearly everyone in our nation is now concerned about what has happened to the once great U.S. educational system. As part of this discontent, we have the opportunity to reestablish our national commitment to the future and to create an interactive, meaning-centered curriculum that can give students the thinking skills we are agreed are necessary for the beginning of the twenty-first century.

To be educated means knowing the depths that wait for us under the surface of things, whatever those things may be. Change, as Louis Pasteur pointed out, does favor the prepared mind. The future may be ultimately unpredictable. But when the educational experience is better suited to the nature of the growing mind, students will do a better job of mapping the potential terrain.

The goal of schooling can no longer be simply reaching for higher levels of basic achievement. Rather, we need to be concerned with creating a *learning culture*, an environment that promotes the wider understandings and mental flexibility that will connect students to fulfilling and socially responsible lives outside of school. Our harvest from the learning culture will be true thoughtfulness, increased community, and new promising possibilities for action. Although improvements in teaching alone will not solve all of our dire social and educational problems, teaching is a factor that has an absolutely vital role to play in successful change.

No one can play it safe and easy when it comes to breaking down the barriers between social problems and educational opportunity. Teachers need the courage and the support to take risks. If given the chance, good teachers, with good approaches, in the right environment, can push the process of more effective thinking and learning forward. They can make a real difference. To do their part in helping our society greet the future, schools' curriculum models and teaching methods must shift to help students critically perceive, analyze, interpret and discover a whole new range of meanings. We need educators and students who can learn to ask insightful questions together, self-monitor, reflect on their own thinking, and be able to plan ahead.

Chapter Three

Cooperative Learning

The age of cooperation is approaching. Teachers and
administrators are discovering an untapped resource
for accelerating students' achievement: the students
themselves.

— *Robert Slavin (1990)*

Cooperative (or collaborative) learning is one of the major developments of the 1980s shaping education in the 1990s. Resting on a solid data base of research and experience, it has been recognized by educators as a successful framework for learning in many disciplines. Building on teacher familiarity with small-group work, it is making its appearance in lesson plans, in-service programs, and subjects from one end of the curriculum to the other. In this chapter, we will review the results of the research and the benefits to students of cooperative learning; give teachers some practical suggestions about the skills necessary for interactive learning, the organization of an interactive learning environment, and specific cooperative activities; and suggest how cooperative learning directly benefits teachers when they collaborate among themselves to evaluate their teaching and pursue professional development.

Individualized Compared to Cooperative Learning

In traditional individualized learning, each student works at his or her own pace and is expected to be left alone by other students. Even when the children self-select appropriate material and pace themselves to complete a work assignment, thus taking on responsibility for completing the task and sometimes evaluating their own progress and the quality of the effort, the biggest drawback of individualized learning remains unaltered. It forces students, who are naturally social, to work in isolation, struggling to piece together fragments of information. Furthermore, a large amount of the teacher's time is spent in correcting, testing, and record keeping—not teaching. In individualized learning, the specific task objective is perceived to be most important, with each student asked to achieve a set goal and the teacher required to be the major source of assistance and reinforcement. As far as this method goes, there is nothing wrong with it. The trouble is that it fills in only part of the learning picture because it fails to tap the learning power and lessons of collaboration. Although elementary school teachers have traditionally used group learning in addition to individualized learning, the customary groups are usually based on "ability" or a skill hierarchy and this ranking gets in the way of collaboration.

Another problematic aspect of traditional learning is competition. Students monitor the progress of their competitors, and compare their own ability, skills, and knowledge. Instructional activities tend to focus on skill practice, knowledge recall, and review, making comparison easy. Assignments are clear, with rules for competing specified. If there is an informal grading curve, then one person's success diminishes another person's ability. Again, the teacher is the major resource and often directs the competitive activity. The competitive atmosphere often induces anxiety, fear of failure, and ultimately withdrawal for many students.

Cooperative group learning takes a different approach. It builds on what we know about how students construct knowledge, promoting active learning in a way not possible with competitive or individualized learning. In a cooperative classroom, the teacher organizes major parts of the curriculum around tasks, problems, and projects that students can work through in small mixed-ability groups. Lessons are designed around active learning teams so that students can combine their energies as they work toward a common goal. If someone else in your group does well, you do well, with the result that social skills such as interpersonal communication, group interaction, and conflict resolution are developed as the cooperative learning process goes along.

Influence on Learning

Some successful cooperative multicultural models view collaborative intimacy as the *natural* condition between teachers and students (Hamm & Adams, 1992). The research bears this out, suggesting that students learn more, increase their understanding, and enjoy learning in cooperative learning groups (Burton, 1987) and that their social and intellectual development is enhanced (Cohen, 1984). A number of studies have pointed to the positive effect of collaboration on student achievement and attitudes towards learning (Slavin, 1989; Johnson & Johnson, 1982). When teachers and students are encouraged to work collaboratively, there is a positive effect on the overall school environment (Renninger, Hidi, & Krapp, 1992). Collaboration produces these results because effective learning is largely a social and often informal activity.

Learning takes place through a child's interaction with his or her environment, family, community members, schools, and other institutions. Language is the means by which learning and meaning are translated, verified, and made conscious. Thus, by interacting with her or his environment, parents, siblings, and classmates, the child comes to know and make sense of the world. This early learning connects to social and cultural experiences to form an experience base. The child then uses language to clarify and extend these connections and construct a more sophisticated base for additional learning.

Cooperative learning builds on this idea that much learning occurs in social contexts. Working in teams provides students with opportunities to talk about what each of them sees in classroom subjects and to participate actively in classroom life. The teacher acts as the students' pilot, selecting meaningful topics for discussion, mapping out opportunities for collaboration, and observing the interaction of the working groups in which students make connections between new ideas discussed in class and prior knowledge. As students are encouraged to jointly interpret and negotiate meaning, learning comes alive. Out of their regular opportunities to talk, read, write, and solve problems together, they construct meaningful explanations for themselves.

It has been argued that expressive language (that is, language that expresses thoughts and feelings) is the foundation of student language and thinking (Adams, 1990). To encourage this natural process of language moving to thinking to continue in the classroom, teachers must allow students to struggle with ideas, informally shaping them for a public audience. Teachers must give collaborative groups time to suggest, share, clarify, and expand concepts. Starting with one student's experiences and background knowledge, the group process can transform those elements to a shared group idea or to a more elegant individual expression. Because unstructured, informal conversations between peers rely heavily on shared experiences for understanding and are expressive in that feelings, beliefs, and opinions are freely stated, this form of communication is students' best starting point for coming to terms with new ideas. Through their informal conversations, learners shape ideas, modify them by listening to others, question, plan, express doubt, and construct meaning. They feel free to express uncertainty and experiment with new language, even if their abilities vary from those of others in the group. Indeed, talking in mixed-ability groups in school has been shown to facilitate and enhance the learning process (Johnson & Johnson, 1989). In our pluralistic society, various mixed racial, gender, ethnic, and ability group structures in the classroom can also help students understand each other.

Small-group discussion provides constant feedback within a supportive environment, allowing individuals to become more at ease with sharing thoughts with others and with examining, comparing, and affixing personal meaning to shared concepts or beliefs. A response group that places its members' ideas into both personal and collective contexts can serve as a powerful motivator for individuals' thinking and discovery, with information being remembered longer because discussion has helped the individual attach personal meaning to information. Ideas take clearer shapes and become more alive. Whether the immediate purpose is building respect for others' points of view, supporting group members, offering constructive criticism, or learning academic material, cooperative learning is so powerful a motivator that there is no better way to jump-start a stalled class.

Specifically, research suggests that cooperative learning has the following positive effects (Slavin, 1983, 1989; Sharon, 1980; Abraham & Campbell, 1984; Levine & Trachtman, 1988; Johnson, 1990; Johnson et al., 1981; Carnegie Foundation for the Advancement of Teaching, 1988; Kagan, 1986):

- *It motivates students.* Students talking and working together on a project or problem experience the fun of sharing ideas and information.

- *It increases academic performance.* Whether students are discovering new concepts, solving problems, or questioning factual information, a collaborative approach has been shown to develop academic skills. Classroom interaction with peers causes students—especially those from diverse cultural and linguistic backgrounds—to make significant academic gains compared to student gains in traditional settings.

- *It encourages active learning.* Years of extensive research and practice have shown that students learn more when they are actively engaged in discovery and problem solving. As students talk and reason together to complete a task or solve a problem, they become more involved in thinking and communicating. Cooperative learning produces the kind of problem solving with others that been shown to spark an alertness of mind not achieved in passive listening.

- *It increases respect for diversity.* Students who work together in mixed-ability groups are more likely to select mixed racial and ethnic acquaintances and friendships. When students cooperate to reach a common goal, they learn to appreciate and respect each other.

- *It promotes literacy and language skills.* Group study offers students many chances to use language and improve speaking skills. This is particularly important for ESL (English as a second language) students.

- *It prepares students for today's society.* Team approaches to solving problems, combining individual energies, and working to get along socially are valued skills in the world of work, community, and leisure. Cooperative learning taps students' social nature, building self-esteem and social understanding.

- *It improves teacher effectiveness.* Through actively engaging students in the learning process, teachers also make important discoveries about the way each student learns and what he or she learns. As students take some of the responsibility for some of the teaching, the teacher's educational power is multiplied.

The literature supports cooperative learning. But the main reason it is catching on is that *teachers can tell that it works*. Cooperative learning works because it promotes interaction through face-to-face communication, and interaction is vital not only in acquiring knowledge but also in developing critical thinking skills. Small groups provide a structure for both personal learning agendas and the joint application of critical thinking skills. Working together, for example, students can teach each other to distinguish hypotheses from verified information and recognize reasoning based on misconceptions.

Cooperative learning works because it links individuals to group success, so that students are supported, encouraged, and given feedback as they critically analyze problems and issues. Cooperative learning works because group members are held responsible individually and collectively. Since everyone has a responsibility to finish all assignments, master instructional objectives, and ensure that all group members do the same, children working in small groups of supportive classmates develop a sense of community and caring. As members of cooperative learning communities, children develop many social skills: the power to communicate, confidence in their overall ability, respect for others, and a sense of value ("I have something to offer").

Cooperative learning works because it teaches skills that are in demand and becoming ever more important in the modern, fast-paced, ever-changing world. In a cooperative classroom, students are frequently engaged in such interpersonal skills as shared decision making, managing conflict situations, and maintaining good working relationships among group members. When a lesson is over, a group typically takes time to reflect on how well its members did as a group—and what could be done better. All these thinking and interpersonal skills will be crucial in the workplace of tomorrow.

Unifying Effects

Cooperative learning is a natural vehicle for promoting multicultural understandings. Positive interdependence, shared responsibilities, social skills development, and heterogeneity result when students at various ability levels cluster together, discuss topics, and learn to take charge of their own learning. They discover how to look for common ground rather than emphasize differences. Recent research supports this view, finding that all members of collaborative groups became more accepting of racially and culturally different classmates (Davidson & Worsham, 1992). Sports teams have long had a similar unifying effect on teammates. Thus, interracial or culturally diverse learning teams can be useful for organizing classrooms in support of multicultural harmony. Studies from social psychology suggest that dividing a class into interracial learning teams reduces prejudice by undercutting stereotypes while encouraging group members to pull together (Costa, 1991). Other researchers (Davidson & Worsham, 1992) have found that cooperative groups are particularly beneficial for Hispanic, African-American, and other minority students. Since many ethnic minority cultures instill strong values of group cooperation, such instruction will build upon their home experiences.

Collaborative efforts also ease the paths of students identified as having impairments. Within a cooperative learning classroom many conventionally defined disabilities integrate naturally into the heterogeneity of expected and anticipated differences among all students. When all students are motivated to actively carry out projects and tasks in their groups, no individual is singled out as being difficult, and no one student presents an insurmountable challenge to the teacher when it comes to accommodating that student's special needs. Once students in a cooperative learning classroom realize that there are many and varied differences among students, no student need be stereotyped. Children whose disabilities make them unable to do a certain tasks will find their differences need not constitute a handicap as cooperative learning is a joint enterprise and all students have information, backgrounds, and skills of some kind to contribute to the learning of others.

The central question is not how naturally social children will adapt to interacting but how individual classroom teachers, already overwhelmed with tasks, can find ways to adapt collaborative techniques, plan thematically, and modify approaches in order to successfully accommodate all students within their classrooms. They must rethink their curriculum structures and seek approaches for teaching students in ways that will build on each child's unique qualities.

Organizing an Interactive Learning Environment

Cooperative learning thrives in an atmosphere of mutual helpfulness where students know *what* is happening—and *why*. For the teacher, this means defining objectives, talking about the benefits of cooperative learning, explaining expectations, and explaining such behaviors as brainstorming, peer coaching, constructive criticism, and confidence building. For the student, this means not only having something meaningful to work on but also learning how to listen well, communicate effectively, and receive constructive criticism.

Learning the skills of engaging in productive conversation, helping a group member without simply telling him or her the answer, and giving and taking constructive criticism requires considerable student effort. Cooperative learning will not take place with students sitting in rows facing the teacher. To facilitate group interaction, desks must be pushed together in small groups (two or more), or students can sit at small tables. Exact group size will depend on the activity, but for many classroom activities, groups of three or four students work better. Resources and hands-on material must be readily accessible. Collaboration will not occur in a classroom that requires students to raise their hands to ask questions, talk, or leave their desks. Instead, students who want help are expected to ask the student next to them. A basic rule of collaboration is that a student has to ask at least two other students before asking the teacher when he or she does not understand something or is stuck on a problem. (Teachers must be aware that cooperative learning will raise classroom noise levels. Placing old carpets and other sound-absorbing materials around the room helps, but teachers and students also need to tolerate higher noise levels.)

Groups often must make several attempts at cooperative learning before they begin working effectively. Like teachers, students must be gradually eased into the process through a consistent routine. The more teachers and students work in groups, the easier it becomes. In particular, some students may encounter initial problems because they are accustomed to being rewarded for easy-to-come-by answers that require little thinking. It may take some time and teacher assistance for them to become comfortable working cooperatively in a more ambiguous situation. Teachers should also be aware that those students with an undeveloped sense of self (personal efficacy or self-esteem) have the most difficult time sharing deeply with others.

Teachers may find these strategies useful in helping students adjust to working in groups:

- *Adjust the group size to suit the activity.* Groups of two, three, or four work well for activities like mathematics problem solving, as well as process writing, prewriting, drafting, revising, editing, and publishing. Groups of five or six often work better for activities like creative dramatics, large social studies projects, as well as for specific writing projects like an integrated thematic unit, mapping the writing journey, personal journals, generating ideas on a project, etc.

- *Experiment with different group patterns and size.*

- *Do not interrupt a group that is working well.* If a group seems to be floundering, ask a group member to describe what the group is discussing or what part of the problem is causing difficulty. (Do not speak loudly to a group across the room. Go to the group if you want to say something.)

- *Interact with the groups from time to time.* Listen carefully to their discussions.

- *Give students rules for group work.* The basic suggested rules are these:

  Individuals must check with other members of the group before they may raise their hands to ask the teacher for help. Help can then be given to the group collectively.

Groups must try to reach consensus on a problem.

All group members should participate in group activities.

Group members should be considerate of others.

Students are to help any group member who asks.

In addition, teachers who are experienced in cooperative learning frequently mention that some student traits that affect success with cooperative learning are being willing to learn from failure, becoming aware of limited economic resources, and working beyond personal limits (Slavin et al., 1985). Moreover, the collaborative process works best when teachers provide students with meanings (or purposes) that go beyond the importance of learning individual cooperative learning skills. Some of these larger meanings are that students of mixed ability, gender, race, and ethnicity can learn to function as a team that sinks or swims together, that groups can take responsibility for the learning of individual members while individuals are held accountable for each group's success, and that learning how to search out, share and receive, and summarize and clarify information to continue progress on a group task are skills useful throughout one's life. Students should be aware of these larger purposes in all their group tasks.

Once upon a time, a second-grade teacher might have three groups: the bluebirds, the blackbirds, and the gorillas. And once you were in the high, medium, or low group you were likely to stay there. Cooperative learning offers the most promising ways out of the ability-grouping maze. A multidimensional collaborative classroom makes learning more accessible to more students, more valuable, and more interesting because the teacher organizes major parts of the curriculum around tasks, problems, and projects that students can work through in active learning teams, not ability groupings. Students then combine energies and abilities to reach common group objectives. As teachers and students organize their interactive learning environments, they all learn to shape questions, interpret data, and make connections between subjects. Students learn to take responsibility for their own learning and to assist the others in their group, combining personal initiative with social responsibility. This allows those with more information to stimulate the students with less and vice versa. The same stimulation will occur when thinking processes like comprehension, decision making, and problem solving are being taught.

The collaborative approaches described in the rest of this chapter are all fairly easy to try, and as students begin helping each other learn, they will see this kind of learning as social, fun, and under their control. With the teacher acting as a resource person, the learners themselves create a climate of acceptance and a spirit of camaraderie. Topical projects, writing assignments, problem solving assignments or journal reaction papers are just a few examples of activities that can benefit from active group planning, negotiating, and the collaborative distribution of work. As each group tries to reach a consensus, its members can create an analysis grid or management plan to compare and contrast the points under discussion as well as students' speculations about outcomes. Within the tension raised by discussion (even heated discussion) of different points of view, learning takes place.

Steps to Structure Cooperative Groups

Johnson, Johnson, Holubec, and Roy (1984) suggest that teachers follow these eighteen steps to implement small-group interactive learning:

- Specify content and cooperative group objectives.
- Determine the size of the group (typically from two to six, depending on the nature of the task and the time available).
- Divide students into groups. (You may assign students or allow students to form their own groups).

- Arrange the room so that you are accessible to all groups and so that group members can sit close enough to communicate effectively yet not disturb other groups.

- Plan instructional materials. (You may wish to give a single set of materials to each group or to give each group member different materials so as to force task differentiation.)

- Assign roles to members of the group; discussed in detail later in this chapter.

- Explain the task.

- Implement strategies such as positive goal interdependence, peer encouragement, and support for learning. For example, you may ask a group to produce a single product or you may put in place an assessment system where rewards are based on individual scores averaged to produce a group score.

- Structure intergroup cooperation.

- Go over the success criteria by explaining the guidelines, boundaries, and roles.

- Specify desired behaviors (taking turns, using personal names, listening carefully to each other, encouraging each other to participate).

- Monitor students (circulate to listen and observe groups and note problems).

- Provide assistance when asked.

- Intervene when groups have problems in collaborating successfully.

- Provide closure to the lesson.

- Evaluate the quality of students' learning.

- Have students assess how well their groups functioned together.

- Give and encourage feedback. Discuss how students and groups could improve.

Here is a more detailed look at specific strategies teachers can use in parts of this process: introducing the task, coaching the groups, and summarizing the work.

Introducing the Task

During the initial introduction, the teacher's objective is to have students understand the problem or skill being addressed and to establish guidelines for the groups' work. The teacher presents or reviews the necessary concepts or skills with the whole class and poses a part of the task or an example of a problem for the class to try. The class then has an opportunity to discuss the concepts or skills. The actual group task or problem is presented after this conceptual overview, and the class is encouraged to discuss and clarify the task. Before breaking the class into groups, it is helpful to have one or two students explain the problem in their own words for the whole class to hear. This student summary of the teacher's directions can clarify the group task, give students practice in thinking skills, and ensure an understanding of the group task. Students then break into their small learning groups, as assigned.

Coaching the Group

As students work cooperatively to solve the problem, the teacher observes, listens to the groups' ideas, and offers assistance as needed. The teacher is also responsible for providing extension activities when a group is done early. If a group is having difficulties, the teacher helps group members discover what they know so far and poses a simple example or perhaps points out a misconception or erroneous idea. Sometimes a group has trouble getting along or focusing on what they are supposed to be doing, and it may be necessary to refocus the group's attention by asking such questions as, What are you supposed to be doing? What is the task? How will you get organized? What materials do you need? Who will do what?

Summarizing

After the group exploration of the task is completed, students again meet as a class to summarize and present their findings or solutions and share their processes. When processes are shared, both group procedures and problem-solving strategies are summarized. Questions for groups to answer might include: How did you organize the task? What problems did you have? What method did you use? Was your group method effective? Did anyone in your group have a different method or strategy for solving the problem? Do you think your solution makes sense? Teachers should encourage students to generalize from the group results, asking, What other problem does this remind you of? What other follow-up could you try based on your findings? Students are encouraged to listen to and respond to other students' comments. It can also be helpful to make notes of students' responses on the chalkboard as a means of summarizing the class data at the close of the lesson.

How Exemplary Teachers Manage the Cooperative Classroom

To be most effective, teaching must respond to students' prior knowledge and ideas. Resisting the temptation to control classroom ideas, teachers must *listen* as much as they speak, so that students get a sense of ownership over their own learning (Bassarear & Davidson, 1992). In a cooperative classroom, a give and take with open discussion and honest criticism of ideas exists between students and teachers, and between students and students.

Studies of exemplary teachers reveal strategies that facilitate and sustain student engagement. Teachers identified as good role models were very successful at controlling at a distance. Moving around the room and speaking with individuals and groups from time to time was also part of their repertoire (Tobin & Fraser, 1989). Their students were able to work independently and cooperatively in groups, developing a surprising degree of autonomy and independence. In classrooms identified as exemplary, students demonstrated the capacity to work together when problems arose, and they knew when to seek help from a peer or the teacher. These teachers were not always worried about maintaining order, nor were they rushing from one student to another, on demand, as hands went up. They had considered all the daily classroom circumstances (broken pencil, confusion about directions, misunderstandings between classmates, and so on) and even had time to reflect on the lesson as it progressed. The key to their successful monitoring was that they had established routines that enabled them to cope with a number of diverse learning needs. In all cases, they prescribed activities that would ensure that each student was active mentally. Students who encountered difficulties were encouraged to try to work them out for themselves, consulting resources and peers (Shulman & Colbert, 1987).

Many exemplary teachers also explained task requirements to the students. When off-task behavior occurred, the teacher quickly spoke to the individual, pairs, or small groups concerned, in a quiet manner that did not disrupt the work of students who were on task. Model teachers also used strategies to encourage students to actively participate. Their "safety nets," for example, allowing students to participate without embarrassment, were found to be especially beneficial among relatively quiet students. Safety nets created a feeling of safety and security. An example of such a safety net is a buddy system for a student new to a school; the buddy shows the student around to alleviate the anxiety of being a newcomer to the school. Using concrete materials to connect learning with thinking and understanding was yet another characteristic that the most successful teachers had in common. Their most effective problem-solving approaches to learning involved direct materials-centered experiences.

By encouraging verbal interactions among groups, these teachers could monitor students' understanding of the content and occasionally ask questions to stimulate thinking. By probing students' responses, they got students to elaborate and clarify their thinking and speculations. However, these teachers also provided examples and additional information to groups who were stuck (Meyer & Sallee, 1983).

Individual and Group Accountability

Teachers can start cooperative group interaction simply by having students help each other in solving problems and completing academic tasks, but it is very important to take the next step of combining this action with positive interdependence among group members and individual accountability. Group interdependence means that each individual plays a unique role. The team loses if individual members do not put out individual effort, that is, members win or lose together. Individual accountability ensures that everyone is contributing to the common goal and gives teachers a way of checking the role that each student is playing in a group's work.

Teachers establish individual accountability through giving group rewards that are based on individual performance (for example, totaling scores on individually taken quizzes to produce the group score); having students make individual presentations on a group project or do unique tasks to contribute to group presentations (for example, in a study of Navaho Indians, one group member can report on the Indians' homes, another can report on foods, another on rituals, and so forth); and providing incentives for students to work together to learn new material but testing students individually.

At the same time, however, teachers must also establish group accountability. If students discuss last night's basketball game instead of working on mathematics, they are not going to get much mathematical knowledge from their group discussion. Teachers must clearly define the task and closely monitor groups to ensure they accomplish the task. Once children learn to expect positive interaction in their groups, they will naturally share ideas and materials and become accountable for their own knowledge, and all group members will be expected to contribute to the group effort. The primary group task can be divided into smaller tasks that are distributed among the members to capitalize on the group's wide range of strengths; however, individuals must be able to expect support for their risk taking in doing the smaller task, and other group members should be perceived to be the major source for that support and assistance.

Defining and Using Group Roles and Other Task Behaviors

When students are new to cooperative learning, teachers may wish to assign certain roles to group members in order to ensure that they all work toward a group goal. Later, the students themselves can assume the charge of making sure that everyone cooperates and contributes. Many teachers identify five basic roles in any group activity (Johnson & Johnson, 1975).

1. *Facilitator.* Organizes the group's work. Makes certain students understand the group's job. Takes the group's questions and concerns to the teacher *after* the group attempts a solution and tries alternatives.
2. *Checker.* Checks with group members to make sure that everyone understands her or his task. Checks to be sure that everyone agrees with the group response and can explain it.
3. *Reader.* Reads the problem or directions to the group.
4. *Recorder.* Writes the group's response or data collection on a group response sheet or log.
5. *Encourager.* Offers support and encouragement to group members. Keeps others feeling good about working together.

For a group of four students, the teacher can combine the facilitator role and the checker or reader role; for a group of three, the checker, reader, and recorder roles can each be assigned to a different person and the encourager and facilitator roles shared, and so forth. However, even teachers who work a lot with cooperative groups do not always assign roles, and students who are used to the process will share the roles naturally. The group poetry reading described later illustrates how a group can be instructed to assign their own roles. Teachers may also ask students to determine what the roles should be.

Organizing a group plan of action is an important part of shared responsibility and shared leadership. Learning how to search out, share, and receive information to continue progress on a group task are important skills in working collaboratively. Students also need the critical thinking skills described in Chapter Two if they are to move the group in the direction of completing their task or goal. Sometimes, it may be necessary to test the consensus of a group, asking how many members agree that a particular direction is advisable or that a particular conclusion is accurate. Other task behaviors to be learned include:

- Getting the group started.
- Staying on task.
- Getting the group back to work.
- Taking turns.
- Asking questions.
- Following directions.
- Staying in the group space.
- Keeping track of time.
- Helping without giving the answer.

Group Support Systems

In addition to helping the group reach its goal and get the job done, a group member also has the responsibility to show support and empathy for other group members and their feelings. The idea is for students to play to each other's strengths and support each other's weaknesses. When a teacher is a part of a support team that encourages others to be openly exploratory and inquiring, he or she has opportunities to affirm his or her understanding and share his or her insights and ways of thinking with others. Both teaching and learning in a cooperative environment require considering ways to encourage ourselves and others to learn. However, students in a cooperative learning classroom do not have to agree about everything. Square holes make for square pegs. Although all students in each group should assume responsibility for promoting and maintaining positive attitudes and a positive group spirit, this does not mean using "team spirit" to suppress dissent or intimidate individuals. Collaboration does not have to equal conformity. To reverse the traditional Japanese maxim, the nail that sticks up should *not* be hammered down. Differences of opinion and conflicting views can actually result in constructive conflict and provide an important source of learning. So it is important for teachers and students to become comfortable with the differing opinions of others, with that which cannot be calibrated or arbitrarily controlled. Agreement is not required, but support is. It is important for everyone to have an opportunity to express ideas, to reflect on the process, and to analyze the feelings and ideas that other group members express.

A complex emotional geometry connects the individuals in a group. When group interactions become tense, a release of that tension is needed; humor is one good way to ease group members' frustrations. Teachers should know and model the following support and maintenance behaviors that help keep activities enjoyable and on an even keel.

- *Empathizing and encouraging:* showing understanding and helping others feel a part of the group.

- *Gatekeeping:* giving everyone a chance to speak in the group, checking to see that no one is overlooked.

- *Liberating tension:* creating harmony in the group.

- *Expressing group feelings:* helping the group examine how it is feeling and operating.

- *Using personal names:* a way to promote security and create a sense of belonging. As students become a part of the social fabric of the class, they are well positioned to grow in self-esteem through successful participation in both the social and the academic aspects of academic life. Having a personal connection with a student by mentioning his or her name—especially if the child is new to the school—helps lay the social-emotional foundation that fosters self-esteem and a sense of belonging.

- *Encouraging students to talk.*

- *Responding to ideas.* Validate a student's idea. One important context for teachers to model curiosity and interest in learning is when responding to questions or ideas from students.

- *Using eye contact.* Even if a child cannot understand a word of what the teacher is saying, the teacher can integrate the student into the class by simply making eye contact occasionally while speaking.

- *Showing appreciation.* Introduce appreciation for a topic or activity by verbalizing reasons why the students should value it. If it has connections with something the students already recognize as interesting or important, these connections should be noted. When the knowledge or skills to be taught have applications to everyday living, these applications should be mentioned, especially those that will allow students to solve problems or accomplish goals that are important to them.

- *Not letting debates and feelings get too heated.*
- *Paraphrasing.* The teacher can help the student clarify her statement by saying, "I think I understand this about what you were saying, but could you elaborate please?" or "Do you mean . . . ?"

Creating harmony, coaching, sharing, and encouraging are learned behaviors. As group members learn to focus energy on the learning task, they also learn to identify with the group process and with support behaviors. When group responsibility and support behaviors are in balance, group members can work collaboratively to achieve important group objectives. When the group task is over, it is also supportive for groups to evaluate their effectiveness and make suggestions for improvement, gaining insights into their own collaborative processes.

Conflict Resolution and Problem Solving

Solving problems and smoothly resolving conflict in the group are important tasks of collaboration and closely related to support tasks. Group members need strategies for negotiating and problem solving in order to successfully defuse conflict and create harmony. The following useful conflict resolution strategies ask students to balance the value of the interaction against the value of relationship between group members:

- *Withdrawing.* One person (or several people) withdraws from the interaction, recognizing that the interaction and its goal are not important enough to justify conflict.

- *Forcing.* Recognizing that the task is more important than the relationship, members use all their energy to get the task done.
- *Smoothing.* Recognizing that the relationship is more important than the task, individuals work at being liked and accepted.
- *Compromising.* The task and the relationship are both important, but there is a lack of time. Coming to an agreement by meeting half way or "giving in," members gain something and lose something but meet the deadline.
- *Confronting.* The task and the relationship are equally important, so the conflict is defined as a situation needing problem-solving techniques, rather than as a conflict between personalities.

Having a formal problem-solving strategy available is useful to groups that must confront and resolve conflicts. For example, cooperative learning groups could use the following five-step process for constructively addressing conflicts.

1. Define the problem and its causes.
2. Generate alternative solutions to the problem.
3. Examine the advantages and disadvantages to each alternative.
4. Decide upon and implement the most desirable solution.
5. Evaluate whether the solutions solve the problem.

For this problem-solving process to work, group members must define exactly what the problem is. On occasion, arriving at a definition can be difficult, but it is worth the effort. Only after the problem is defined do group members suggest alternative solutions and explore the consequences of each alternative. Group members then make a decision to *try* an alternative and to review the results within a stipulated period of time.

It may also be important to teach students confrontation skills and specific techniques for successful conflict resolution. As part of learning to collaborate, students should learn to:

- Describe behavior. Do not evaluate, label, accuse, or insult.
- Define the conflict as a mutual problem rather than a win/lose situation. The goal is to make the outcome a win/win situation.
- Use "I" statements not "you" statements (for example, say, "I think this idea will not work," rather than, "You are wrong").
- Communicate what they think and feel.
- Be critical of ideas, not people; affirm others' competence.
- Give everyone a chance to be heard.
- Follow the guidelines for rational argument.
- Make sure there is enough time for discussion.
- Take the other person's perspective.

Students engaged in cooperative learning must also learn negotiating as part of problem resolution. Negotiating involves mutual discussion and arrangement of the terms of an agreement. Learning to "read" another person's behavior for clues to an acceptable problem solution is crucial for determining what will appeal to that person and making a deal in which each participant's preferences and needs are considered.

Complementing task, support, and problem-solving behaviors are communication skills, particularly active listening. This latter skill involves both attending to and responding to group and individual efforts. Active listening allows all group members to be fully in tune with each other while allowing for discussion and elaboration. When group members acknowledge (perhaps by paraphrasing) the content, feelings, or meaning of other members' communications, they promote good will in the group and deeper understanding between themselves and others. When everyone is given a chance to express her or his ideas, participation of all members of the group is ensured, and group members feel secure in the knowledge that they are contributing to the group.

Peer Coaching

Peer coaching is a model that provides opportunities for students to assist and receive assistance from other students (and teachers from other teachers). When team members are peer coaches, they provide feedback, plan projects, help implement teaching suggestions, offer support, and give constructive criticism. They serve as a caring support group, assisting individuals over rough spots. They help individuals reflect, check perceptions, and share frustrations and successes. The give and take among group members will be constructively critical at times—good coaches are honest about peers' work. Peer coaches work together and share their ideas with other members of the collaborative team.

When team leaders are peer coaches, they learn how to promote positive learning transactions in the classroom. As active problem solvers and analytical thinkers, they strive to see all parts of a problem and the ways peers are thinking, delving deeply into inquiry and possible solutions to problems. The dialogues of all peer coaching are an interplay between feeling and thinking. When built on trust and the ethic of caring, these dialogues become an integral tool of learning, fulfilling learning's purpose, which is to "come into contact with ideas, to understand, and work cooperatively" (Noddings, 1984, p. 186).

Two Examples of Cooperative Activities

The following examples of a group poetry reading and a group problem-solving task illustrate how students can learn specific content
and bring their real-life problems into the classroom through collaborative learning, while also learning how to use roles in group
assignments and to apply critical thinking skills, consensus reaching skills, and a problem-solving model.

Reading and Analyzing a Poem

This activity involves teamwork in which students take specific
roles and illustrates a structure that is useful when students are to
analyze videos, newspaper articles, or literary works. The activity,
as shown here, works particularly well for analyzing poems because
they are often more open to interpretation than other literary works
and are typically short so that a single poem can easily be discussed
within a classroom hour. The poem by Langston Hughes (Hughes,
1990) used in the following example can provoke a lively discussion in which students learn about constructing a coherent argument and supporting a particular point of view through debate and
compromise. As an extension of the activity, groups could be
assigned to argue conflicting points of view and to gather evidence
to support their particular arguments.

For this activity, the class can be divided into groups of three,
consisting of a checker-animator, who makes sure everyone understands the directions and keeps the discussion lively but also
focused on the questions; a reader who reads the poem and the
directions to the group; and a recorder who explains and/or defends
his or her group's interpretation of the poem to the rest of the class.
Or the students can decide what roles there are. Students may
begin by reading the poem orally in their groups. On the second
reading, they assign roles.

Mother to Son

Well son, I'll tell you:
Life for me ain't been no crystal stair.
It's had tacks in it.
And splinters,
And boards torn up,
And places with no carpet on the floor—
Bare.
But all the time
I'se been a-climbin' on
And reachin' landin's,
And turnin' corners,
And sometimes goin' in the dark
Where there ain't been no light.
So, boy, don't you turn back.
Don't you set down on the steps
'Cause you finds it's kinder hard.
Don't you fall now—
For I'se still goin', honey,
I'se still goin' honey,
I'se still climbin',
And life for me ain't been no crystal stair.

by Langston Hughes

After students have read the poem, each group's reader reads instructions that ask the group to write three different answers to the following questions and try to reach a consensus on the best possible solution. The group is asked to work cooperatively and told that everyone must agree on and be able to explain the group's responses to the questions. Each group should write answers to the following questions:

1. What are the emotions/attitudes expressed by the mother in the poem?
2. What are your reactions (feelings and thoughts) to the poem?
3. What do you think are three key words in the poem?
4. What is the poem saying?

Solving a Problem in Management

For this activity divide the class into groups of three. Explain that the students will be involved in solving a problem experienced by some schoolchildren living in Trenton, New Jersey (specifying who has the problem makes problem-solving activities more realistic). These children have a real problem: every day, they complain about slow service in the cafeteria grill. The groups' task is to help them solve their problem. Explain how the problem-solving procedure works and that it is divided into sections: fact finding, problem finding, brainstorming, coming up with solutions, and coming to consensus. Join the students in solving this real-life problem. This group activity could be brought to closure by forming a panel or round table to discuss the issue and try to find solutions or even producing a video that can be put on the local cable television public access channel. Each group could also be assigned the cooperative task of meeting with another group so that group members could explain their conclusions. All of this positive group work involves face-to-face interaction, social skills, individual accountability, and group processing.

In addition to directions for the students and questions that they should ask, the activity shown here includes sample answers that the students might supply. Have students follow these steps (adapted from Dalton, 1991):

1. Find the facts. Ask these questions to get started:

What do we know? *Lunch time is a problem.*

What would we like to know? *Whether other people see it as a problem (teachers, principal, cafeteria workers), and why they see it as a problem.*

What resources might help us? *Talking with children and adults involved in the noon hour service and checking with other schools that have a similar lunch service.*

2.   Find the problem. Ask, What do we see as the problems?

Older children pushing in.

Too many children buying things.

Not enough cafeteria helpers.

No teachers on duty at the grill.

Students getting tired of waiting.

Bad manners.

Slow grill service.

What is the most important problem? *Slow grill service.*

Restate the problem so that you can work on ideas for it: *How to improve grill service so that it is fair to all children, teachers, and helpers.*

3.   Brainstorm as many ways as you can think of to solve the problem. Remember, accept all ideas, do not judge.

Schedule times students can use.

Get more volunteers for the grill.

Open the grill only on certain days.

Use fast food service goods in the grill.

Open two grills.

Teach students better manners.

Write to school council and ask them to pay for more helpers.

4. Come up with a possible solution by evaluating the list of brainstormed solutions. Ask, How will we judge or analyze ideas? What criteria will we use?

A. *How much will the solution cost?*

B. *Is the solution fair to everyone?*

C. *Is the solution difficult to organize?*

Using an analysis grid or scaffolding (Exhibit 3.1), assign points to your brainstormed solutions. Ask how well each solution meets each item of your criteria. Give 3 points to a good solution, 2 points to a fair solution, and 1 point to a poor solution. The solution with the highest number of points is probably your best solution.

5. Come to a consensus. *Get more volunteer helpers.*

Ask, How will we put our plan into action? Define the action steps. After defining the steps, ask, What problems might we have? How can we deal with them?

Step 1. *Interview principal, grill helpers, and students. Do a survey and graph the results.*

Step 2. *Present a verbal and a typed report to the principal and the grill supervisor. Gain support for plan.*

Step 3. *Design posters to hang in community places.*

Step 4. *Write and duplicate letters to send home with each student.*

Step 5. *Write a report on the grill investigation and its outcomes for the school newspaper and local newspaper.*

Exhibit 3.1. Sample Analysis Grid.

Solution	Criterion A	Criterion B	Criterion C	Total Points
Set up a schedule of times				
Get more volunteer helpers				
Open two grills				
Teach better manners				
Have school council pay for more helpers				

Assessment and Professional Development

Evaluating cooperative learning requires a variety of procedures. In spite of new evaluative techniques on the horizon, schools will probably continue to measure and evaluate some learning outcomes by such instruments as standardized tests, quizzes, and written exams. Fortunately, new performance-based tests that have open-ended questions and problem-solving functions are starting to be used. The collaborative classroom can make use of these perfor-mance-based tests and of such measures as portfolios and holistic grading (see Chapter Five). It is also important for students to be involved in evaluating their own learning products, the classroom climate, and their individual skill development.

Self-evaluation and peer evaluation must also be a part of teacher assessment in the cooperative learning classroom. Teaching is a dynamic act that creates and realizes decision-making power over what happens in the classroom. Teachers are autonomous problem solvers and, as such, require a professional work environment. The new wave of school reform changes top-down management organizational structures to structures based on teacher empowerment.

This professional power must go hand in hand with responsibility. As students of teaching, teachers cannot put in their class time and skip the homework. Assessing and coaching colleagues is now part of the job description. Professional development and peer coaching work best when they, too, are based the concept of cooperative learning. A small support group of colleagues, bound by an ethic of caring, can go over the work done by individual teachers, offer constructive criticism, and give suggestions. Professional development and support is for *everyone*, and schools are now offering counseling from outstanding teachers and remedial intervention programs to teachers who are having trouble.

Changing classroom organizational patterns and teaching strategies requires systematic staff development and the association of like-minded colleagues. It also takes time, practice, and systematic support for the vital energy inherent in new skills to become part of teachers' repertoires. Such basic changes in the organization of learning also require a school environment where it is safe to make mistakes and safe to learn from those mistakes.

Hands-on, "minds-on" interaction with peers raises awareness and instills confidence in a way that reading or hearing about a new teaching strategy cannot. After some initial experiences with cooperative learning, teachers' rough edges can be smoothed with additional reading, practice, and on-site peer mentoring. Teacher workshops and university classes can help—especially when teachers try activities, share experiences, and give and receive assistance within a collegial structure that supports collaboration. As group members become comfortable with sharing their concerns, teachers can discover each other's personal and professional roles. As peers help with planning, implementation, and feedback, and as teachers experience the various processes of cooperative learning themselves, they come more fully to understand the power of the technique (Johnson, 1990).

Simply putting students in heterogeneous classes and teaching the same old curriculum is not good enough for educational reform. Other aspects of instructional practice must also be meaningfully changed—deepened, extended, and strengthened. As schools focus on the depth and quality of thoughtful work, classes will be far more useful for students and teachers. Teachers need methods, materials, and time to plan before they can make untracked classes work up to their potential. To move toward untracking the curriculum requires patience, cooperation, thorough planning, and professional development.

The Future of Collective Learning

Cooperative learning brings students to the edge of many possibilities, sharing visions and understandings that can enhance individual learning. By actively engaging students in the collaborative process, teachers have been able to integrate the teaching of social skills and critical thinking with academic content. With the support of teachers and a solid research base, collective learning is becoming this nation's most widely used instructional innovation (Clarke, Wideman, & Eadie, 1990), destined to make a real difference in U.S. education.

Chapter Four

Electronic Learning

New ways of relating to information require a break from habit. Thousands of years ago, we developed the written word to record information. Next, we developed the printing press. Today, we are learning multimedia computing, the coming together of computers, video, sound, and animation. Every new development in information handling has dramatically affected the way we educate our children.

Computers and television have a tremendous impact on children. We shape technological advances, and they shape us— not always for the better. Some, like television, are often written about as Lady Caroline Lamb wrote about the poet Byron, "mad, bad, and dangerous to know," and both computers and television are sometimes seen as particularly dangerous enemies, creating a culture of electronic peeping Toms that has no moral foundation (Kiesler, Siegel, & McGuire, 1984).

Yet the yeast of knowledge, openness, and enterprise raises the need for a multiplicity of learning media and technological tools. In spite of the dangers, it is the authors' belief that schools can use technology to support and strengthen the best in student learning, helping students harness these powerful tools on behalf of worthwhile human endeavors. Our schools can also teach students to recognize how poorly used technology can undermine social values, human goals, and national intentions.

This chapter concerns not only specific ideas for selecting and using computers, television, and multimedia programs to teach the subject matter, critical thinking skills, and cooperative learning skills the future will demand from our students but also the ways educators must respond to the changes that television and computers are making in our world. We must take on the responsibility for teaching students how to understand and evaluate the information, much of it in the form of entertainment and advertising, that parades for hours daily on our television and computer screens.

Media Symbol Systems and the Character of Education

Print and video (film, television, or computer visuals) take different approaches to communicating meaning. Print relies upon the reader's ability to interpret abstract symbols. The image on a video screen is more direct. The screen's life-like visual symbol systems are made up, in part, of story structure, pace, sound track, and color and other connotational concepts. Computers, distant data bases, and television, in an array of guises, are rapidly becoming our dominant cultural tools for selecting, gathering, storing and conveying knowledge in representational forms (Bagdikian, 1987). Each communication medium makes use of its own distinctive technology for gathering, encoding, sorting, and conveying its contents associated with different situations. The technological mode of a medium affects its interaction with its users just as the method for transmitting content affects the knowledge acquired. However, broadly speaking, in both print and video, thinking and learning are based on internal symbolic representations and the mental interpretation of those symbols. What is more, the impact of either print or video can be amplified by the other. (The idea of print as an immutable canon is a historical illusion.)

Symbolically different media presentations vary in the mental processing skills they require, and each individual learns to use each medium's symbolic forms for purposes of internal representation (Bianculli, 1992). To even begin to read, a child needs to understand thought-symbol relationships. To move beneath the surface of video imagery requires some of the same understandings. It takes skill to break one's mind free from the effortless wash of images and electronically induced visual quicksand on the video screen. Training is required to develop students into critical video consumers who are literate in interpreting and processing the visual images they receive watching twenty-five-plus hours of television every week at home and working five hours a week at school on computers.

Learning does seem to be affected more by *what* is delivered than by the delivery system itself. In other words, the quality of a learning program is key (Anderson, 1983). But different media are more than alternative routes to the same end. Studies also suggest that specific media attributes call on different sets of mental skills and, by doing so, cater to different learning styles (Saloman, 1979). The video screen *is* changing the texture of learning. Processing must always take place and it always requires skill. The closer the match between the way information is presented and the way it can be mentally represented, the better it is communicated and the easier it is to learn. Better communication means easier processing and more transfer. Recent research suggests that voluntary attention and the formation of ideas can be facilitated by electronic media, with the concepts taught becoming part of the child's repertoire (Brown, 1988). Thus, new educational choices are laid open by electronic technologies. Understanding and employing these choices well will require us to interpret the new technological literacies from a critical perspective. We would also do well to remember that historically, while certain educational principles have remained constant, each step along the way from speech to handwritten texts to printed texts required major changes in teaching and learning.

Since the field of education seems to be entering a unique period of introspection, self-doubt, and great expectations, theoretical guidelines are needed as much as specific methods. If we want to give teachers the freedom to reach educational goals, we must know what those goals are. It is dangerous to function in a goalless vacuum, because rituals can spring up that are worse than those drained away. As electronic learning devices flood our schools and homes, we need to be sure that we link findings about these devices to teaching practice and that we define educational needs in both theoretical *and* practical ways. If theory and practice are not integrated, then one will get in the way of the other.

A wide range of intellectual tools can be used to help students understand social and physical reality. Technology can be one of these tools, or it can be an instrument to subvert human integrity. To avoid the latter fate, adults and children need to have control over the technology they are using. The research suggests that for students to be creative in print they must read good literature, know how to search out information, write for a real reader, tap their personal experiences, and cooperatively edit their material. Students' learning about electronic communication technology can follow a similar pattern, reaching students by opening their eyes to things they might not have thought of on their own. Students can come to understand technology while technological tools help them tap into real experience, fantasies, and personal visions. A combination of thoughtful strategies and the enabling features of video tools can achieve lasting cognitive change and improved performance (Riel, 1989). Through a mind-eye approach, previously obscure concepts can become comprehensible to students, with greater depth, at an earlier age.

Print, writing, and hand-drawn pictures (the oldest technological media) have been the cognitive tools that Western culture has traditionally chosen to teach children. Good theoretical and practical techniques developed for understanding how these traditional communication media interact with human learning will be helpful in understanding the new media—even after we have gone beyond the current technological horizons. As print, computers, and video merge, children and young adults can develop explicit metacognitive strategies as they search for data, solve problems, and graphically simulate their way through multiple levels of abstraction.

Television and Telecomputers: Change and New Values

Information and communication technologies are reshaping the face of our social institutions and the world of work, with very little planning or control being exercised by anyone over the ingredients or the outcome of this change. Entertainment programming on television may well be our single most important source of cultural and political information. Truth has become what clever advertising says it is, blocking out reality and affecting the core of our democracy. And advertising is by no means only for goods and services—special interest groups now run ads that promote their views and discredit the views of others. Some social and political analysts, however, see light at the end of the tunnel. They argue that citizens are becoming more politically and culturally aware and are demanding more choice. They view the promised new age of interactive television, the telecomputer, as a way around passivity, releasing Americans from the hold of the mass media (Guilder, 1992). But interactive television will not automatically be an improvement over today's television unless we educate students to use this new medium to advantage.

Democracy becomes what it pays attention to. A democratic community is defined by the quality of its educational institutions and its public conversations. Our national values, supported by our Constitution, require educated citizens who can think and respond to leaders, and who are actively willing to go beyond the kind of patriotism that largely follows the flag and stern rhetoric. We need the kind of patriotism that supports a thinking, decent, and literate society that exercises citizenship. Ignoring the increasing role of technology in our political and social processes means ignoring both looming changes and bright possibilities. A world of accelerated change requires our full, thoughtful attention if we are to preserve our humanity and our human values. Technologically induced passivity can lull us, as can the seductive, simplistic belief that technology by itself will solve our problems. To avoid this fate, we must help people gain a heightened awareness of human and technological possibilities, and that can occur only through the educational process.

The long-term implications of the ongoing changes in the communication media are important, if not frightening. The convergence of technologies is causing a major change in societal behaviors, life styles, and thinking patterns. With few people monitoring the change—or theorizing about its healthiness—electronic media are creating vast knowledge highways. And the human race is being forced to communicate through an electronic web of ideas before any quality assurance tests have been performed on the system. Bill McKibben (1992, p. 42) paints the problem this way: "We have come to worship 'communication' and the technology that enables it to occur at unprecedented rates and volumes. What is missing is information about the physical limits of a finite world. About sufficiency and need, about proper scale and real time, about sensual pleasure of exertion and exposure to the elements, about the need for community and solid, real skills."

In the latter part of the twentieth century, there is little question that our reality is being shaped by electronic information *and* electronic illusions. *The future will be televised.* The question is, How might the cathode ray tube be used to spark a renaissance in human learning, thinking, and communication? In the last decade, research on educational technology has begun to provide some understanding of how new communication media affect cognitive and affective development.

Visual Models and Learning

Studies confirm that the power and permanency of what we learn from the printed word is greater when visually based mental models are used in conjunction with that print. Inferences drawn from visual models can lead to more profound thinking (Dorr, 1986). There are indications that the perception of reality as it appears on a video screen is a mediating factor in forming personal behavior and social attitudes across age groups (Dorr, 1986). Children learn to rely on their perceptual (visual) learning even if their conceptual knowledge contradicts it. The video screen's potent visual experiences push viewers to accept what is presented even when the images run contrary to verbal explanations or personal experience.

Children can become adept at extracting meaning from the conventions of video production—zooms, pans, tilts, fade-outs, and flashbacks. But distinguishing fact from fiction is more difficult. Piaget showed how certain notions of time, space, or morality are beyond children's grasp before certain developmental levels are reached. Research on television viewing suggests that it is not vocabulary limitation alone that impedes children from grasping some adult content (Dede, 1985). Young children can usually distinguish between fantasy and reality, but they do not know what is needed to understand the subtle meanings often assumed by adult television. The result is that a child's response to adult programming is typically skewed toward his or her own distinct needs (Tripp & Hodge, 1986). Children lack the fundamental integrative capacities needed to "chunk" (or group) certain kinds of information into meaningful groups of the kind obvious to adults. Thus, children who need help in developing strategies for tuning out irrelevancies may be especially vulnerable to unwanted adult content (McKibben, 1992).

Most of the time, children construct meaning for television content without even thinking about it. They attend to stimuli and extract a meaning from subtle messages. The underlying message that children (and many adults) receive from most television programming is that viewers should consume as much as possible while changing as little as possible. If we want children to construct better, more useful meanings from their viewing, we must help them to understand the conventions of the television screen and to turn these conventions into new tools for handling information and exploring the world. We must increase their ability to critically analyze, interpret, and extract meaning from video messages and help them become intelligent video consumers who understand the specific techniques and philosophical nuances of the dominant electronic medium in our society (Adams & Hamm, 1987).

Sorting through the themes offered up to viewers requires carefully developed thinking skills. What viewers perceive on the screen they place within their framework for concept formation. Individuals who possess an adequate conceptual framework and can respond thoughtfully rather than uncritically to what they perceive are becoming ever more central to learning and to our society. For better or worse, broadcast television has provided us with a common culture. When viewers share a common culture, they ought to share similar sets of tools and processes (abilities to construct meaning, process information, interpret, and evaluate) for making sense of cultural artifacts such as television programs. In addition, generalized world knowledge is important for processing and using televised information. Like print, visual imagery from a television (or telecomputer) screen can be mentally processed at different levels of complexity. The greater the viewer's experiential background, the greater his or her understanding. The ability to make subtle judgments about video imagery is a developmental outcome, growing out of an accumulation of viewing experience. Thus, as mentioned earlier, different age groups reveal varying levels of comprehension when they view television programs. Eight-year-olds, for example, retain a relatively small proportion of central actions, events, or settings of typical programs. Even when they do retain explicit content, younger children fail to infer interscene connections. Improvement in comprehension occurs with maturity. But for children to acquire a substantial understanding of the medium of television, they must be trained, as must their parents and teachers.

For children, this training can occur during lessons structured around the medium of television, and should be designed to assist and encourage children to become intelligent video consumers. Many public television stations are now offering special workshops for teachers in the effective classroom use of educational television programs. One technique from these workshops includes selecting a short segment from a program for viewing, designing carefully crafted questions about the segment, getting students to talk together about what they watched, replaying the tape with the sound off, and encouraging students to come up with two or three things they found out from the segment and to share that information with others. Have students look for and identify propaganda techniques and act them out or make up some propagandizing material or advertisements of their own in order to understand the devices better. Evaluation of television viewing can also promote important comprehension skills. Encourage students to analyze and rate what they view.

People learn best if they take an active role in their own learning. Relying upon a host of cognitive inputs, individuals select and interpret the raw data of experience to produce a personal understanding of reality. Ultimately, it is up to each person to determine what she or he pays attention to and what she or he ignores. How elements are organized and how meaning is attached to any concept are individual acts that can be influenced by a number of external agents. The thinking that must be done to make sense of perceptions ultimately transforms the "real world" into different things for different people.

What an individual understands while viewing depends on the interplay of images and social conditions. Physical stimuli, human psychology, and the information processing schemes taught by his or her culture help each person make sense of the world. In this respect, reacting to and learning from television and its content is no different from learning from any other experience in life. The cathode ray tube can be as valid a source of information as the street or the school. It is just as possible to internalize ideas from electronic visual imagery as it is from conversation, print, or personal experience. Television is not exclusively a passive or mindless entertainment (marketing) device. Whether positive or negative, video imagery is an object of thought on which children can exercise their growing mental capacities.

Reflective thought and imaginative active play are an important part of the growth process of a child. Research has shown that, contrary to popular belief, children must do active work to watch television, make sense of its contents, and utilize its message (Anderson, 1983). Their evaluative activities include judging and assigning worth, assessing what is admired, and deciding what positive and negative impressions should be assigned to the content.

In some studies, it has been shown that, through an emphasis on show business values, fictional treatments, and magical effects, television is likely to distort awareness of reality (Hawkins & Pingree, 1981). Heavy television viewers have a vision of the world that is more like what they watch than it is like the real world. Data from U.S. Department of Health and Human Services (1982) research also suggest that the children most heavily oriented toward television viewing are likely to be less imaginative than other children and that children already predisposed to imaginative activities were the ones less attracted to the television medium. However, heavy viewing does not automatically result in stunted personal growth or poor academic achievement. And although broadcast television viewing may be inappropriate for certain children—it has been linked with aggressive behavior in a few and has harmed young viewers by displacing reading—some students have profited from television. An 1993 study by the National Research Center on the Gifted and Talented at the University of Connecticut suggests that television's unstructured and flexible nature should be "considered as a viable learning tool rather than as a detractor of attention, literacy, and learning skills." Several Japanese studies have found that many students who viewed a great deal of television actually got better grades than those who did not. Television, it seems, is too diffuse and contradictory in content to push viewers in a particular direction on its own, and this is why education is so important.

Thinking Tools to Assess Media Messages

Parents, teachers, and other adults can significantly affect what information children gather from television. Research shows that students' social, cultural, educational, and family contexts influence what messages students take from the medium, how they use it, and how literate they are as viewers (Bryant & Anderson, 1983). Anderson (1983) supports the view that today's students should be able to:

- Understand the grammar and syntax of television, as expressed in different program forms.
- Analyze the pervasive appeals of television advertising.
- Compare similar presentations or those with similar purposes in different media.
- Identify values in language, characterization, conflict resolution, and sound/visual images.
- Identify elements in dramatic presentations associated with the concepts of plot, storyline, theme, characterizations, motivation, program formats, and production values.
- Utilize strategies for the management of duration of viewing and program choices.

Both parents and teachers can engage in activities that affect children's interest in televised messages and teach them how to process video information. In particular, the length of time parents and siblings spend watching television, the kinds of programs they view, and their attitudes toward programming messages all have a large influence on a child (McLeod, Fitzpatrick, Glynn, & Fallis, 1982). Modeling good viewing behavior, interacting with the child during viewing, explaining content to show how it relates to the child's interests, and having rules about what may or may not be watched are just a few examples of the positive viewing motivation adults can provide. Adults can also exhibit an informed response, point out misleading television messages, and take care not to build curiosity for undesirable programs. If parents are heavy watchers of public television or news programming, then children are more likely to respond favorably to this content. (If adults read and there are books, magazines, and newspapers around the house, children will pay more attention to print.) Influencing the settings in which children watch television is also important. Turning the television set off during meals, for example, sends a message about family priorities. Families can also seek a more open and equal approach to choosing television shows, interacting before, during, and after a program. Parents can also organize formal or informal activities outside the house that provide alternatives to television viewing.

It is increasingly clear that the education of children is a shared responsibility. Parents need to be connected with the lessons taught in the schools. But it is teachers who will be called upon to make the educational connections between varieties of print and visual media on the one hand and language arts, reading, mathematics, science, and art on the other.

Activities to Make Sense of Television

Like an understanding of the conventions of print, an understanding of the conventions of television can cultivate tools of thought, giving the viewer new ways of handling and exploring the world. Interpretation of the action and messages on a video display terminal requires going beyond the surface image to the deep structure of the medium. Consumers' understanding of both the practical and philosophical nuances of a medium moves those consumers in the direction of mastery. Teachers can encourage students to become intelligent consumers of visual media through the following activities. As students carry out these and similar activities, they will also build a common body of experiences, humor, and feelings, and will work on critical thinking skills and the collaborative learning process. (Note that teachers do need to preview any videos before they are used in the classroom because some parts may not be appropriate for children. Teachers can also, as is suggested for the activities described here, select particular elements and record them on a separate tape so that the classroom tape contains only the useful segments.)

- *View television critically.* Decoding visual stimuli and learning from visual images requires practice. Seeing an image does not automatically ensure learning from it. Students must be guided in decoding and critical viewing. One technique is to have students "read" an image on various levels. Ask students to identify individual elements of the image and classify them into various categories, then relate the whole to their own experiences, drawing inferences and creating new concepts from what they have learned. Encourage students to look at the plot and story line and to identify the message of the program. What symbols (camera techniques, motion sequences, setting, lighting, and so forth) does the program use to make its message? What does the director do to arouse audience emotion and participation in the story? What metaphors and symbols are used?

- *Compare print and video messages.* Have students watch a current event as shown on the evening television news and compare that report to the same event as described in a major newspaper. A question for discussion might be, How do the major newspapers influence what appears on a national network's news program? Encourage comparisons between the two media: What are the strengths and weaknesses of each? What might the reasons be behind the different presentations of a similar event?

• *Evaluate television viewing habits*. After compiling a list of students' favorite television programs, assign students to analyze the reasons for these programs' popularity and to examine the messages these programs send to their audience. Do the same for students' favorite books, magazines, newspapers, films, songs, and computer programs. Have students look for similarities and differences between the media.

• *Use video for instruction*. Make frequent use of three- to five-minute video segments to illustrate different points about video messages. Focusing on a short segment is often more effective for teaching purposes than showing long videotapes or a film on videocassette. For example, you can show a five-minute segment from a videocassette movie to illustrate how one scene uses foreshadowing or music to set up the next scene and to influence the viewer.

• *Analyze advertising messages*. Advertisements provide a wealth of examples for illustrating the way media messages affect people. Move students progressively from advertisements in print to television commercials, allowing them to locate features such as packaging, color, and images that influence consumers and often distort reality. Analyze and discuss commercials in children's television programs, asking, How many minutes of advertising appear in an hour? How have toy manufacturers exploited the medium? What is the broadcasters' role? How should we respond to that role?

• *Create a scrapbook of media clippings*. Have students keep a scrapbook of newspaper and magazine clippings about television and its electronic associates. Have them paraphrase the articles or draw a picture or otherwise map out a personal interpretation of the articles and share the results with other students.

• *Create new images from old*. Have students take a mundane photograph and multiply the image, or combine it with other mundane images, in a way that makes the photograph interesting. Have students reflect on the new image and discuss why it is more interesting than the original image.

- *Use debate for critical thought*. Debating is a communication model that can serve as a lively facilitator for concept building. (Formally debating a current and relevant topic also serves to extend speech and language skills.) For example, the class can debate the real or potential role of the mass media in supporting political tyranny, public conformity, or the technological enslavement of society. The discussion can serve as a blend of social studies, science, and humanities study while encouraging thought about media roles.

- *Include newspapers, magazines, literature, and electronic material (brief television news clips for example) in daily class activities*. Use of the media and literature can enliven classroom discussion of current conflicts and dilemmas. Neither squeamish nor politically correct, these sources of information provide readers with something substantial to think and talk about, and they can be used to present the key conflicts and dilemmas of our time in ways that allow students to enter the discussion. With these sources of information, teachers can structure lessons that go beyond the delivery of facts to stimulate reading, critical thinking, and thoughtful discussion. By not concealing adult disagreements, teachers help students take responsibility for promoting understanding, engage them in moral reflection, and provide a coherence and a focus that help turn controversies into advantageous educational experiences.

- *Have students make their own video production*. Many Americans today videotape their own scenes with a camcorder (video-camera recorder). The results can be edited and then "dumped" into a standard VCR for playback. These new "video pencils" can transform the landscape of student visual creations. (They may also have a major impact on our society as more and more once "invisible" events are documented.)

Planning, visualizing, and developing a video production allows students to critically sort out and use video techniques to relay meaning. Young video producers should be encouraged to open their eyes to the world and visually experience what is out there.

By realizing their ideas through video production, students learn to redefine space and time, and use (and understand) media attributes such as structure, sound, color, pacing, and imaging. Video production gives students a powerful framework for evaluating, controlling, and creating in the video medium.

Computers: Making the Most of Technology

Computers are both evolutionary *and* revolutionary. They help us do some things (like typing and numeric calculating) better, *and* they conjure up new possibilities for critical thinking, collaborative learning, and creativity. In the 1980s, most personal computers were designed to run letter- and number-based programs, such as word-processing programs or spreadsheets. The new multimedia computers run programs containing still photos, video clips, and sophisticated graphics. This technology can have a liberating effect on individuals' imaginations and encourage fresh perspectives. Its positive effect on creative work goes beyond simply forcing communication patterns off established roads. Related electronic devices are also becoming common in the classroom. There are VCRs, camcorders, and palm-sized personal communicators that recognize cursive handwriting and can, among other things, send and receive wireless facsimiles. All these interactive conveyers of visual imagery, sound, and print give students and teachers another tool for manipulating imagery on video display screens and for understanding. Multimedia computing adds a new dimension to learning, assisting students' imaginative spirit of inquiry and making lessons sparkle—and as we struggle with school reform, we need all the help we can get.

As technological and human horizons change, we must find in ourselves a flexible drive and intent for innovation and progress. Technology helps us kick against educational boundaries; however, it will not do this without our being willing to actively use and experiment with it, realizing that our initial visions may be too narrow. Alexander Graham Bell thought when he invented the telephone that it would be used to listen to distant symphony concerts. Thomas Edison thought that the phonograph record would be used to send messages. Some of our best thinkers have missed the potential of their inventions. Physicist Heinrich Hertz was the first to generate and detect radio waves, yet he dismissed the notion that they might ever have practical value. Is there a relationship between preparation or predictive thinking and luck? Do we increase our chances of success by trying more avenues and being prepared to take advantage of what is offered to us to work with? We should also recall the lordly condescension of the British post office's chief engineer toward Bell's invention: "the Americans may have need of the telephone, but we do not, we have plenty of messenger boys" (Clarke, 1992). We should not dismiss the new technology as irrelevant to education, thinking we can already do what it does in other ways.

It is often difficult to detect subtle happenstance and to know how we make room in our own lives for positive accidents to happen, but exposing ourselves to different experiences and paying attention opens up all kinds of possibilities. A healthy prescription for future-oriented thinking is to follow your curiosity, leave doors open, and use technological tools, making room for good luck to happen. Training your eye to notice things goes a long way toward making unpredictable visions and advances happen. Each new finding can open up fresh questions and possibilities, breaking the habits that get in the way of creative thinking and change. Anything that changes perspective, from travel to technology to human teaching, can help generate new ideas. Motivation is also present, because it is usually more fun to do things in which the unexpected may turn up than to stick with the predictable. The playful gleam in the eye is often an engine of progress, increasing the individual's capacity to fashion novel ideas or products. Creatively playing with ideas, some of which may seem silly at the time, may result in getting lucky with one or two of them.

Technological tools for education should be designed to open multiple doors to reality and provide a setting for reflection. Progress in school reform will be limited if teachers are forced to use traditional instructional delivery tools or models. "Ask and tell" and "tell and ask" are limited patterns, with or without a computer. The new computer-based multimedia programs are more interactive, profiting from findings regarding cognitive development and collaborative learning. Computer-based activities can have problem-centered structures that wrap learning experiences around problems in new ways as students visually enter the human body as a blood cell or explore another planet. Using such multimedia activities in the form of either computer programs or interactive television, students learn to refine and use knowledge meaningfully. If we allow new technologies to fulfill their promise in the classroom, students will become active participants in knowledge construction across a variety of disciplines, passing through a technological gateway to learning in the twenty-first century. As state-of-the-art pedagogy is connected with state-of-the-art technological tools, we will change not only the way knowledge is learned and stored but also the way new knowledge is constructed.

Computers: Hardware and Students' Capability

Having an idea of the technical platform that computer programs, especially multimedia programs, require makes it easier for those who are using these programs to visualize the programs' effects. The hardware for multimedia is simply a computer with a videodisc player and speakers plugged into it, and sometimes a speech synthesizer. Each CD-ROM (compact disc—read only memory) or videodisc has room to store the contents of many video tapes. Most importantly, videodiscs have a random access feature that allows users to move quickly to any part of a video that they wish to view. With this technology, for example, a user can set her or his computer to access a particular section of a video, play that section, then access a different file to view printed material describing the imagery on the video. If the user wants to replay the section or switch to another part of the disk, she or he can do so with a few strokes on the computer keyboard.

New computer programs use windowing techniques that can place several images from different programs on the screen, allowing users to move easily between types of information. In some systems, a viewer can even zoom in on an item or pull away from it, turn it, or flip it to get a closer view. When a telecommunications modem is added to the computer, students can communicate with libraries and schools across the country. Some multimedia workstations even have built-in videocameras so that users can hold video teleconferences with people in distant locations and construct their own video compositions on videodisc. Although currently many of the best multimedia programs are designed to run on a Macintosh computer, versions for IBM compatibles are starting to arrive on the software shelves.

Students should also be acquiring personal technical platforms as they go through school. By the time they get to high school, they should be able to access information, process words, create images, and solve problems with computers.

Computers as Tools and Tutors

When microcomputers first appeared in schools in the early 1980s, most instructional computer work consisted of learning programming languages or using drill and practice software as a kind of electronic worksheet. By the mid 1980s, we started to see educational software that used the unique characteristics of the medium to enhance students' learning. For today's students a computer can be a great help with everything from essay writing to mathematical applications to brushing up on subject information. Two types of software are of particular interest: multimedia and hypertext.

Multimedia

The vivid images of multimedia can stimulate students as they move quickly through mountains of information, pulling out important concepts and following topics of interest. This process changes students' relationship to information by allowing them to personally shift the relationship of elements across time and space. In the natural and social sciences, computer simulations allow students to learn from experiments that they would not get to perform otherwise. Computer applications in biology, chemistry, engineering, ergonomics, physics, psychology, and physiology allow teachers to create simulations that conform to and illustrate the normal laws of the universe. Research shows that students benefit when they are given control over system parameters and can explore their effects (Stark & Metz, 1988). It is even more helpful when children can choose their own routes for information gathering and analysis. The computer materials that are most effective and most popular provide social interaction along with problem solving. Using computer platforms with multimedia possibilities, learners can follow a topic through more than one standard classroom subject, reading something here and viewing a video segment there, changing and controlling how the information they receive is structured. This process gives students more control of the technology than in the days of computerized drills and makes students take more responsibility for their learning.

Capitalizing on computer-controlled interactive activities, teachers can reach a child through many senses. Information can be embedded in visual narratives to create contexts that give meaning to dry facts. For example, computers can use mathematical rules to simulate and synthesize life-like behavior of cells growing and dividing. Multiscreen videodisc systems allow students to become involved in distant, dangerous, or rare situations: to tour rare archaeological finds in China or simulate running a nuclear power plant or even, with a program like *Voyager: The*

Interactive Desktop Planetarium, simulate a journey into outer space. Instead of listening to a lecture or looking up information in a book, they can investigate what is out there themselves, using the sound, graphics, and video capabilities of multimedia computers. Children will often pass up passive television viewing when they can use a computer or game controller to interact with a visual medium. Many children, for example, are already familiar with the courseware *Where in the World Is Carmen Sandiego*. They learn geography by electronically rushing around the world, trying to catch up with Carmen. When the computer-controlled version goes up against the linear PBS television program of the same name, the interactive version usually wins hand down because of its higher levels of personal involvement.

Software is becoming available that helps students understand imagery, solve problems creatively, and apply these solutions to real life situations. A recent ABC news program, for example, showed how inner-city children applied the concepts of city planning by solving such problems as crime, unemployment, and transportation for imaginary cities via computer software. They could apply what they learned by suggesting solutions to real world problems of actual cities. And they could explore how things would look from street level if their city plan were built.

With a grant from the Annenberg Foundation and help from the University of Pennsylvania, the National Gallery of Art recently distributed 2,500 videodiscs with visual and print information about the gallery's collection to schools in areas with the greatest need. Thus, students in juvenile detention centers, in the inner city, and in homeless shelters got a chance to experience the power of art. Like the majority of U.S. youth, most of these students have never set foot inside an art gallery. At the 1993 Association for Supervision and Curriculum Development (ASCD) Conference, Robert Coles spoke of helping these struggling children by "going for the contact" and building on the motivating potential of art. He used such gallery paintings as Edward Hopper's

"Midnight Cafe" to help students understand connections between themselves and universal human emotions like loneliness, observing that his goal was "to reach the heart so that the mind will become awakened."

Hypertext and Interactive Literature

Is the print medium a doomed and outdated technology? In the future, will books be found mainly in dusty museums that were once libraries? No, the modern era is not the end of books. But there is a new electronic kid on the block who takes traditional narrative and places it in randomly accessible blocks of text and graphics. Some of the new computer-based programs even add sound and video to these equally empowered chunks of meaning. This new writing is called hypertext. It is a remarkable new way of putting students in touch with what they are reading or viewing, because it puts students in charge of the story. They are able to change the sequence of events, change or make up a new beginning or ending, or choose to find out additional information.

Navigating stories with no fixed center, beginning, or end can be very disconcerting to the uninitiated. Because interactive literature asks the user to break down some of the walls that usually separate the reader from what is being read, hypertext requires reading skills different from the linear skills required by most books. To make sense of the resulting anarchy and chaos, hypertext readers have to become creators, discovering new themes, concepts, and outcomes as they choose their own paths through a web of information.

Interactive Storytime, for example, tells stories with narration, print, music, sound effects, and graphics. Using a mouse, children can click on any object shown on the computer screen and connect the spelling of the object's name to its pronunciation. In the story *Just Grandma and Me*, children can click on a dozen or more different objects to affect the story line. Click on the window, and

Grandma's dog wakes up and enters the story; click on the mailbox, and the letters come out; click on a flower, and out comes a new character, a bee to bother Grandma.

Traditional literature is structured as a linear progression worked out in advance by the author. The reader brings his or her own background and unique interpretation to what the author has written, but the author provides the basic sequential structure that pushes all readers in the same direction. Computer-based literature is quite different. Each hypertext fiction allows the reader to choose what to look at next. The reader shapes the story line by choosing the next expository sequence from a vast web of printed text, which may also include (and more and more often does include) sound, graphics, and life-like video. As key words or images are highlighted on a computer screen, the reader clicks what he or she wants next (either with a mouse or, in some systems, by putting a finger on the screen) and hops into a new place in the story and a new set of outcomes.

The forking paths in this electronic literature pose new challenges for readers—for example, how do you know when you have finished reading when you can just keep circling through the web on new paths? When you can no longer follow someone else's predetermined path, good reading and writing skills become more important than ever. Judy Malloy's hypertext fiction *Its Name Was Penelope* shuffles 400 pages of a fictional woman's memories so that they come together very differently every time you read it. If you do not like one ending, you can loop back and change it to another. Hypertext authors Carolyn Guyer and Martha Petry include suggestions to help new readers through the patterns, layers, and rhythmic looping of their *Izme Pass*. Some readers will need all the help they can get as they travel in a continuously shifting web of incidents. However, today's children are used to television programs (from "Sesame Street" on up) that move quickly among short segments of information. In addition, many of the educational computer programs found in elementary schools require students to wander in a maze of ideas. As a result, students may not be as disoriented as many of their elders are by the various forms of interactive literature.

While many of the early hypertext efforts were more like interactive comic books than literature, the new programs are more sophisticated and provide us with hints of a new literary genre. However ill-defined it may be at this moment, *something* important to the future of literature is happening. Schools will have to build some of the elements of the new genre into their reading and language arts curriculum and be prepared to help both teachers and children explore the new meanings of literacy in our contemporary computerized culture.

Sources for Software

The following list contains the authors' current multimedia favorites, all convincing ways to bring the schooling process to life.

> *Apple Early Language Connections* (available from Apple Computer). Literature-based product for K–2.
>
> *The Chicago Art Institute* (available from Voyager Company).
>
> *Computer Visions: The Electronic Instructional Media System for Teaching Computer Literacy* (available from South Western Publishing Company).
>
> *English Express* (available from Davidson; Teaching Tools for Teachers).
>
> *The Great Solar System Rescue* (available from Tom Synder Productions). Simulation.
>
> *Interactive NOVA* (available from Scholastic Software). Specifically recommended titles in this series are *The Race to Save the Planet, Animal Pathfinders,* and *Miracle of Life.*
>
> *Introductory Games in Spanish, Introductory Games in French,* and *Playing with Language* (available from Syracuse Lan-

guage Systems). Multimedia language instruction for children.

Just Grandma and Me (available from Broderbund Software). A title from the Living Books Series.

The Macmillan Dictionary for Children—Multimedia Edition (available from Maxwell Electronic Publishing).

Martin Luther King, Jr. ABC News interactive videodisc.

Multimedia Beethoven (available from Microsoft Corporation).

Multimedia Grolier Encyclopedia (available from Grolier Electronic Publishing).

National Air and Space Museum Archives (available from Smithsonian Institution). Three videodiscs containing still photographs of rockets, airplanes, and important events and people in the history of aviation and space exploration.

National Gallery of Art (available from Videodisc Publishing). A narrative history of the National Gallery of Art collection and a tour of the gallery plus 1,645 color images of the art work in chronological order. A print index orders the frames by author and title.

Science 2000 (available from Decision Development Corporation). Thematic approach to science study.

Prices and general sources of software for the classroom will, of course, be changing as the technology evolves. However, here are some observations that will give you ideas about where software is available, now or in the not-too-distant future. Some hypertext pieces can be found, free of charge, on electronic bulletin boards. Bought off the shelf, some are comparable to a traditional book in price, but the ones that use multimedia are fairly expensive. For example, the electronic fiction *Agrippa,* by science fiction writer William Gibson, is packaged with copper etchings (which change over time when exposed to light) and sells for more than $500. On a more affordable scale, a New York publisher is working with cable operators to set up a channel so that hypertext works can simply be downloaded and used at home. More than a dozen texts of fiction, humor, and politics have already been put into an interactive literature format that can be carried on cable. In addition, the Simon & Schuster Education Group has formed a partnership with Franklin Electronic Publishers in order to accommodate educators' desire to use textbook funds to purchase a mixture of electronic and print materials. A more "California dreamin'" kind of approach is a proposal for a hypertext network, to be called Xanadu—from the people in Marin County, in particular Ted Nelson, who brought you the terms hypertext and hypermedia (which has faded into multimedia).

You might also consider writing your own material. Writing original hypertext is not as hard as you might think. Nearly everyone with a Macintosh computer has Apple's HyperCard program, which electronically shuffles the chunks of narrative and graphics in hypertext works. More complex programs for producing hypertext, such as Storyspace and Intermedia, are also available, though favored more by commercial writers than educators. (There is no need in any of these programs to do any computer programming.) Using these tools, a few schools are even encouraging students as hypertext writers and artists.

Evaluating Software

In an informal survey of public school children, the authors found that those most familiar with computers were also most excited about educational computing. Familiarity with good programs seemed to breed positive attitudes toward evaluating software, modifying existing programs, and incorporating computer-based instruction into instructional plans.

The teachers in our survey who indicated that they were familiar with educational computing also felt that it was possible for microcomputer courseware to stand side by side with books as an

Exhibit 4.1. Teachers' Software Evaluation Checklist.

1. Does the program meet the students' age and attention demands?

2. Does the program hold the students' interest?

3. Does the program develop, supplement, or enhance curricular skills?

4. What examples does the program use to teach these skills?

5. What prerequisite skills do students need to use the program?

6. Does the program require adult supervision or instruction?

7. Children need to actively control what a program does. To what extent does the program allow this?

8. Can the program be modified to meet individual learning requirements?

9. Does the program have animated graphics to enliven the lesson?

10. Does the program meet instructional objectives, and is it educationally sound?

11. Does the program involve higher-level thinking and problem solving?

12. What activities would serve as a follow-up to this program?

13. How will students' performance be evaluated?

14. Do the students like the program? Teachers should reserve their final opinion about any courseware until they have seen it used by the students. Some teachers may find particular courseware motivating and easy to integrate into their instructional program; others may disagree. The bottom line is, Do you like it?

important instructional tool. And, like books, software programs were viewed as good, bad, or indifferent. It takes training to be able to tell the difference. The checklist in Exhibit 4.1 will help teachers evaluate software in relation to their students' needs. Moreover, as they observe students using technology in informal and formal sessions, teachers are conducting a kind of action research that will teach them as much about applying technology as any textbook.

An additional way to evaluate software for classroom use is to have students do it. Given the tools, children are capable of more penetrating evaluative thinking and intensive inquiry than has traditionally been allowed for in our schools, and the child's view is an important consideration because the program must make sense to the child. Having students work together on software evaluation can be turned to an excellent learning experience. Moreover, even the most technologically advanced teacher does not have time to review all the programs that come down the pike. Teachers can give a new program to a couple of students, have them figure it out, teach it to two others—and then show the teacher how it works. Allowing students to have a hand in constructing the learning process can both assist the teacher and help build a learning community.

Multimedia, simulations, Logo microworlds, word processors, interactive literature, spreadsheets, data base managers, expert (artificial intelligence) systems, and modem/software combinations (telecommunications) that put the computer in touch with the outside world—all these formats and options increase the potential for influencing impressionable minds. But they also represent time-consuming points to be evaluated, constituting too large a universe for the teacher to figure out alone. Teachers can and must help each other here, of course, but the task becomes much more approachable when students take some of the responsibility.

A curriculum should be a cooperative and interactive venture between students and teachers. On both an individual and a social level, those directly involved with the process must be taken seriously. Working together, they can decide what benefits are gained from particular software programs. After all, the software user is in the best position to decide if the program takes learners out of the process or lets the learners be in control of the computer. Good software programs let students learn together at their own pace—visualizing, talking together, and explaining abstract concepts so that they can relate them to real-life situations.

Children can learn to critique both computer software and television programming much as they learn to critique books. One of the first tenets of book review criticism is to critique what is usually taken for granted. Another is that a critic must have at least a little affection for the medium being critiqued. Why not have students produce "book reports" on computer software programs? This is the most interesting way to approach the software evaluation process. Similar concerns tend to run through all evaluations even though the process is very subjective and personal; thus, students can use sample book, theater, television, and movie reviews from newspapers as models.

Students can begin their software evaluation by sifting through professional software evaluations and advertisements in magazines and journals, checking to see if the flow of a program makes sense. Next they can try out the software as they think a peer would use it, asking, What happens when mistakes are made? How are the graphics? Do I think I can learn anything from this? Is it exciting? The students' software evaluation checklist in Exhibit 4.2 can guide students through a review process.

Data Highways and Interactive Media: The Shape of Things to Come

Before many of us have understood what our relationship with the current technology should be, major technological advances are recasting the potential of that relationship, combining television, computing, and telecommunications in new ways. These advances are emerging at a time when the Federal Communications Commission (FCC) and the government are encouraging information highways that will connect our homes, schools, and workplaces and give us more control over what flows through our television sets and computers. Visions of a global "communicopia," an international computerized information network with hundreds of channels, electronic shopping, simulation games, visual libraries, and

---

Exhibit 4.2. Students' Software Evaluation Checklist.

Name(s) of student evaluator(s)_____

Name of software program_____

Publisher_____ Subject_____

1. How long did the program take? _____minutes

2. Did you need to ask for help when using this program? _____

3. What skills do you think this program tried to teach? _____

    _____

    _____

4. Please circle the word that best answers the question.

    Was the program fun to use?   yes   no   somewhat not very

    Were the directions clear?   yes   no   somewhat not very

    Was the program easy to use? yes   no   somewhat not very

    Were the graphics (pictures)
good?   yes   no   somewhat not very

    Did the program get you
really involved?   yes   no   somewhat not very

    Were you able to make
choices in the program?   yes   no   somewhat not very

5. What mistakes did you make? _____

6. What happened when you made a mistake? _____

    _____

    _____

---

fax services may soon become reality. For example, Apple Computer's EZTV system, a device to make your television interactive, enables users to call up batting averages during a baseball game or view a house on their television set as they discuss mortgage rates with a real estate agent. The add-on system sells for about $500 and lets users navigate—using Macintosh-style icons—through hundreds of channels, services, and interactive games. America Online is just one example of a network for personal computers. Subscribers can tap into libraries, access the international Internet, have conferences, and play games with users in other cities.

7. What was the most interesting part of the program? _____
   _____
   _____

8. What did you like least?_____
   _____
   _____

9. What's a good tip to give a friend who's getting started with
   this program? _____
   Extended activities:
   Make up a quiz about the program and give the questions to
     other students in the class who have used the program.

   Create your own soundtrack for part of the program.

   Make up a student guide for the program. Use your own direc-
     tions and illustrations.

   Write or dramatize a TV interview with one of the characters
     in the program.

   Interview other students who have used the program and write
     their responses.

   Write a review of the program for a magazine.

   Call for information about tapping into *Prodigy* (an electronic
     subscription service): (800) 776-3449. Some of the best edu-
     cational software can come to you over the telephone line
     (*Reading Magic Library* and *Where in the World Is Carmen
     Sandiego* are just two examples).

A change of this magnitude in communication possibilities is
bound to have implications for education. By the year 2000, many
millions of U.S. households and some schools will have these services. The convergence of broadcast television, cable services, computer networks, and telephone systems with video games,
educational software, film libraries, and publishing will offer many
opportunities to entertain for profit, to inform, and to educate. This
explosion of technological advances can enslave our youth with
mindless video games (as they attempt to stave off boredom) or
empower them to learn and to think in new and interesting ways.

From an educational standpoint, the best new efforts will build on children's natural interest in television and video games to make learning fun.

The new communication technologies can serve as great public resources, and commercial profit alone should not determine how these new technologies will be exploited. The airwaves, after all, are owned by the public. Emerging public utilities must show a concern for learning and responsible social action. Any new media system is a public trust that should enable students to become intelligent and informed citizens. The FCC provides licenses to broadcasters only if they "serve the public interest." Now is the time to define what is meant by public interest and to devise rules to ensure that our media provide our children with a foundation for formal learning.

Unfortunately, quality programming appears to be the last thing to be considered in designing the new media. It is lagging well behind the hardware possibilities, but if intellectual depth and educational concerns are not factored in at the creation of the information superhighway, it will be much harder to incorporate them later on. However, amid all the commercial maneuvering by cable, telephone, and computer giants, there are developments that would exploit the new technologies for educational purposes. General Instruments, Intel, and Microsoft are working on a cable converter that has a built-in microcomputer. Set-top cable conversion boxes are also being developed by Scientific-Atlanta and Toshiba. Both converter possibilities can bring dazzling special effects into the home or classroom and enhance the interactive quality of television, allowing interactive storytelling and writing. The new technology not only can make information visually intriguing but also can provide two-way communication with live experts or computers with artificial intelligence. Tutoring, for example, might be done by live, recorded, or computer-composed experts.

Companies already beginning to tap into the educational potential of these new technologies are Motorola, Kaleida Labs, and Scientific-Atlanta. They are working with an Apple-IBM joint venture to develop software and hardware for the delivery of interactive and multimedia services to homes and schools. In addition to supplying interactive entertainment, these services *should* also allow for electronic field trips and the downloading of the educational simulation that will become ever more informative and attractive to use thanks to the virtual reality technologies now seen largely in video games. For example, one video game design from Silicon Valley's 3-D Company includes a computerized version of the 1992 presidential campaign. Users control computerized versions of Bill Clinton and others, interview reporters and officials, and access important speeches and news footage of key events while making strategic decisions that affect the outcome. The result can cause candidate Clinton to cry (lose) or laugh (win).

In virtual reality simulations, players put on glove controllers and a helmet-like device, to move inside a game or learning situation. Instead of manipulating images on a flat screen, players can move their bodies around, pivot up, and duck down as they capture or escape villains. Head-mounted displays have separate liquid crystal display screens for each eye in order to create three-dimensional effects, and stereo earphones for high-quality sound. When the gloves are used, wearers feel their hands grip objects. Tank commanders and pilots used virtual reality simulators to prepare for the Persian Gulf War. In 1993, astronauts started using virtual reality programs to train for missions in which they must use jet packs to move around in space. As the technology improves and the cost drops, virtual reality is moving from an expensive military/space program to arcade attraction and home entertainment possibility and a potential tool in education.

Social Considerations

Technology in and of itself is not the solution to our educational problems. But it *is* an essential element in the solution because it allows us to put together electronic components of lessons in ways that create truly individualized sets of learning experiences for students. As we do so, however, it is important that we develop a modern philosophy of teaching, learning, and social equity. While the new educational communication technology has the potential to make society more equal, in practice it frequently has the opposite effect. As we enter the world of computers, camcorders, interactive television, satellite technology, and data bases, the poor have less access than ever to our society's opportunities. What Jonathan Kozol (1991) calls "savage inequalities" are coming to be viewed as a form of violence that cuts deep personal and social wounds. School reform? We need equal access to technology to get there.

Most inner-city and rural school districts lack the money to train teachers to use computers effectively, so in poor schools children are still taught to use the computer primarily for typing or drill and practice, while the students in affluent schools are using computers for creative exploration—designing multimedia presentations and collaborating with classmates in problem-solving experimentation. To become an equal instrument of educational reform, computers must do more then reinforce a two-tier system of education. A user's access to faculty, other students, data bases, and library resources changes the way he or she creates, accesses, and transmits information. Those denied access to the new ways of handling information will fall farther and farther behind, their academic ambitions stifled. Thus, there are serious social consequences when the more wealthy school districts have greater access to telecommunications and advanced information technology. Everyone deserves access to a provocative and challenging curriculum.

Electronically connecting the human mind to global information resources will result in a shift in human consciousness similar to the change that occurred in the world's societies as they moved from oral to written cultures. The challenge is to make sure that this information is available for all, in a twenty-first century version of the public library. The convergence of communication technologies will be a catalyst for transforming the learning process and making people more creative, resourceful, and innovative in the things they do. While learning to use what is available today, we need to start building a social and educational infrastructure that can travel the knowledge highways of the future. Experts may disagree about the ultimate consequences of innovation in electronic learning, but the development of students' basic skills, habits of mind, wisdom, and traits of character will be increasingly affected—one way or another—by the new technology.

Professional Development in Technology

There were only about thirty thousand microcomputers in the schools in 1980. Today, there are well over four million. Most schools now have at least a few computers and a VCR. In an unpublished report on technology in U.S. public schools, Quality Education Data reports that the number of Macintosh computers in K–12 schools has doubled over the last two years. With the phenomenal growth of both hardware and software, there is a greater than ever need for teachers to combine knowledge of effective instruction with the effective use of computer technology. Professional knowledge about children, learning, curricula, and schools goes hand in hand with the competencies needed to use computers to advantage. Armed with new ideas and technological tools, teachers can meet the challenges of school reform head on.

Mark Twain once wrote that he wanted to be in Cincinnati when the world ended, because everything happens ten years later there. A few educators feel the same about using new media— "Can't it be put off until I retire?" Recent surveys show that the majority of teachers are not up to speed in educational computing (Office of Technology Assessment, 1988). In addition, some colleges that prepare teachers still do not prepare them to use technology effectively. The result is that school districts (Washington, D.C., for example) may still spend twice as much on staff development as they do on hardware and software (Harasim, 1990).

The successful use of computers in the classroom will not solve our most serious educational problems. But if teachers are not able to use and teach the use of this technological medium, the schools will become even less able to cope with the existing problems. It is relatively easy for school districts to buy computer equipment— and even to interest children in it. The difficult thing is to engage teachers and principals. In the world outside the school, computers are seen as real tools for real people. A similar view would be appropriate for schools. Teachers will have to make some changes in how they teach, but computers will never be electronic teachers or administrators of learning. The computer can be a facilitator of thought, but bypassing the teacher would be a serious mistake. Schools of the future will need more adults than ever: teachers' aides, parents, older students, and more. However, they will also need computers, because computers are proving indispensable in just about any intellectually significant enterprise. Teachers do need to be able to use computers to solve problems and communicate, to give and receive information. To help teachers become competent and confident users of these smart machines, schools, and teachers themselves, must maintain a professional development effort.

Many schools are mired in unproductive routines that prevent teachers from making creative breakthroughs. However, before we get too critical, we should recognize that it is difficult to redesign the plane when you are the pilot and flying at 30,000 feet. Seldom is enough time taken to go back to the drawing board and use good data and experience to get something right. Educators need time, space, support, and professional development to make all the changes required.

However, while some school districts are working hard on staff development, teachers also frequently complain that schools are notorious for bringing in hardware and software and then avoiding staff development. Sharing with peers is crucial to any literacy learning process, and teachers seem to agree that working on computers in pairs is usually better for beginners than working alone. Helping teachers become more comfortable with technology also means providing direct assistance and letting them take computers home to practice. A cross-section of the teachers the authors interviewed in three schools wanted to know how to use a computer and CD-ROM and videodisc players, hook up a modem for distance learning and telecommunications, attend a conference or professional development workshop on the topic, and have computer resources such as books and professional journals available. Nearly everyone was interested in training if the district paid for it, release time was provided, and the training was in a convenient location. Teachers genuinely seemed ready, willing, and eager to learn new skills, although they were not ready to forgo a weekend with their families in order to spend that time at a college.

Because teachers are increasingly being called upon to become more sophisticated managers of students' learning, professional development in using computers has to be given the highest priority, so that students can be directed by knowledgeable teachers aimed at achieving an instructional purpose. This purpose must go well beyond having a few computer programs in a learning center at the back of the room where a student goes when everything else is done. In addition, like any good learning material, computer software needs to be enhanced and extended by the instructor. The computer program with the best instructional design is no better than the classroom teacher who integrates it into the curriculum. Most teachers would not think of assigning a chapter from a history or science book without some kind of follow-up activity. They should feel the same way about computer lessons. Every other subject incorporates some kind of teacher intervention. There is no reason why students should be left to fend for themselves when the computer enters the process.

In today's world, children grow up interacting with electronic media as much as they do interacting with print or people. Unfortunately, much of the programming, from video games to television, is not only violent, repetitious, and mindless but also distracts students from more important literacy and physical exercise activities. Dealing with the new digital realities requires a new approach to teaching basic reading, writing, and computation skills. It also requires a heightened sense of social responsibility on the part of those in control of digital programming.

Television and computers are now present in most schools. As the 1990s usher in a brave new world of technology in which television and its computer-controlled associates are being designed for interacting, shopping, ordering movies, exploring digital environments, and playing long-distance video games, the resulting nationwide information pipelines should be used for education as well, permitting students to explore a much broader world of knowledge and learning. Making better use of computers and interactive television means going beyond thinking of them as electronic workbooks to collaboratively exploring problems and disparate ideas. As artificial intelligence comes along, it too can be used to enhance the real thing.

Harmonizing the present and the future will require more than reinventing our schools. We must attend to support mechanisms, and we must develop habits of the heart and habits of the intellect that link society together, so we can sail the crosscurrents of a transitional age together. The teacher is the foundation of educational change, but technology can lead to a reexamination of what to teach and how to teach it. And it can end the isolation of teacher and student.

The future may be bumpy, but it does not have to be gloomy. What we need is a controlling vision that explains media innovation *and* pedagogical principles. In the meantime, we can educate the whole person to be productive in a democratic society, attending to learning style, group process, and the skills for learning in an expanding electronic world.

Chapter Five

Assessment Alternatives

Many teachers have a vision of what should be happening in their classes. It goes something like this: students work independently or in small groups, doing investigations or tasks and using tools such as manipulative materials (blocks, beakers, clay, rulers, chemicals, musical instruments, calculators, and computers), assorted textbooks, and other references. Students consult with each other and with the teacher, keeping journals and other written reports of their work (Gill, 1993). Occasionally the entire class gathers for a discussion or presentation. The class is rich in problem solving and ideas. Unfortunately, traditional assessment methods do not support this vision. Standardized tests measure isolated facts. Moreover, many school districts use standardized achievement tests that are poorly matched to textbooks or the instructional approaches of particular teachers, but when a curriculum and a test are not aligned, incorrect conclusions will be drawn. In the authors' view, curriculum goals should determine the test used and not vice versa.

Of course, the first use of assessment must occur in the classroom, to provide information to the teacher on which he or she bases instructional decisions. Teachers have always depended on their own observations and examination of student work to help in curriculum design and decision making, and teachers need support in their efforts to set high goals for student achievement. However, equally important is the use of assessment in the world outside school, where people are valued for the tasks or projects they do, their ability to work with others, and their responses to difficult problems or situations. To prepare students for future success, both classroom curriculum and assessment must encourage the performance and the skills that are valued in the adult world. In order to meet this new goal for assessment, many groups of educators are exploring and creating exciting new assessment possibilities under a new name: *authentic assessment.*

This term is meant to indicate that students are doing worthwhile, meaningful tasks. Authentic assessment means evaluating students by asking them to demonstrate the exact behaviors that the teacher wants to produce in them with her or his teaching. It means that the criteria for success are public knowledge. Students need to know what is expected and how their product will be evaluated. Their successes should be evaluated in ways that make sense to them and allow them to show off what they do well. Authentic assessment searches out students' strengths and encourages integration of knowledge and skills learned from many different sources. It encourages pride. Authentic assessment may include self- and peer evaluation, and the products that students generate for assessment may include portfolios, writing, investigations, and verbal responses to open-ended questions.

Maps for Reflection, Assessment, and Change

Learning requires communication with self, peers, and knowledgeable authorities, and it requires effort, but it also requires meaningful assessment. A lesson from twentieth-century physics is that the world, ultimately, cannot be objectified. The same is true of the people who live in the world. Still, in both science and education, we need to say where we want to go, how we are going to get there, and periodically, how far we have progressed. To move on school reform, we have to know the desired outcome of that reform at various levels of schooling. Once we know where we are going educationally, teachers must be given freedom and an equal chance to get there. To both help them get there and determine how well they are getting there, we must objectify. We must come up with a quality assessment system.

Standardized multiple-choice tests have not been all that helpful in answering the complex and multifaceted problems facing
U.S. education. In fact, they may even be counterproductive, brow-
beating schools by putting them under enormous pressure to raise
test scores, often at the price of deadening students' critical thinking or aesthetic appreciation. Higher-level thinking goes beyond
simply recognizing that a mistake was made, as students are asked
to do in some standardized test questions, to imagining *why* the
mistake was made, getting feedback from others, and finding practical ways to correct the mistake. Performance assessment helps us
get closer to the teaching of higher-level thinking that we ought
to be doing. Portfolios, for example, help teachers and students
become actively involved in evaluating and providing examples of
their own learning. They are encouraged to create, evaluate, and
act upon material that is valued by themselves and others. Portfolio benefits and functional design are discussed in detail in this
chapter, along with the assessment methods of curriculum investigations, open-ended questions, holistic scoring, observations of performance, and interviews. Ways of implementing and gaining
support for authentic assessment are also suggested.

Portfolios

The portfolio is a container of evidence that demonstrates a student's skills and dispositions. It might be described as a powerful
tool for guiding conversations with teachers and peers about what
the student is thinking. Therefore, a portfolio must be more than
a random folder of student work. It should be a deliberate, specific
collection of student accomplishments. The focus is on what a student can do, not on mistakes.

Portfolios themselves are not new. They have long been used
by artists and photographers as a means of displaying representative samples of their work. What is new is the interest in using this
performance assessment technique across the curriculum. Portfolios have now been used for several years by various reading and

writing projects (Graves, 1983). For over five years, Harvard University has had a successful arts program that uses portfolios for instruction and evaluation (Mitchell, 1989). In addition, the National Assessment of Educational Progress has recently suggested using portfolios to assess students' writing and reading abilities (Finch, 1991). Increasingly, colleges and universities are asking students to submit portfolios as part of their entrance requirements (Farr, 1990). Some schools are even starting to evaluate faculty through teaching portfolios.

Portfolios can document the probing questions that students have asked, identify students' thinking, and help connect that thinking to real-world understandings. Portfolios can also measure elements of the thinking process: ability to work independently, keep journals, collaborate in small groups, discuss ideas, brainstorm, and listen. As learners express their ideas and reveal examples of their thinking in their portfolios, teachers can gain insights into how to design instruction to match their needs. As teachers become knowledgeable about assessing the change in students, they will become more knowledgeable in directing the change process in themselves and in their schools (Graves & Sunstein, 1992).

Portfolios can be used in the classroom to bring students together, to encourage discussion of ideas, and to provide evidence of understanding and accomplishments. By taking an evaluative look at their own work and the work of peers, students develop an ability to reflect, a sense of different ways of looking at their own work. This reflection can be rich with insights into ways of thinking and understanding, and it can suggest directions for the future (Farr, 1990). The connections the student learns to see among instruction, learning, and assessment are strengthened when a portfolio links the teacher and student in a very personal and meaningful way. Far from squelching inspiration, as many fill-in-the-bubble tests do, portfolio assessment promotes creativity and self-reflection. The procedure of gathering work encourages students to work collaboratively to analyze, clarify, evaluate, and explore their own thinking. Assessment of the portfolio invites students to invent, organize, predict, represent, visualize, and genuinely reflect on what they are learning.

Critics of this kind of assessment contend that portfolios can get in the way of standardized comparisons like national assessment exams. Portfolios are more time consuming and expensive to compile and maintain. The critics are right. Filling in the bubbles is easier. But most educators agree that the effort of keeping portfolios is worth it because it produces a realistic measure of performance.

Choosing Evidence

Although gaining popularity in art, language, and reading, increasingly, portfolio assessment is also making inroads into other curricular areas. Teachers in math, science, and social studies are just beginning to look at the possibility of using these processes to collect, organize, reflect on, and display selected work samples. Whatever the discipline, the evidence chosen for a portfolio can be the means through which educators gain a more powerful understanding of student achievement, knowledge, and attitudes. At the same time, this evidence makes the student aware of his or her own learning history, because a portfolio is not a one-time collection of examples but a means of bringing together representative material over time. Each element can represent a different form of expression and means of representing the world. The purpose is to gain a more accurate understanding of students' work *as it develops and grows*.

Gaining Support

How do teachers explain portfolios to parents? To begin with, they can explain the rationale behind portfolios to *everyone*—parents, students, principals—*before* they start using this assessment method.

They can be ready to discuss student progress and explain why portfolio assessment is an asset. Everyone should know that the portfolios are not to be a collection of test scores. It is also important to develop a year-long plan for using the portfolios, including the dates, times, and places the portfolios will be used in individual conferences with students, parents, and supervisors (principals).

Determining Purpose and Design

Some educators maintain that students should keep almost all their work in the portfolio while others design a portfolio with carefully selected items. There is no single formula or right way to design portfolios. However, because portfolios sketch pictures of students' understanding and because the intent is to capture the past in order to shape the future more effectively, careful attention should be given to the definition of what is to be assessed, the appropriateness of the contents to the outcome or behavior that is to be assessed, and the audience for which the portfolio is intended. In short, the purposes behind the portfolio should determine its design. The range and the depth can be determined by the teacher, the student, and the nature of the content. Involving students in the selection process gets them directly participating in their own learning and their own evaluation, thus promoting intellectual autonomy and self-respect. For example, teachers could ask students to choose two examples for each category in the following list.

- Work that reflects a problem that was difficult for you
- Work that shows where you started to figure the problem out
- Evidence that you learned something new
- Work that shows you reached a solution
- Work where you needed to keep searching for ideas
- Things you are proud of
- Things you would like to forget

A more general list of what might go in a portfolio (on paper, tape, computer disk, and so forth) is the following (adapted from Mumme, 1990):

- Writings
- Journal entries, reactions to one's own work, and personal reflections and feelings
- Attempts at solving problems, ideas about projects, and investigations
- Art, audio- and videotapes, photographs, or other creative expressions
- Selected samples of specific content presented over time
- Student logs, collected data entries, and research
- Group recordings, assignments, projects, and ideas
- Rough drafts and polished products
- Teacher comments and assessments

To help the person reading the portfolio identify and organize the contents, a portfolio should include a table of contents (or index) and some background information about the student. A cover letter by the student, dates and brief captions on all items, and a description of specific assignments or tasks that the evidence represents are other ways of assisting the reader. The contents of a portfolio can be added to, improved, revised, edited, or even discarded over time.

Evaluating

In an accepting environment, portfolio assessment can go hand in hand with the development of students' intellectual autonomy. Having students select what they want to represent their work can be a powerful educational experience in its own right. Portfolio contents can reveal a surprising depth of thinking and provide personal insights that touch students' personal and academic lives and, like all performance assessment tests, can be used to assess analyzing, predicting, estimating, problem-solving and other reasoning skills. Once challenging questions about students' intellectual autonomy and critical thinking skills become part of the formal evaluation process, the teaching of such skills will be considered more than an evaluation frill or something for gifted students. In this sense, portfolios can legitimize what good teachers want to do anyway.

The information accumulated in an assessment portfolio assists the teacher in diagnosing the learner's strengths and weaknesses, knowledge and attitudes. In the process, as the learner becomes aware of his or her own learning history and directly involved in assessing his or her progress, the barrier between the learner and the *assessment* of the learner starts to crumble. The portfolio evaluation process broadens when the portfolio is used as a conferencing tool with children, parents, and supervisors. This part of the process is also a powerful educational experience for the student (Quinta & McKenna, 1991), and teachers, parents, and even learners themselves can gain a better understanding of the learner in and out of school because of the insights portfolio contents reveal. As students collect, organize, and reflect on their school experiences and those of their peers, they communicate who they are and how they view themselves in relation to others.

Criteria for evaluating student portfolios fall into four primary categories. They are listed here with suggestions of specific items for which students, teachers, and parents should look.

1. *Evidence of critical and creative thinking.* Does the student's work show that he or she has:

   Demonstrated an understanding of the responsibilities of citizenship?

   Organized and displayed data? (This material should go beyond the statistical data to include information about such other project/problem items as gathering the data. For example, the data could be from a statistical graphing assignment based on a student survey.)

Conjectured, explored, analyzed, and looked for patterns?

Made use of the intellectual tools of analog and inquiry?

Evidenced an understanding of democratic values and social responsibility?

Used concrete materials such as video excerpts, computers, graphics, calculators, and/or drawings or sketches as an aid in interpreting and analyzing problems/issues?

Searched out information, explored, and critically examined research data?

2. *Quality of activities and investigations.* Will the student's activities or investigations help him or her develop an understanding of significant concepts in the discipline (social studies, science, or language arts, and so forth)? Do the activities cut across several areas of the discipline?

3. *Variety of approaches and investigations.* Does the set of portfolios provide evidence that students used a variety of approaches? Do portfolios include a variety of resources and provide evidence of research to support opinions and differing approaches to solving a problem? Do the portfolios include different activities or investigations?

4. *Evidence of understanding and skill in situations that parallel prior classroom experience.* The portfolio should provide evidence that students know why they are using certain procedures, what they are looking for, and what the data they find mean.

Assessment of these categories should be integrative and oriented toward weighing students' critical thinking and problem solving, not simply their recall.

Other integrative assessments that can be added to portfolios include teachers' observational notes, students' self-assessments, and progress notes written by the teacher and student (often these are written collaboratively).

Adding Project Assessment

To function in the twenty-first century, students need to become actively involved in evaluating their own learning. Constructing projects for portfolios can promote an attitude of efficacy, wonder, and curiosity that stirs an appetite for lifelong learning. As students learn to work cooperatively in small groups, writing about and discussing their ideas, keeping journals, brainstorming, sharing, and constructing projects, they expand their knowledge, horizons, and possibilities. Through such collaboration, in a caring community, students construct meaning as they document and build their knowledge of themselves and the world. Thus, project work is important because assessment should not simply measure decontextualized skills but show that the student can apply a learned skill in a new context. It is more important to demonstrate actual *understandings* than to do well in a rote, ritualized performance. After graduation, many of us spend more time working on things that resemble projects than we do answering true/false questions or filling in the blanks on a test. About the only time we take anything like a multiple-choice test is when we go to get a driver's license. Projects help students stretch their knowledge and show that they can really use what they have learned. To assess students' projects, ask these questions:

- How was the project conceptualized?
- What techniques were used?
- Is it accurate? (There must be individual accountability.)

- How has the presenter collaborated with others? (Working together with others is a plus, so collaboration is something students can and should describe honestly.)

- How is the project presented? (Humorist Woody Allen has said that 80 percent of any job is showing up. Here 80 percent of the project is the presentation.)

Conclusions

The demand is increasing for authentic assessment alternatives to multiple-choice testing. Portfolios are often mentioned as one means of providing genuine, practical, performance-based assessment that can aid teachers and others to assess students' ability to *apply* facts, concepts, knowledge, and higher-order thinking skills. Portfolios can stimulate ongoing conversations with students, parents, and educators about processes relating to teaching and learning. They can help us attend to subjects that do not lend themselves to traditional testing methods—like the arts (Mitchell, 1989). Portfolios also encourage students to explore and teachers to assess what goes both *in* and *across* subjects. Portfolio contents drawn from different times and contexts can get people talking and learning across disciplines, a necessity for critical and creative thinking.

Finally, portfolios are proving useful in linking assessment with instruction, allowing students and teachers to reflect on their movement through the curricular process (Mumme, 1990) and to pay attention to students' ideas and thinking processes. Traditional testing still has a place in the classroom, but we must respect its limits and search for more connected measures of intellectual growth. Coupled with other performance measures, portfolios can make an important contribution to educational reform and serve as a stimulus for new paradigms in learning.

Curriculum Investigations

One of the best ways to assure the connection between instruction and assessment is to embed assessment into instruction. When students become involved in practical tasks that can be easily evaluated, assessment can be both natural and invisible. Assessment activities or questions can be presented to the students without their being aware of a difference between the assessment and other classroom work.

The investigations students carry out may be related to a subject area, such as science or art, or may be explorations of purely mathematical questions. Although the most typical material for assessment is a collection of student writings, diagrams, tables, or maps, there are also opportunities for observing or videotaping student performance.

In reviewing students' investigative work, ask whether students can:

- Identify and define a problem and what they already know.
- Make a plan—creating, modifying, and interpreting data.
- Collect needed information.
- Organize the information.
- Discuss, review, revise, and explain results.
- Persist, looking for more information if needed.
- Produce a quality product or report.

Opportunities for investigation are endless. Here is a brief list of topics for student investigation that also offer opportunities to assess performance. Students can be asked to understand maps; use tools; monitor traffic patterns near school; discuss sports statistics; analyze collected litter; measure plant growth; compare population statistics; prioritize availability of resources; make a chart of the parts of the body; organize diet, exercise, and health programs; or create sound waves and music patterns.

Open-Ended Questions

Questions may be more or less open, depending on how many restrictions or directions are included. Open-ended questions add assessment to classroom questioning strategies. An open-ended question is one that asks the student to respond (in most cases, in writing) to a situation. The needed student response may range from a simple clarifying of the student's thinking to writing directions or making generalizations. Here are several examples of open-ended questions or requests for responses:

- Look at this graph. Explain what the graph might mean.

Name	Age
David	_____
Nancy	_____
Bill	_____
	1 2 3 4 5 6 7

- Linda wants to paint one wall of her room. The wall is 8 meters wide and 3 meters high. It takes one can of paint to cover 12 square meters, and the paint is sold at two cans for $9. What else will Linda need to consider? Make a plan for this painting job.
- The air in Plain City is warm and contains a great deal of water vapor. During the night the temperature drops to 20° C. What would a person be likely find outdoors in the morning? Give a rationale for your thinking.

There is a wealth of information to be gained from this kind of assessment. The variety of acceptable thinking reflected in student responses will go far beyond what may be imagined, and misconceptions can be detected. Teachers learn whether students can:

- Recognize the essential points of the problem involved.
- Organize and interpret information.
- Report results in words, diagrams, charts, or graphs.
- Write for a given audience.
- Make generalizations.
- Understand basic concepts.
- Clarify and express their own thinking.

For a classroom teacher to read all of the papers generated by frequent writing in response to open-ended questions might seem burdensome. Teachers who have had their students write, however, say that the results are worth it because they learn more about student understanding and the gaps in student knowledge than they do from traditional assessments, and students have a chance to show more of what they know and to exhibit a wide range of problem-solving approaches.

Holistic Scoring and Setting Rubrics

A random sample of papers can reveal what a class as a whole understands. One of the simplest yet most effective ways to grade student writing for understanding is to use a holistic scoring method. For example, the teacher may first sort papers into stacks labeled "acceptable," "missed the point, " and "has some special quality." Looking again for students' thinking rather than small bits of knowledge, the teacher then divides each stack into two further levels. This grading method minimizes the need for teachers to structure questions to draw forth identical predetermined responses.

Before adopting holistic grading, however, the teacher must define a rubric, a description of the requirements for varying degrees of success in responding to each open-ended question. The rubric should reflect the specific important elements of the problem and also allow for the uncommon responses often seen in students' investigative work. For an example of the kinds of factors to be considered, see Exhibit 5.1, which shows a general rubric with the six categories of grading just mentioned.

Performance Assessment and Action Research

The object of performance assessment in the classroom (also called action research) is to look at how students are working as well as at their completed tasks or products in order to begin a pattern of sustained improvement. The pattern is: observe, reflect on what has been observed, plan to use the information, and act on the plan. Teachers may carry out action research through observation in the classroom or in interviews.

Classroom Observation

An observer or interviewer may stay with a student group or make periodic visits, and/or activities may be videotaped, audiotaped, or recorded in writing by an outside adult, the teacher, or the students themselves. Observing actual student performance gives teachers additional information about students' abilities to reason and raise questions. It gives insights into how well students are concentrating, how they communicate, and how well they work together, organizing and presenting information.

The key to fundamental sustained change is the involvement of teachers in the change process, and teachers are faced with dozens of problems or important questions about their teaching and students' performance every day. Taking time for informal reflection on these problems and questions in order to determine what should be changed is one thing, taking time for a full-blown action research project is quite another. In deciding on a performance problem for study, the teacher should choose one that will not take

Exhibit 5.1. General Rubric for Scoring Open-Ended Questions.

Demonstrated Competence

Exemplary Response: Rating = 6
Student gives a complete response with a clear, coherent, and unambiguous explanation; shows understanding; identifies all the important elements; presents strong supportive argument. (For example, if third-graders had been asked to write about how to build a swing, you could actually build the swing from this paper.)

Competent Response: Rating = 5
Student gives a fairly complete response with reasonably clear explanations; presents solid supporting arguments.

Satisfactory Response

Minor Flaws, but Satisfactory: Rating = 4
Student completes the problem satisfactorily; uses ideas effectively; may have confused explanations; may have unclear argumentation. (The swing might get built if you read this paper.)

Serious Flaws, but Nearly Satisfactory: Rating = 3
Student begins the problem appropriately, but may fail to address significant parts of the problem; response may reflect an inappropriate strategy for solving the problem.

Inadequate Response

Problem Begun but Not Completed: Rating = 2
Student writes explanation that is not understandable; shows no understanding of the problem situation. (There is little chance that anyone could build anything from this paper.)

Problem Not Effectively Begun: Rating = 1
Student chooses words that do not reflect the problem; makes no attempt at solution; fails to indicate which information is appropriate to problem.

No Attempt: Rating = 0
Adapted from Stenmark, 1989.

so much time that it interferes with teaching and the environment she or he wants to sustain. The teacher should also make sure that the chosen problem is one she or he really *cares* about and can potentially *do* something about.

Additionally, all research projects require that the problem be formulable, that is, capable of being stated as a question. They also require the researcher to focus on the relationship between variables and to have some way of objectively testing her or his hypothesis. Variables other than the one being investigated should be kept constant, otherwise they may influence the outcome, making the research invalid. Potential variables to watch for and control include time of day or week, time allotted to a project, and make-up of a work group.

The observation itself, to be dynamic and insightful, should be sharply focused, allowing the observer to make inferences about individuals and the group process. The observer should ask, Do the individuals consistently work with others, try to assist others, and become actively involved in the problem? How does the group divide the tasks, agree on a plan, and provide support for each member? Attention to students' learning styles will give many of the answers. Focused observers also zero in on students' ideas by asking, Are students able to explain their ideas, support their arguments and give evidence, and consider the ideas of their peers? Observers should be particularly mindful of the ways students verbalize in the group. Do the students talk for self-clarification? Are they good listeners?

Interviews

Teachers can assess student understanding through interviewing students (assessment questioning). When assessing understanding, the teacher tries to get a picture of the student's own thinking rather than whether the student can provide a "correct" answer. In essence, the teacher is finding out how students are making sense of their work. The interviews can be as brief and informal as most other typical classroom interactions between teacher and students; however, it is necessary to arrange the logistics of time, people, and curricular planning. The interviewer must find a level of understanding at which the student is comfortable; thus, it is generally better to start by asking broad general questions rather than specific narrow ones. Follow-up questions should gradually become more specific as the teacher centers on what makes sense to the student.

Ethnographic Research

A less formal type of research, commonly called ethnographic research, adds student and teacher interpretations of what is occurring in individual classrooms to direct observations of events. Its most important elements are the shared meanings participants take from the learning experience. Ethnographic research provides systematic, reliable information about a teacher's classroom environment (Doyle, 1981). Like active research, it usually involves an analytical description of what participants actually say and do in a particular classroom setting, but it is deliberately interpretive, identifying important patterns of events and trying to explain interrelationships. Ethnographic studies can be simple or complex: some focus on carefully selected aspects of instruction, and others attempt to explain the classroom culture.

Encouraging Teachers to Develop Assessment Skills

Being curious about how students *think* and learn has always been part of a teacher's job description. What is new is that professional educational and social science researchers are now systematically investigating the effectiveness of methods of assessment and widely sharing the information they discover, helping us see, for example, that the causes of some learning problems may be locked deep in the human personality, the intimate processes of the family, subtle aspects of popular culture, or the "savage inequalities" (Kozol, 1991) of U.S. social and educational life.

But if we ever want to move from educational reform talk and analysis to action, we need the involvement of informed teachers in the assessment process because, even if the information a teacher garners from his or her classroom research is to be used to improve practice only in his or her classroom, it is vital that the information be valid. It is also vital for teachers to share the information and ideas they gain from assessment activities. Some teachers find it best to work with another teacher to collect assessment data, organize them, and then figure out a way to share them with others. Sharing might involve graphing results, mapping out a teaching strategy, videotaping illustrative classroom events, giving informal readings of class essays, or simply making a few overheads to share at a faculty meeting. In addition, teachers' ability to make better informed choices about learning activities and teaching methods goes hand in hand with teachers' ability to share activities and communicate with students. Student input about learning processes builds the knowledge of all concerned about those processes and helps build students' internal commitment to learning.

The exposure of teachers to new knowledge and their thoughtful reflection upon all manner of assessment projects can do much to enliven teaching. When teachers become students of their own learning, they find the discrepancies between what they believe about learning and how they practice learning. Discoveries they make themselves are more convincing to them and make them much more willing to change what they do. Thus, thoughtful interpretation of the results of assessment can play a major role in teachers' professional learning, helping them become reflective and autonomous professionals.

Part Two

Content in the Classroom

Chapter Six

Integrated Language Arts

Integrated language arts describes a literature-based approach to language learning that connects students to real communication situations and is built on critical thinking and cooperation. In contrast to basal reading programs that provide step-by-step guidelines, integrated language arts programs call on teachers to become independent decision makers about activities in the learning process. While such an approach may be considered as much a philosophy as a methodology, instructional method is essential to carrying out the philosophy successfully, and this chapter focuses on those ideas, issues, and practical methods that are useful in meaningful language arts teaching and learning.

Many of these ideas and methods are based on the notion that language is learned holistically (in context) rather than in bits and pieces. Learning from practice exercises is viewed as less effective than learning from real, existing literature or writing for a real audience. In addition, a literature-based language arts approach has a profound effect on children's writing. If children *read* good literature, it has a positive effect on their own writing (Burns, Roe, & Ross, 1988). A fundamental premise is that students should read, write, and speak frequently throughout all areas of an integrated curriculum.

This chapter is designed to help teachers (or prospective teachers) make the transition from traditional teaching of reading and writing to helping children read and write through encounters with real text. Those who are already familiar with this process will learn ways to refine their literature-based program, and all educators will find new ways to make the learning of language arts more active, dynamic, purposeful, and fun. In addition to describing ways to construct activities around poetry and newspapers and to use readers theater and creative drama, the chapter discusses the role of collaborative learning in the integrated language arts classroom, the critical thinking skills that are developed, assessment ideas, and helpful technology.

Traditional Teaching: Textbooks and Fragmentation of Learning

If a literature-based approach is more effective, why do some educators still insist on using traditional reading series? For one thing, the textbook-centered approach to teaching does not require as much preparation time, thought, or training as an approach that asks students to experience real situations and solve real problems. If the teacher is not well prepared, the textbook provides an approved outline for lessons. Some administrators support the use of reading series because they believe this approach ensures that specific skills will be learned in a particular manner or sequence. But neither workbook nor fragmented basal exercises connect to real literature or to students' experiences, in other words, to the world students will encounter out of school. Worse yet, students' interest in workbook and exercise materials has to be artificially induced. (However, there is reason for some optimism even about the traditional approach: some textbook publishers have taken these kinds of criticisms to heart and are working to develop literature-based material.)

And we do not *have* to throw out the textbook when we organize a classroom for an integrated approach. If teachers feel the need to supplement their literature-based programs with textbook materials, they can use the enrichment or follow-up activities found in many reading series' teacher's editions for that purpose. A creative teacher can take the best of the textbook materials and create a positive environment for a literature lesson.

Organizing Classrooms for
Literature-Based Learning

A positive environment for integrated language arts teaching is one in which literature is an important focus and in which children experience good poetry and prose and make connections across aspects of language and the arts—poetry, drama, writing, song, and visual art. Teachers frequently read stimulating stories and poems aloud so that they become essential literary tools. In organizing the curriculum, teachers build on topics or themes (Goodman, Goodman, & Hood, 1989). Teachers' overall goals in this classroom include providing pleasurable learning experiences, stimulating students' imaginations, promoting creative expression, and helping students explore a variety of literary styles and recognize the function of language.

Individual integrated language arts classrooms will differ as much as do textbook-based classrooms. Much depends on the teacher's or the school's acceptance of the concept. Still, there are certain themes that run through literature-based instruction. In an effort to give children time to listen, talk, write, read, and create, the teaching day is often divided into larger blocks. Teachers also read to younger children and share reading experiences with them through tools like big books—very large copies of books (available from many publishers)—or enlarged stories, poems, or chants the children have composed and illustrated. (Exhibit 6.1 describes how to make a big book for children in the lower grades.) Big books provide many opportunities to expand younger children's concepts of language, composition, and critical response.

The physical environment is of utmost importance to integrated language arts instruction. Organizing the classroom so that students can talk as part of the reading and writing process requires easily accessible learning materials or learning centers and spaces for group and individual work. Teachers new to such an approach may want to begin with one or two learning centers and add more as things move along well and the library centers, writing centers,

---

Exhibit 6.1. How to Make a Big Book for Shared Reading.

Determine the content. Is your big book going to be a new version of a published book, a completely original story, or a poem?

Gather materials: sheets of 18" x 30" paper; 12" x 18" white construction paper; yarn, clips, or metal rings to bind it together; and markers, paint, crayons, and collage materials.

Have the students prepare the text on the construction paper, gluing or taping it onto the larger pages in a way that leaves plenty of room for illustrations. Have students use various art techniques to create illustrations to go with the text. Both the print and the pictures must be big enough to be clearly seen by children sitting fifteen or twenty feet away.

Assign a group of students to make the cover, back page, and "copyright page" (with all the authors and illustrators listed). A statement about what the book is based on, a dedication page, and a page about the authors are other possibilities.

If possible, laminate the pages (so that they will last) before binding them. Be sure that the finished big book is left out on display.

---

theme centers, and so on become organizations or structures for language learning (Swartz & Pollishuke, 1991). The idea is to arrange for children to have many encounters with a wide range of imaginative devices that communicate the intellectual and emotional value of writing and reading.

Language Arts and Collective Learning.

In a literature-based framework for literacy instruction, the environment is also collaborative. Students are encouraged to discuss the work they are doing on writing projects and make connections to the books they are reading. Teachers encourage talk and collaboration because they recognize its value and importance in learning. A child's whole range of language skills can improve when students form literacy circles to discuss what they are reading and composing and to receive immediate feedback during the reading, writing, and revision process. At other times, peers can structure the framework for discussion by evaluating evidence, making predictions, or developing a line of thought. The most competent readers tend also to be the most competent talkers, listeners, and writers (Barr, Kamil, Mosenthal, & Pearson, 1993); therefore, developing fluency and strength in one area of communication supports the growth of fluency and strength in another.

Collaboration and peer tutoring are proven components of an integrated language arts classroom. In such learning environments, children can develop skills for responding to literature and can progress from simply telling a peer that the peer's story "has a good introduction," to asking, "How did your story answer the expectations your introduction set up?" They can learn responses of appreciation ("I like the way you . . ."), classification ("Can you explain how . . . ?"), definition ("This is about . . ."), and extension ("Can you tell me more about . . . ?"). Having children share brief passages from stories can also heighten group members' interest in certain kinds of reading and writing.

The nature of the critical thinking and the peer support found in any reading or writing task depends on the time allowed to students for reflection, group discussion, and holistic language processing. In the literature-based language arts classroom, the teacher sets the framework within which students use good literature, their own writing, and authentic oral language. The focus is on meaning and the communication process, and teachers treat students as if they are all members of the same literacy club rather than textbound pupils searching for correct answers (Smith, 1985).

Reading

Various national reports, including *Becoming a Nation of Readers*, point out that children spend less than 7 percent of their time in the classroom actually reading (Anderson, Hiebert, Scott, & Wilkinson, 1985). This practice contradicts the fact that, the more time students spend reading books they like, the better they do on reading achievement tests (Conley, 1987). And since children's interests can motivate them to raise their reading levels, it makes sense to let them choose some of their own books and spend more time actually *reading* them.

Current research and theory support the use of literature for the development of student literacy (Nagy, 1988). Further, the use of whole, meaningful works—rather than excerpts or revisions—helps develop better readers and better writers (Conley, 1987). However, in spite of sufficient evidence that there are more effective methods, many reading programs in elementary schools still depend on the basal reading systems that focus on discrete skills and the use of contrived stories. Basals have a controlled vocabulary and pay far more attention to form than they do to function. It is to make these programs work (more or less) that students are frequently segregated by "ability"—with those in the lower tracks getting a double dose of subskills and a watered-down curriculum. The results are abysmal. Thus, the shift to literature-based programs is meant to bring practice in literacy instruction into harmony with current knowledge, since "the way students are asked to respond to literature in school influences their development as readers, writers, and thinkers as well as their enjoyment of literature" (Routman, 1991, p. 87).

Teachers are adopting a variety of approaches to literature-based reading. Some use a literature-based language arts or reading series; others make extensive use of trade books (children's literature). Some start by devoting at least two or three days a week to literature-based reading instruction. Others accelerate the process and institute a complete whole language program, in which students are assessed by how well they use the reading strategies of guiding, monitoring, adapting, and responding to what they read.

Writing

Good writing has more to do with language and the reading of good literature than it does with any collection of rules. Many of the best resources and models for children's writing are implicit in well-written stories and children's literature. Improved communication is a goal that can be reached through developing students' critical thinking, innovative thought, concern for the audience, and social skills. Students can collaboratively build a mastery of writing conventions by encouraging each other to communicate more fully and critically (Perfetti, 1985). The sharing of ideas helps each child develop a better understanding of the writing process and stimulates student conversations around literary pursuits.

A consideration of students' learning of oral language is helpful here. Unlike reading and writing, oral language has always been treated holistically. It is usually viewed as a naturally occurring phenomenon that, under normal circumstances, develops on its own, and few efforts have been made to teach the subskills involved in speaking, because children come to school able to talk and exhibiting mastery of those subskills. In developing their oral communication skills, children are left to focus their attention on the communicative function of language rather than its form (Stahl & Miller, 1989). Why not let some of this approach filter into the teaching of writing?

In an integrated language arts program, writing connects all the language activities of the classroom. The desire to use language to convey meaning is something that children bring to school with them and that can be a means of connecting language activities. Writing that is exciting and challenging combines words with the volatile elements of the writer's soul. Even students living in the most dire circumstances, in neighborhoods marred by gangs, drugs, and violence, sometimes describe the fierce, liberating power that comes from penetrating their world with language (Scott, 1993).

On one level, therefore, students' writing can be a focused and edited version of inner speech. Beyond the revision of speech, the teaching of writing can draw upon students' fantasies, memories, sensations, and reflections. Additionally, students' knowledge of literature, insights from peers, stored information, and ideas drawn from interviews can be important materials and examples as students write to learn (as opposed to learn to write) (Murray, 1990).

Broadly speaking, students' writing to learn might begin with groups of between four and six students each generating ideas by brainstorming, discussing issues in the news, or sharing a book they have read as part of the prewriting process. Listening to and generating new ideas can help individuals or pairs of students contribute possibilities to the overall group writing project. After written material has been developed by the individuals or pairs, it can be revised and edited in the small group. Here, students exchange drafts and solve overall writing problems in response to questions and suggestions made by peers and the teacher. There is both a risk and an advantage in viewing writing as work in progress, as this collaborative process does, because such a view always leaves open the possibility for change and the possibility that others can add to the meaning of the writing or polish its presentation to an audience (Andrasick, 1990). Even if students are simply comparing short essays that explain the solution of a problem or writing in personal journals and sharing the results, they are able to collaboratively focus on critical and creative thinking in the context of that writing (Dyson, 1989).

Teachers must take students' social skills development into account as they incorporate literature-based writing into classroom routines. For younger students, the writing process can take the form of jointly produced stories about experiences. These can be placed on large charts with the teacher or an upper-grade student doing the writing. As soon as they can write on their own, the children can keep a private journal with labeled drawings, experiences, and writing samples. As students learn to expand their perspectives, they can begin to carry a story from one page (or day) to the next, and time may be set aside each day for a personal journal entry.

In an integrated curriculum, writing is not just for language arts or English class. It is a form of creative thinking that enlivens learning in the arts, mathematics, social studies, and sciences. Additionally, the give and take of writing with peers helps students share, and thus learn, subject matter across the curriculum. By turning their language arts classrooms into collaborative ventures, teachers find that students are more willing to select their own topics and explore subjects of real interest to themselves and their peers (Gere, 1985). Being allowed to draw on ideas from class, their personal lives, and their reading is a powerful catalyst for students' thinking and their development in the art of writing. As children get together to discuss their writing, they can compare its quality to ideas expressed in existing literature. They can construct meaning by using all the sources of information they find in personal experience, written texts, and social contexts.

One way to organize a classroom for writing is to have students write for a variety of audiences within a structure like a writing workshop, learning to draft and revise their writing until it meets the needs of an audience. Exhibit 6.2 contains a third-grade teacher's lesson plan for an interactive writers' workshop approach to a writing assignment.

Also, just as teachers must read good literature to teach reading, the best writing teachers write, and they share their drafts with students (Heath & Margolies, 1991; Perfetti, 1985), so the students can see that mature writers, too, go through a series of messy drafts before what they have done is ready for an audience. The hard reality is that revision is one of the keys to good writing. A process folio can show an adult's efforts at each stage and help students understand more about the writing process and the thinking that goes into it. The fact that the best adult writers may revise their work half a dozen times usually comes as a surprise to students.

The overall approach to writing discussed here emphasizes *process* over *product*. Product becomes important only in the final sharing or publishing. This approach shows promise for improving students' fluency, giving them control over their writing, and increasing the complexity of what they write.

Exhibit 6.2. Writer's Workshop Plan.
(45 Minutes Daily in the Autumn)

1. Students begin by making a list of all the topics they know anything about. You can model this for them on the overhead or chalkboard. Then, they circle the ten topics they are most interested in. Of those ten, students are to star two that are the most interesting, choose one, and begin writing everything that pops into their head about that topic. This is day one. At the end of the period, ask for volunteers to share a couple of their best sentences. Ask the class to make *positive* comments about the shared sentences. Students file their writing each day in a folder and keep their topic list to be added to as new ideas come to them. This process occurs daily.

2. Each day, students choose to continue writing upon that topic or to begin something different. The rules are that they only write on one side of the page, they never erase—just put a line through— they skip lines, and their names and the *date* appear each day.

3. Writing is kept in a folder, never taken home, and never graded. It is *imperative* that the author maintain ownership!

4. Writings are shared in small groups or pairs or among the whole class at informal times. The teacher has students schedule a conference whenever a student desires. The teacher roams the classroom to keep up with each student's progress.

Classroom Writing Communities

The development of a writing community is a very powerful way for students to collaborate in developing their writing voices (Heilbrun, 1989). Whether writing is self-, peer-, or teacher evaluated, teachers must not lose sight of the psychological reality that what is valued becomes what is valuable. Jointly developed folders, or portfolios, have a major role to play in student writing assessment, providing a running record of students' interests and what students

5. The teacher models good writing from her or his own efforts and shares many books in mini-lessons, to call attention to a variety of genres and styles of writing techniques. One mini-lesson is given at the beginning of each writing workshop period.

6. Mini-lessons can also be delivered to individuals, small groups, or the whole class.

7. After several weeks of writing, students are taught to use peer editing skills with partners or in small-group settings.

8. By the first of November, the students are to select one of their favorite writings to develop into a final product through a revision process of peer editing and teacher editing until the written work is ready for a parent to type. Students may illustrate their work or collaborate with a partner to illustrate it. The work is then bound and becomes part of the classroom library. Students can take these books home to share with others.

9. In February, the class holds a formal Young Author's Day to celebrate all of the students as published authors. Parents, friends, grandparents, and administrators are invited to hear the students read from their books. It is a big day!

This plan was developed by Jeanette Jones, a third-grade teacher at Cayuse Prairie School in Kalispell, Montana. Jones developed her own ideas and also adapted models from Donald Graves (1993) and from Tom Newkirk, Susan Stires, and Nancy Atwell.

can and cannot do, and helping them take more responsibility for their own learning, so the teacher can exert less control. The ability to evaluate does not come easily at first, and peer writing groups will need teacher-developed strategies to help them process what they have learned about being a member of a peer writing team. (As Calkins, 1991, points out, reflecting on team membership is a form of metacognition—students are learning to think about thinking.) The skills of productive group work may have to be made explicit. This can be done by gathering the students together (in a seating arrangement that allows them to see each other) and asking them these or similar questions for evaluative social processing:

- How did group leadership evolve?
- Was it easy to get started?
- How did you feel if one of your ideas was left out?
- What did you do if most members of your group thought that you should write something differently?
- How did you rewrite?
- Did your paper say what you wanted it to?
- What kind of a setting do you like for writing?
- How can you arrange yourself in the classroom to make the writing process better?
- What writing tools did you use?
- How do you feel when you write?
- Explain the reasoning behind what you did.

Remember, it is as important for students to write down their reasoning as it is for them to explain their feelings and preferences.

Ensuring the Success of Peer Editing Groups

Peer editing requires comprehension, reasoning, and reflection. To be effective evaluators, student editors should come to a piece of writing with specific questions in mind. The questions on the following checklist can be applied to any kind of writing:

- What is the focus or main idea of the draft?
- Are the supporting details related directly to this focus?
- What additional details should the writer add?
- Does the draft have a clear organization?
- Is there anything I find confusing?

- Are there any awkward or unclear sentences or paragraphs?
- What do I think or feel after reading the draft?
- Are these the effects the writer intended?
- What do I like best about the draft?

Peer editors should also learn to be sensitive to the writer's feelings and needs, be courteous, point out strengths as well as weaknesses, supply constructive criticism and offer suggestions for improvement, and focus on ideas and form rather than proofreading.

Most of the editing work can be left to the students—shaping sentence structure, paragraphing, or determining which paper is to go first, second, or third in the final group product. This has proven a better learning process than having the teacher collect the first draft and suggest revisions (Hansen, 1987). Sometimes when working with a coauthor (or two), students will form a creative unit that depends on a balance of personalities to produce good writing.

Assessing Students' Writing

At times, teachers may intervene in students' writing as part of the learning or assessment process. For example, although it is important that journal entries be in a student's own words, the teacher can make comments about that writing, without formal grading. There are also times when teachers must intervene to assess students' writing or to do some final editing before a written work is widely shared. (Remember to stamp "draft" or "creative writing—work in progress" on anything that might go home before it reaches its final form. A work-in-progress stamp can save you a little embarrassment when a misspelled word or some bad grammar reaches parents.)

Writing activities can also be restructured on an ongoing basis according to what is learned about students' writing abilities from the assessment features of journals, writing folders, and peer conferences (Applebee, Langer, Mullis, & Jenkins, 1990). When children grow up in literate cultures, the emergence of written language is a gradual process. At various points in that process, both the teacher and the students should ask questions that assess students' whereabouts. For example, How well was the student able to communicate his or her ideas through writing? How well did the student use the composing strategies of planning, drafting, revising, and editing? What collaborative strategies did the student use for getting help with his or her writing?

As described earlier, holistic scoring, rather than concentrating on mechanical errors, looks at how well students develop overall concepts (Stotsky, 1989). It is now frequently used to grade writing across all grade levels and has been successfully used from the first grade to graduate school. (The method of holistic scoring is described in detail in Chapter Five.)

Holistic scoring can be used in conjunction with students' writing folders, helping students learn to assess their own progress and the progress of peers. A folder can include holistic scores from peers and teachers on the student's writing samples as well as the student's final drafts. The student, the teacher, and the parents can then look over the student's writing history and assess the range (and fluidity) of the compositions. Exhibit 6.3 shows the kind of writing stimulus that can get students started on creating writing samples for their folders.

Students who assess themselves can be asked to look for these elements in a sample of their writing.

- *Fluency.* This measure involves such factors as length of sentences. In general, the longer the sentences, the higher the fluency.
- *Sentence types.* The goal is to combine fragments into sentences and also to vary sentence types.

Exhibit 6.3. Sample Writing Stimulus.

If you think about it, you're really not the same person you were four or five years ago. Your ideas, tastes, attitudes, and perhaps even your goals have changed—probably in several ways. Choose any one person (a relative, a teacher, a friend, or anyone else) or any event or experience (a course, a trip, a conversation, or any other event or experience) that has made a difference in your life and explain as fully as you can how the person or event has changed you. Be specific in showing how you are different now because of the person or event. In writing your composition be aware of the following elements:

- *Ideas:* the extent to which the thoughts and content of the essay are original, insightful, and clear
- *Supporting material:* the extent to which the ideas of the essay are supported by examples and details that are specific, appropriate, original, and well developed
- *Unity:* the extent to which the parts of the essay are connected to each other and help achieve the goal of the essay
- *Style:* the extent to which the language of the essay is used creatively and correctly and how it helps achieve the writer's goals

---

- *Vocabulary.* Assessment determines whether word choice is limited and whether the student makes good use of unusual words in a passage.
- *Structure, sequence, and grammar.* These are important in the final product.
- *Ideas.* Ideas should be interesting, original, and to the point.

Structured and Unstructured Experiences with Poetry

A twentieth-century American might disagree with Wordsworth, a nineteenth-century Englishman, who explained poetry as "emotion recollected in tranquility." People reach for poetry today because, in its own way, poetry tells truths that other communication techniques often miss.

Preparation

Teachers must have some basic knowledge of the vocabulary of poetry in order to help children enjoy it and mature in their understanding and appreciation. Reading or writing poetry in an integrated language arts classroom involves student awareness and understanding of the elements that make poetry unique.

- Poetry uses condensed language, so *every* word becomes important.
- Poetry uses figurative language (for example, metaphor, simile, personification, and irony).
- Poetry often uses rhythmical language (regular, irregular, or specific metrical forms).
- Words may be rhyming (through internal, end-of-line, or run-over rhymes) or nonrhyming.
- Poetry uses a language of sounds (alliteration, assonance, and repetition).
- Poetry uses a language of imagery (such as sense perceptions reproduced in the mind).
- Poetic units of organization are lines arranged in stanzas or ideas arranged in a story—also, balance, contrast, build-up, and surprise (Denman, 1989).

Students should also have some understanding of the major strains of fixed form verse and free verse. Nell (1989) suggests these distinctions: fixed form verse can be categorized as narrative or storytelling; literary, with a prescribed structure (for example, limerick, ballad, sonnet, or haiku); and lyric. Free verse can be analyzed according to its tone (humorous, serious, nonsensical, sentimental, dramatic, didactic), its content (humor, nonsense, everyday things, animals, seasons, family, fantasy, people, feelings, adventure, moods), and its time of writing (contemporary or traditional).

Since what we read influences how we write, there is a natural connection between students' written poetry and the richness of the literature they are exposed to. By leading students to appreciate literature and poetry across time and cultures, the teacher can enhance their ability to write it. A variety of children's literature and poetry presented to students is a source of vocabulary, metaphor, and conceptual material for them. Experiencing the language and rhythm of good poetry gives students the building blocks for creating their own poetic patterns. In addition to reading published poetry to their students, teachers can share their own efforts at poetry with the class.

Writing Collaboratively

The collaborative writing of poetry intertwines process with content and students with learning. The cooperative linking of poetic concepts will often turn mundane work into poems rich in detail, sentiment, and humor. Having the group as an audience for their poetry will help students become more responsible in communicating their understanding to others and more attuned to the need to change and build ideas. When the writing of poetry is fused with collaborative dreams, emotions, and sometimes comedy, the process can foster personal and intellectual growth. Students should learn that poetry is more than just printed words on a page. Poetry comes alive when the reader and the words connect in a way that speaks to the reader's experience and generates meaning. Poems can be built on external stimuli, like sights and sounds, or internal ones, like thoughts and tensions. Unsaid inner meanings can be revealed in the "music," or rhythm, of a poem. Poetry often happens as sensibility encounters control of language and rhythm. A good subject for students beginning to write poetry is one that offers a meta-physical possibility.

Students can also be introduced to the way many real writers write. Beethoven would write fragments in notebooks that he kept beside him; later he would develop these themes. He received ideas from every conceivable direction, including the works of other composers, folk music, and myths. Like other writers, he needed a thorough knowledge of the language he used (music) and a broad range of experience to build upon. Children can emulate real writers by keeping a notebook of ideas about experiences they have had, books they have read, and changes in their thinking about various subjects. Beyond having some mastery of language, being able to think in images is essential, as is the ability to concentrate. It is also important for students to learn to get something, almost anything, down and go from there. The process of sketching out an idea and developing it into a clear vision can foster student language growth and help illuminate the reading and writing process.

There are various methods for the collaborative writing of poetry. For example, when students are ready to write, each team or partnership can be given a short time (one or two minutes) to compose the first line of a poem. On a signal from the teacher, each team passes its paper to the next team and receives a paper from another team. Each team then reads the line that a preceding team has written and adds a second line. The signal is given, and the papers rotate again—each time, each group reads what is already on its paper and adds another line. Teams are encouraged to write what comes to mind; even if it is only a team member's name, they must write something in the time allotted. After eight or ten lines have been written, the papers are returned to their original teams. Each team adds another line, if it chooses, and then revises and edits the poem it started. The poems can then be read orally, with team members alternating reading the lines. Later, some of the poems can be turned into optical poems (pictures made with the words of the poem) or put to music or illustrated, as described in the following activities.

Activities

These suggested activities will give students developmental experiences with both their own and others' poetry.

- *Poetry with movement and music or with illustrations.* Poems can be put to music and movement. One student can read the poem and the rest of the group can use streamers, or penlights in a darkened room, to move with the words and the music. Students can also illustrate picture books to go with poems that they can later share with younger children. A classroom anthology of poetry can be illustrated and laminated.
- *Daily oral reading of poetry.* Students sign up and read aloud each day. Other students "point," commenting on parts of the poem that catch their attention.
- *Free writing period.* A period of one-half hour to one and one-half hours is set aside each day for students to write on any topic, in whatever form they choose, including poetry. A sharing time follows this period, so that students may respond to each other's writing by pointing and asking questions.
- *Literature sharing time.* Students gather in small groups once a week to share books, including poetry, that they have been reading. The groups are structured so that each student reads the author and title of a book, tells about it, reads one or two pages aloud, and receives responses from members of the group, who specifically point out parts they liked and ask questions.
- *Wish poems.* Each student writes a wish on a strip of paper. The group's wishes are read all together. Students then write individual wish poems and share them.
- *Group work with metaphors.* Poems containing metaphors are read aloud. Collectively written poems that make comparisons are written on the board. Students also write individual comparison poems and share them with the class.
- *Poetry-based lessons.* Lessons can be based on poetry books for children. For example, *Dinosaurs,* a poetry anthology for chil-

dren edited by Lee Bennett Hopkins (1987), inspired this four-step lesson:

- Teacher reads poems about dinosaurs aloud.
- Students brainstorm reasons why the dinosaurs died and words that relate to how the dinosaurs moved.
- Models of dinosaurs and pictures are displayed and talked about.
- Students write poems about dinosaurs and share them.

- *"The fame to the name."*[1] This simple activity can be adapted to suit class and curriculum needs. It integrates whole language, cooperative learning, and poetry and also the subject areas of social studies, history, and mathematics. Students write a poem in the form of an acrostic, based on a name from their studies. The name chosen is written vertically on a chart pad or on the board. Then for each letter in the name, the class brainstorms a sentence or phrase that tells something about the name. Here is an example, based on the name Alaska:

> *A lot of fresh air*
> *Land of the frozen*
> *Athabaskans, Eskimos, Aleuts,*
> *Seals, bears, moose and more*
> *Kaleidoscope in the night sky*
> *A state to be proud of.*

Model the first acrostic poem with the class to give the children an idea of how it is to be done. Using alliteration can add excitement. Once the acrostic form has been modeled, incorporate cooperative learning by breaking the class into small groups. Each group can work on one letter of an acrostic poem or invent a topic for a

[1]This activity was contributed by Debra Emerson, in cooperation with Karen Baloh, Fairbanks, Alaska.

complete poem. Be sure to allow time for group presentations. For a parental involvement activity, have each student and his or her family write a poem using the family's last name. Families with two last names can be encouraged to use both, or students can write poems using their own names. This fun activity can be used throughout the whole year. To incorporate writing across the curriculum, pull names or subjects from the children's life experiences and science, social studies or history, and math classes. Encourage the students to write about animals and their habitats or about the weather or scientific facts about the state or city. Suggested social studies topics include peoples, their cultures, and the history of places. Children may also wish to include personal school or family history in their poems. Math can be incorporated by using population figures or the actual size of a state. To instill such traits as patriotism, pride, school spirit, and self-esteem, have the children focus on the positive elements of each name used.

- *Creating poems from words in the environment.*[2] This activity is designed to increase students' observation of words in their environment as they create poetry from printed words they observe around them in the classroom, elsewhere at school, on field trips, at the bus stop, or walking down the street. Pair children up or have them form groups of three. Set physical boundaries, limiting them to the classroom, hallway, playground, and so forth. Set expectations based on the needs of the class. Each group, armed with writing and/or sketching supplies, is instructed to gather from the environment words or phrases that appeal to group members. The words do not need to be related in any way. They may be words children like the sound of, like because of what they stand for, or associate meaning with. It is helpful to set a time limit for the word search.

After the words have been collected, instruct the groups to cut out all the words and phrases they have written on their paper and

[2]This activity was contributed by Leslie Markham, in cooperation with Karen Baloh, Fairbanks, Alaska.

ask them to rearrange the words to make some kind of sense and to add illustrations, and so on. With group consensus, words can be added or deleted, and when students are satisfied with the word order, they glue the words in place. Allow time for students to practice reading the resulting "poems," to establish some sort of rhythm. It might be fun to put a poem to music and collaborate in making a rap song out of it. Alternatively, students can have fun with the visual presentation of the poem. Show them various ways that poets have physically arranged their poems to add meaning and impact. Shel Silverstein's poems are one example.

If one of the goals is to have a finished product to publish, instruct students to revise, edit, and rewrite their final poems. Rough drafts can be saved in a portfolio until a later date. At that time, students can reread all their poems, revise if necessary, and choose their best ones for publication. An important part of the writing process is to read the poetry aloud to an audience. One group of third-grade students who tried this activity read their poems to classmates, school secretaries, parent helpers, and a fifth-grade class. The fifth-graders provided excellent feedback because they were more experienced with the writing process and knew how to make positive suggestions. The students really enjoyed collecting the words for their poems, creating a new meaning from their data, and sharing the end product. Working in collaborative groups added excitement to the activity and increased involvement with the writing process. Teachers who try this out can modify it to suit their needs. Listen to the students; they often come up with their own extension projects.

Reading Newspapers for Group Discussion and Writing

Newspapers can be an excellent supplement to literature, original documents, and oral histories. With students in the upper grades, newspaper articles spark ideas for group discussion and provide writing models for analysis. As they read, students see how a composition is organized. They can also compare videotaped television news segments with written reports on the same stories. *The New York Times*, the *Washington Post*, the *Los Angeles Times*, or the local newspaper can be more stimulating than a textbook. For younger children, simple pieces with pictures and publications like the *Weekly Reader* can replace more difficult newspapers.

The daily newspaper, particularly if it is in a student's second language, can be an intimidating document for a student to tackle. To early readers, accustomed to materials geared toward their competency levels, a newspaper is imposing in format and vocabulary. By preparing imaginative exercises, such as the comparison between a newspaper story and the same story on a news broadcast, a teacher introduces newspaper reading and demystifies those pages filled with newsprint. The televised news items or conversations should be shown first so that what the students have listened to and seen is then applied to print.

Newspaper reading can also be approached through the newspaper scavenger hunt, an exercise that can be modified for a variety of reading levels. Teachers draw up a list of words, short phrases, cartoons, and pictures extracted from a newspaper and hand it out to pairs of students along with a copy of the newspaper, in which the students hunt for the items on the list. When they locate an item, they put the number of the page on which the item is located on an answer sheet and then circle the item in the newspaper. A time limit is set, and when time is up, the students can compare their success rates.

In addition, the teacher can go over a newspaper with the class as students collaboratively search for connections with a nightly news program the students were asked to watch as homework. Small groups can also make up a creative story composed of headlines, subheadings, and a few connections of their own. Political cartoons with the captions removed can also be presented to groups of students who are then asked to come up with their own captions.

Readers Theater: Connecting Literature, Writing, Speaking, and Listening

Readers theater is the oral presentation of prose or poetry by two or more readers. The goal is to use a highly motivating technique to engage children in a whole range of language activities and literate behaviors. This approach can be a good informal cooperative learning activity, in which students not only respond to each other as character to character but exhibit spontaneous responses that tie the group together with the situation of the text. Typically, performance in front of an audience will intensify the experience.

For this form of integrated language arts learning, students can be given complete scripts, or they can be asked to write scripts in small groups after reading a story or a poem. The story or chapter to be read might be ten or twenty pages long; the finished readers theater script only two or three pages. Try some prepared scripts first in order to show students the basic idea. Once students have had a chance to read prepared scripts for an audience, they can make a script of the text of a story they like. The focus is on sharing and extending authentic text. In this way, readers theater combines the effectiveness of rereading and writing to enrich children's reading comprehension and appreciation of literature (Wolf & Heath, 1992).

The typical readers theater lesson involves scriptwriting, rehearsal, performance, and follow-up commentary for revision. The rehearsal is important; children should have a chance to practice and refine their interpretations. Lines, gestures, intonation, and movement should be worked out in advance. The idea is to carry the communication of plot, characterization and theme through vocal qualities, facial expressions, and gestures. There are no props, and "acting" is not involved. Individual interpretations are negotiated between group members. Everyone should have a copy of the script to hold; roles are read, not memorized. (A few mistakes in reading can be good for a laugh.) One way to stage the presentation is to have the children seated in the presentation area. When reading they stand up, and when their turn is over they sit back down. Or they can stand with their backs to the audience, turning to face the audience when it is their turn to read. If there are more children than roles, some children can share roles, reading aloud together.

Teachers are always looking for ways to make poetry interactive and stretch its learning possibilities, and readers theater achieves that goal. Students can divide a poem up into speaking roles in several ways, read each version aloud in their small groups, and discuss which division lent dramatic effect to the piece and which script has the best logical breaks or shifts. Exhibit 6.4 contains sample scripts and follow-up questions for two distinctly different readings of the same poem.

Exhibit 6.4. Readers Theater Poetry Scripts.

Script One

Reader 1: "Abandoned Farmhouse," by Ted Kooser.
   He was a big man, says the size of his shoes
   on a pile of broken dishes by the house;
   a tall man too, says the length of the bed
   in an upstairs room; and a good, God-fearing man,
   says the Bible with a broken back
   on the floor below the window, dusty with sun;
   but not a man for farming, say the fields
   cluttered with boulders and the leaky barn.
Reader 2: A woman lived with him, says the bedroom wall
   papered with lilacs and the kitchen shelves
   covered with oilcloth.
Reader 3:   And they had a child,
   says the sandbox made from a tractor tire.
Reader 2: Money was scarce, say the jars of plum preserves
   and canned tomatoes sealed in the cellar hole.

(Continued)

Exhibit 6.4. (*Continued*)

And the winters cold, say the rags in the window frames.
It was lonely here, says the narrow country road.
Reader 1: Something went wrong, says the empty house
  in the weed-choked yard. Stones in the fields
  say he was not a farmer;
Reader 2:   the still-sealed jars
  in the cellar say she left in a nervous haste.
Reader 3: And the child? Its toys are strewn in the yard
  like branches after a storm—a rubber cow,
  a rusty tractor with a broken plow,
  a doll in overalls. Something went wrong, they say.

Script Two

Reader 1: "Abandoned Farmhouse," by Ted Kooser.
Reader 2: He was a big man,
Reader 4: [Echoes]:   a big man,
Reader 1:   says the size of his shoes
  on a pile of broken dishes by the house;
Reader 2: a tall man too,
Reader 4: [Echoes]:   a tall man,
Reader 1:   says the length of the bed
  in an upstairs room;
Reader 2:   and a good, God-fearing man,
Reader 3: [Echoes]: good and God-fearing,
Reader 1: says the Bible with a broken back
  on the floor below the window, dusty with sun;
Reader 2: but not a man for farming,
Reader 1:   say the fields
  cluttered with boulders and the leaky barn.
Reader 3: A woman lived with him,
Reader 1:   says the bedroom wall
  papered with lilacs and the kitchen shelves
  covered with oilcloth,
Reader 4:   and they had a child,

Reader 1: says the sandbox made from a tractor tire.
Reader 3: Money was scarce,
Reader 1:   say the jars of plum preserves
    and canned tomatoes sealed in the cellar hole.
Reader 2: And the winters cold,
Readers 3 and 4: [Echoes]:   oh, so cold,
Reader 1:   say the rags in the window
    frames.
Reader 3: It was lonely here,
Readers 3 and 4: [Echoes]:   so lonely,
Reader 1:   says the narrow country road.
Everyone: Something went wrong,
Reader 1:   says the empty house
    in the weed-choked yard.
Reader 2:   Stones in the fields
    say he was not a farmer;
Reader 3:   the still-sealed jars
    in the cellar say she left in a nervous haste.
Reader 4: And the child? Its toys are strewn in the yard
    like branches after a storm—a rubber cow,
    a rusty tractor with a broken plow,
    a doll in overalls.
Everyone: Something went wrong, they say,
Reader 4 [Echoes]: Something went wrong.

    Ask these questions following each reading:
    • Does each reader have an equal share of the poem?
    • Why do you think the characters in the poem left the farm?
    • Does this readers theater version of the poem help you get to
      know more about the characters?
    • How would what your conception of what happened to the
      characters influence how you would divide the poem up?
    • What are the dramatic or thematic advantages to this division
      of lines? Explain the thinking behind your preferences.

Kooser, 1980, p. 64.

Students can also write scripts for stories, including stories from children's literature. Exhibit 6.5 presents a script of a story for beginning readers.

Creative Drama

Engaging in literacy-related creative drama should be part of every language arts program. Teachers can use creative drama to integrate language learning experiences and make important contributions to children's literacy development (Johnson, Christie, & Yawkey, 1987). For example, dramatic play can be used to bridge the gap between written and visual forms of communication. Students might work in small groups to script, act, and even videotape a one-minute commercial or to pick a topic, develop a skit, practice it, and perform it for the class. To follow-up, they can critically examine the reasoning behind each group's presentation to the class. Commercials developed by students can be compared to those on television.

Like many of the activities in this book, creative drama emphasizes the fundamental educational goals of self-realization in unified learning experiences, firsthand experiences in democratic behavior, functional learning related to life, and comprehensive learning. More specifically, it helps students construct their own meanings in response to literature and writing, encouraging the clarification of ideas and values. On the practical side, creative dramatics can be carried out by small groups with few props, no memorization of lines, and no chance for failure. It does not need to emphasize performance; it can be adapted to many types of books, lessons, and subjects; it evokes contributions and responses from students who rarely participate in standard discussions; it assesses how well students know the material being enacted (characterization, setting, plot, and conflicts); and it can be a stimulating prewriting exercise.

Exhibit 6.5. Readers Theater Prose Literature Script.

Chicken Little

Roles

Narrator	Chicken Little
Cocky Locky	Goosey Loosey
Turkey Lurkey	Ducky Lucky

Narrator: One day Chicken Little ran into the garden. She wanted to find something to eat. She looked under a big tree. Whack! Something fell on her tail.

Chicken Little: Oh! Oh! The sky is falling. The sky is falling. I will run. I will run to tell the king.

Narrator: Away ran Chicken Little to tell the king. She ran and ran. Chicken Little met Ducky Lucky.

Chicken Little: Oh, Ducky Lucky! The sky is falling. The sky is falling!

Ducky Lucky: How do you know?

Chicken Little: I saw it with my eyes. I heard it with my ears. Some of it fell on my tail. I am going to tell the king.

Narrator: Ducky Lucky looked at Chicken Little.

Ducky Lucky: I will go with you. We will go to tell the king that the sky is falling.

Narrator: Away ran Chicken Little and Ducky Lucky to see the king. On and on they ran down the road. Chicken Little and Ducky Lucky met Cocky Locky.

Chicken Little: Oh, Cocky Locky, the sky is falling! The sky is falling!

Cocky Locky: How do you know? How do you know the sky is falling?

Chicken Little: I saw it with my eyes. I heard it with my ears. Some of it fell on my tail. We are going to tell the king.

Cocky Locky: I will go with you.

Narrator: Chicken Little ran. Ducky Lucky and Cocky Locky ran. They all ran to tell the king. Chicken Little saw Goosey Loosey coming down the road.

Chicken Little: Oh, Goosey Loosey! The sky is falling! The sky is falling!

(Continued)

Exhibit 6.5. *(Continued)*

Goosey Loosey: How do you know the sky is falling?

Chicken Little: I saw it with my eyes. I heard it with my ears. Some of it fell on my tail. We are going to tell the king. Ducky Lucky is going with me. Cocky Locky is going with me. Will you go with me?

Goosey Loosey: I will go with you.

Narrator: Away ran Chicken Little. Away ran Ducky Lucky. Away ran Cocky Locky. Away ran Goosey Loosey. They all ran to tell the king that the sky was falling. Chicken Little and Ducky Lucky went on down the road. Cocky Locky and Goosey Loosey went on down the road. They met Turkey Lurkey.

Turkey Lurkey: Where are you all going?

Chicken Little: Oh, Turkey Lurkey, the sky is falling! The sky is falling!

Narrator: Turkey Lurkey looked at Chicken Little.

Turkey Lurkey: How do you know that the sky is falling?

Chicken Little: I saw it with my eyes. I heard it with my ears. Some of it fell on my tail. We are going to tell the king.

Narrator: Turkey Lurkey looked at Cocky Locky. Then he looked at Goosey Loosey. He looked at Ducky Lucky. Then he looked at Chicken Little.

Turkey Lurkey: No, no, Chicken Little. The sky is not falling. We will not go tell the king. We will go to the garden. We will see what fell on your tail.

Goosey Loosey: I will go to the garden.

Cocky Locky: I will go with you.

Ducky Lucky: I will go with you.

Chicken Little: Well, I will *not* go to the garden. I *know* that the sky is falling.

Turkey Lurkey: Come, come. We will all go to the garden.

Narrator: Turkey Lurkey and Goosey Loosey ran. Cocky Locky and Ducky Lucky ran. They all ran to the garden. Turkey Lurkey looked up at the sky. He looked under a big tree. He saw something under the tree.

Turkey Lurkey: Oh, Chicken Little, the sky is not falling. A nut fell on your tail.

The way students are asked to go about the creative drama process influences their development as readers, writers, and thinkers. Suggestions for a successful process include the following:

- Do not rush students. Coach from the sidelines if necessary, telling students, "Take your time," or "You're doing fine."
- Maintain an environment in which each student can find his or her own nature without imposition. Growth is natural to everyone.
- Remind students that individuals who act, agree, and share together create strength and release knowledge surpassing the contribution of any single member.
- Treat student restlessness and static behavior as a danger sign. Refreshment and a new focus are needed.
- Become familiar with the many resource and game books useful in this work.
- Be flexible and able to alter your plans on a moment's notice.
- Observe audience reactions as well as the drama. The reaction of the audience is part of the creative dramatics experience.
- Avoid giving examples. Too often the students become bound to the example and do not try new things.
- Allow the creative drama experience to be joyous and free of authoritarianism so everyone will engage in it in an open manner.

Story Dramatization

The following steps are useful in teaching students to dramatize stories and create their own scripts:

- Select a good story; read or tell it to the group.
- With the class, break the plot down into sequences, or scenes, that can be acted out.

- Have each student group select a scene group members wish to dramatize.

- Instruct groups to break the scenes into smaller sequences and to discuss the roles, motivations, characterizations, props, and so forth. Encourage students to involve themselves in the developmental images of the characters—what they did, how they did it, why they did it. Have groups make notes on their discussions.

- Meet with groups to review and discuss their perceptions. Then let them go into conference and plan in more detail for their dramatization.

- Have the whole class watch the production of each group. Instruct audience members to write down five things they liked and five things that could be improved in the next playing.

- Let the players return to their groups at the end of the group performances and evaluate their own drama for five things that they liked and five things that could be improved.

- Ask groups to present their group evaluations to the whole class. Discuss findings, suggestions, and positive group efforts.

Activities

There are many ways to develop creative drama activities for student active learning teams. In the following suggested activities, students can be viewed as performers required to demonstrate their collective knowledge. The teacher's role will be that of a coach, helping students interpret the material in meaningful ways.

- *Personifying.* Each student draws the name of an inanimate object (pencil sharpener, doorknob, waste basket, alarm clock, and so on). Then students pick partners, and each team creates an improvisation involving the objects they picked.

- *Showing emotions.* Assign an emotion to each student (anger, jealousy, shyness, nervousness, nerdiness, arrogance, and so forth). Students must act out the emotion without actually naming it. The class notes significant details and discusses which emotion was being portrayed.

- *Extending a story.* Creative drama can extend a story. Try blocking (working out movement for) a play as it is read aloud in class. Giving a visual perspective increases concentration.

- *Increasing research and journalism skills.* Using techniques of role-playing and creative drama, have student groups show *how* to conduct interviews, giving both good and bad examples. Short excerpts from television news or radio information programs also provide good models for discussion and creative drama activities.

- *Increasing vocabulary.* Assign five words to a group and have group members use them in a skit.

- *Creating character transpositions.* Students can imagine a story they have just read taking place in a town or city that they have seen. For example, they can design a skit that takes a character from a historical period and presents him or her with a present-day dilemma. If they have been reading the tales of King Arthur, for instance, they might think of Merlin working in a used car lot, Sir Lancelot at a rock concert, Guinevere at a NOW meeting, or King Arthur interviewing for a job on Wall Street.

- *Redefining history.* Send students back through time by asking them to design a skit around what would happen if they found themselves transported to an earlier period. If they are reading Arthur Miller's *The Crucible*, for example, they could imagine what would happen to a present-day teenager (with Walkman and black T-shirt) who somehow lands in Salem, Massachusetts, at the height of the witch-hunting hysteria.

Literacy, Critical Thinking, and Prediction Strategies

Stretching students' minds means developing readers and writers who can think critically and creatively, who have been taught to infer meaning, anticipate story outcomes, discuss higher-level questions, and extrapolate to other situations. The teaching of these critical thinking skills, especially the skill of predictive and inferential thinking, benefits from directed reading and thinking activities (DRTAs) and directed writing and thinking activities (DWTAs). These directed thinking activities can be a positive influence as schools move from the traditional emphasis on reading skills to a collaborative-learning, literature-based approach that emphasizes creativity and thoughtfulness.

Inferential skills can be thought of as "reasonable reflective thinking that is focused on deciding what to believe or do" (Ennis, 1987, p. 65). In general, the better you are at making inferences, the better you are at reading. In DRTAs, students try to predict what will happen in a story on the basis of a few clues that they have been given. The stories can be students' or teachers' true experiences or can be taken from literature. As the students read, they continue to jointly speculate about the story and form hypotheses. Divergent responses are encouraged—although opinions must be justified on some logical basis. After the story has been read, students demonstrate their understanding by using story elements rather than simply recalling important points.

In the early grades, predictable books, like *Henny Penny* or *Curious George*, can teach thinking and prediction skills. Big books are particularly useful when using a DRTA with younger students. The teacher simply shows the page and asks the students what they think is going to happen next. Exhibit 6.6 contains a sample DRTA strategy (this one drawn from a real incident) for older children. Reading activities also include having partners read to each other and then make predictions based on visual (or written) clues or having partners construct summaries after reading an entire story.

DWTAs serve as vehicles for allowing ideas to come to fruition and for helping students decide where to go with their stories. Peer conferences occur during the planning, revision and editing process. Small cooperative groups help students learn to listen, question, resolve conflicts, share resources, and make decisions.

Exhibit 6.6. Directed Reading and Thinking Activity.

Directions. Place a dozen lines from a story on an overhead projector, uncovering them one at time as students guess what might happen next.

My big dog went down to the supermarket. What do you think he did? (Pause, ask for predictions before continuing.)

He stood up, leaned against the window, and looked in. What did he see? (Pause, ask for predictions before continuing.)

A leg of lamb. What happened next? (Pause, ask for predictions before continuing.)

The window broke. What did he do? (Pause, ask for predictions before continuing.)

He jumped in and grabbed the leg of lamb. What did he do with it? (Pause, ask for predictions before continuing.)

He ran for home. The police saw him. What did they do? (Pause, ask for predictions before continuing.)

They chased him, red lights flashing. I had just gotten home from work and I heard a knock on the door. Who was it? (Pause, ask for predictions before continuing.)

It was the police. What did they say? (Pause, ask for predictions before continuing.)

"Is he yours?"
"Yes."
"Do you know he just broke into the supermarket and stole a leg of lamb?"
"Noooo. How do you know you have the right dog?"
"He's chewing the evidence."
What happened next? (Pause, ask for predictions before continuing.)

I got a $365 bill from Allstate Insurance. But did they ever bill me for the leg of lamb? (Pause, ask for predictions before continuing.)
No, but for that price, I could get a side of beef.

Group support also increases the willingness for risk taking that is so important in language learning. Exhibit 6.7 illustrates an exercise combining predictive thinking and the writing of a story. Intensive social and affective forces can result in some very creative arrangements of the items in such exercises.

It is also valuable to use mixed-ability reading and writing groups in combination because reading good literature shows how adult writers go about setting the scene for the presentation of ideas. In addition, research suggests that collaboratively reading and writing together prompts more critical thinking and imaginative storytelling (Marcel & Carpenter, 1987). Directly connecting reading and writing programs also proved effective in achieving multiple perspectives and a greater depth of understanding (Weintrab, 1988).

Critical Thinking Across the Language Arts

Literature is not read in isolation. It must be integrated with the other language arts. Students use oral language to talk about what they are reading. They also listen to others, write in their response journals, and dramatize stories. When students connect a story they have read to creative drama and writing activities, they share imaginative ideas with their peers, creating an atmosphere in which unconscious thought flows freely. Students can also be asked to record how they think and make inferences about what they read.

A specific suggestion for expanding critical thinking across the language arts is to have students explore how community or historical figures developed their ability to read, write, and think imaginatively. Children can use the whole range of language skills by inviting five elders in for an oral history project. Each elder is assigned to a small group of students who interview her or him and who take notes and later write up the history. This project can also be connected to social studies by asking questions about specific events and times: for example, What was it like during World War

---

Exhibit 6.7. Predicting and Writing a Story.

Directions. Place each of the following items under one of the category headings below:

Items

Fillipo	honor
Florence	dinner
Mona	marriage
a falcon	Lisa
poverty	illness

Category Headings

Setting   Characters   Problem   Solution   Ending

Make up a story with this setting, these characters, and this problem, solution, and ending. Share the story with the whole class.

II? This activity connects generations and makes history come alive. A local newspaper might even be willing to come in and cover the event. In a small town, the newspaper might even carry the final version of what the students write about each visitor.

The integrated language arts approach encourages long periods of self-selected reading, teachers reading aloud to students, and the sharing of reading and response projects that emphasize reflection and interpretation rather than plot summaries. These analytical approaches to literature also help teachers uncover special student interests in an author, illustrator, or theme. Students and teacher might even plan a unit together, choosing books around a topic or person of interest and planning reading and response activities. Students can keep response journals and focus on a few favorite books through writing, art, or creative drama activities or through a particular line of research.

Some teachers use what they call a think-aloud. Choosing one or two thinking strategies to teach—such as predicting, visualizing, confirming, elaborating, or summarizing—they talk about how they use those strategies for constructing meaning and activating their own prior knowledge as they read. Then they have the students practice the same meaning construction strategies, working with partners as they read, think out loud, and jot down a few notes. This exercise helps students develop their critical reading and writing skills.

Technological Tools for the Literacy-Intensive Future

Littera scripta manet (the written word remains), said Horace. The digital book may not replace the printed variety in the third millennium, but it will alter the literary landscape. Print culture will continue to be important because, among other things, it connects us to a rich literary tradition and provides a unique communication tool, but it is time to teach nonprint literacy along with what Seymour Papert (1993) calls "letteracy." So far, teachers have had only glimpses of the technological possibilities for interactive communication and computer-assisted language learning. But those glimpses are impressive. Word-processing programs can facilitate the collaborative writing process. Using their classroom computers, children can select their topics, write drafts, interact with peers in reading and writing projects, and revise, edit, and publish their work for real audiences. They can use computers with multimedia capacities to compose with print, images, and sound. Furthermore, the research suggests that rich social interactions can occur around writing on the computer screen (Cochran-Smith, Kahn, & Paris, 1988; Mehan, 1989). And once our nation develops its information superhighways, the materials in large libraries will no longer be in some distant location but in the cyberspace of our computers, available to all. Already some schools are using the Internet electronic data network.

And there are other applications. Interacting with sounds and with objects on the screen while alternating between English and another language makes electronic books a powerful way to learn both English and other languages. Students can also see and hear models for high-quality reading. Words or concepts can be highlighted so that the reader can clearly understand options or hear how a written word or sentence is pronounced. In this way, phonics can be taught in the context of whole texts while students focus on meaning. For example, instead of providing an electronic worksheet on the letter O, a good program might bring up a poem with a lot of O sounds in it. Thus, computer-based stories can make it easier for teachers to incorporate subskills into the literature and writing program.

As argued in Chapter Four, computers are dynamic tools that should not be confined to computer labs or serve as expensive flash card systems. In an integrated language arts classroom, the computer can be used for word processing, reference retrieval, simulation, multimedia production, and telecommunication. And many children's books with enriching accompanying information (for example, interviews with authors) are now coming out in CD-ROM format, adding yet another rationale for integrating reading, writing, speaking, and listening into our language arts classrooms, since "reading" the new electronic texts more and more requires all those language skills. The computer has transformed the possibilities of text in a way that allows the reader to converse with characters, learn the subskills needed to read, and construct nonlinear journeys through literary space. Interactive electronic novels are being written for the computer in a multisensory mode that appeals to the current generation of visual learners. Publishers are developing joint ventures with computer software companies to create electronic versions of libraries of children's titles. The result is higher literary content and a greater variety of electronic titles. Will these high-tech developments influence the school reading program? You bet.

Teachers are discovering that electronic stories allow readers to think, create, and construct meaning in a way that encourages further adventures in literacy. A visually and personally enriched contextual setting for reading, language learning, and communication will help students think critically and grasp the meaning of printed material. The best titles in this new literary genre value dialogue, inquiry, puzzlement, and student autonomy.

Hypertext, the nonlinear writing discussed in Chapter Four, is more than a literary fad. It is part of a technological shift that will irrevocably change the teaching of reading. The multimedia children's books *Arthur's Teacher Troubles* and *Just Grandma and Me* are among the top ten selling computer CDs. Children can spend hours upon hours working their way through a title that would be disposed of quickly in the traditional format. Interactive stories allow readers/viewers to structure the plot, create character attributes, solve problems, and find solutions. They can also see the consequences of their decision making and can circle back to restructure their experience over and over.

Hypertext both strongly demands and powerfully teaches literacy and critical intelligence. As more and more PCs are equipped with CD-ROM players, electronic book sales will expand, and children will see these intriguing and demanding works as normal parts of the reading experience. Book stores will be drawn inexorably into selling electronic texts, and as electronic literature gains momentum, larger libraries will stock this literature, and hypertext will become a natural choice for reading. Even Hollywood is getting into the interactive mode by starting to produce a new type of film/book/video game in which the plot is guided by the "reader." In some of these efforts, captioned video images are used to improve students' reading comprehension, vocabulary, and motivation.

At their best, hypertext works help the reader to go beyond the limitations imposed by the linearity of conventional print and to participate in a virtual community of literary characters. In the world of hypertext and computer networks, time and space take on different dimensions. When children in different locations can participate in the same hypertext story or electronic data base, the concept of literary community takes on new meaning. A good example here is the undertaking by the Library of Congress and a consortium of institutions across the United States to create a digitized Leonard Bernstein archive as a contribution to the information superhighway. Among other things, the archive contains a vast collection of correspondence, musical recordings, video interviews, photographs, and musical manuscripts. Students can interact with the digitized material and each other, and even hear how it would sound if they changed a composition. The whole project is in keeping with Bernstein's background as an educator and master of media. The educational consequences of having numerous such resources available are enormous.

If some of today's visual learners are given a curriculum that is too book-intensive, they lose interest. For those children who prefer that print be reinforced by visuals, hypertext is a great motivator. As students struggle to link concepts and ideas, hypertext can heighten awareness of story structure and interject a new element of excitement into reading. Since their personal decisions have significant consequences in electronic stories, students must really pay attention. Of course, no text closes the door on rethinking or rereading. When reading traditional literature, readers constantly make individual interpretations, revise their thoughts, and reread. The reader always has an obligation to be an active participant in the text. Still, hypertext forces the issue by refusing to let the reader sit back, fade away, or mentally wander. Passivity and short attention spans are less likely to get in the way of this literary medium.

Hypertext fiction connects to the roots of literary tradition. In many ways, the ancient world of the oral tradition is closer to the new electronic narrative forms than the world of print. Myths, fables, and various forms of folktales often relate basically similar stories in different ways or create many tales around a central figure, as the literature of classical Greece testifies. A similar pattern of variations occurs when our children use today's technology to get away from prearranged sequences and to build new cumulative pictures by making new links among events or episodes and wondering about the consequences of different decisions.

Whatever literary current we find ourselves in at the end of the twentieth century, literacy and critical thinking skills will remain constant prerequisites for further learning and for living a productive life in a democracy. What will change most are the instructional vehicles and the manner in which knowledge is gained. How children will read, learn, and entertain themselves is changing, and because of their familiarity with computer games and computer-based activities at school, many children have less trouble adapting to interactive reading than adults. Moreover, conventional literature will not be diminished. There will still be times when it will be best to be caught up and transported by a traditionally told story.

There is, however, another important issue to be addressed. Who will shape our new interactive literature? If our best writers avoid creating interactive literature and allow the field to be controlled by today's crass video producers or by computer programmers more interested in technique than content, it will become more difficult than ever to motivate students into reading and writing because we will lack the right electronic texts. Worse yet, literature will be increasingly consigned to and isolated in the schools. The competition for people's time is fierce, and fewer and fewer Americans spend as much time reading as they do watching television. Exposed to the insistent power of our rampaging electronic media, many Americans have lost the discipline to read more than brief passages in print. What novel have *you* been reading during the last month? Have you spent more time watching television? Hypertext may be able to help reverse our nation's slide into functional illiteracy. The technological advances now occurring can bestow a cornucopia of educational and informational possibilities upon us or leave us all in a cultural wasteland.

Hypertext can play a major role in reversing our population's move away from the intellectual depth of print by offering an abundance of compelling literature. But as the physical form of information expands, the way it is taught must also change. Whether we call electronic literature hypertext, multimedia, or hyperfiction, its arrival means that soon computer-mediated reading will become a staple of life in classrooms. The new interactive children's books can help balance the seductive power of television and strengthen literature's appeal in the fierce competition for a child's time. Language made us human; literacy made us civilized; technology will make us powerful in our language and literacy.

Modeling Literacy

Beyond the activities in the literature-based integrated language arts classroom, beyond the potential of electronic learning and literacy, lie some simple truths about literacy that all teachers must bear in mind. Children learn about reading and writing and using language to construct meaning in active ways; for example, they interact with peers by using meaningful stories to accomplish genuine purposes. The goal of adult mediation should be to provide information that students need to know when they need to know it. It is up to both teachers and parents to create a literate environment and mediate the learning that goes on by modeling the use of literacy activities.

Whatever adults want to make important to children, they must make important to themselves as well. For example, it is hard for a teacher to teach reading if he or she does not (at least occasionally) read books. Likewise, it is hard for a parent to instill a love of literature if there are no books, magazines, and newspapers around the house. Reading the environment precedes reading the word. Yet some parents today cannot read, and those who can are most likely to be working outside the home. If parents also do not know what is going on at school, then there is likely to be little help at home for students struggling to become literate.

When teachers change their methods and classroom organizational structures, they need the understanding of administrators, other teachers, *and* parents. Some teachers meet with parents before school starts to set cooperative goals and ask about each child's strong and weak points—what works for her or him and what does not. Parents can make a big contribution to their children's success in school by helping them use reading, writing, listening, and speaking for real purposes, and teachers can encourage practices that promote literacy at home and are similar to those that work in the classroom. As this chapter has emphasized, language learning at its best is a shared experience. At home, this means stories at bedtime, discussions of the day's news, adults who read, museum excursions, and library visits. Such creative language experiences help develop children's capacity for an aesthetic response to literature. At school, it is up to the teacher to make sure that literacy instruction builds on the students' outside experiences, adding to them the strategies necessary for meaningful reading and writing.

The kind of language arts program and activities described in this chapter are built on a belief in collaborative learning and a complementary belief that literacy instruction should be natural, holistic, and connected to a strong literary base. This powerful approach to literacy development requires activities that are intrinsically motivating because they help students draw on their own cultural and personal resources as they develop productive habits of the mind. Engaging youngsters in an active group exploration of ideas is exciting.

For the seeds of literacy to grow, teachers must take themselves seriously as agents of change who arrange classroom environments for cooperation, problem solving, and engagement. Providing a rich, engaging, literary environment for all children also means recognizing that children have different pathways to literacy, but that taking *some* path is essential because only literacy will give students the tools they need to reflect on a whole range of communication possibilities, thinking critically and participating meaningfully in learning. It will also give them new capacities for personal and social action.

The methods a teacher chooses to teach language skills will reflect her or his unique combination of professional knowledge, policy requirements, student background, and personal choice. A teacher's degree of success in using an integrated language arts approach to learning will depend upon her or his philosophy of teaching and learning and her or his enthusiasm (Routman, 1991). To paraphrase William Blake, *energy is an eternal delight.* If teachers are energized and really believe in literature-based language instruction, they usually do just fine—even if they have to wait for their school systems to catch up.

Chapter Seven

Mathematical Power

There was once a state legislator in Wisconsin who
objected to the introduction of daylight saving time
despite all the good arguments for it. He maintained
sagely that there is always a trade-off involved in the
adoption of any policy, and that if daylight saving
time were instituted, curtains and other fabrics
would fade more quickly.

—*John Allen Paulos (1992)*

The more technological our world becomes, the more often we find
ourselves in situations that require us to think and communicate
mathematically. Whether we are making sense of newspaper
graphs, predicting results at work, or planning for a trip across the
country, mathematics filters into our lives. Computational skills,
the ability to express basic mathematical understandings, to estimate confidently, and to validate the reasonableness of estimates,
are part of what it means to be literate, numerate, and employable.
Yet there is little doubt about the discrepancy between school
mathematics and mathematical applications in the real world. Our
real mathematical problems have little to do with what has traditionally been taught in many classrooms or the information found
in most math textbooks. It is our human tendency to do mainly
those things that we view as having some general utility; thus,
many students do not see the point in mastering material that is
detached from the world outside of school. In school, students usually do math alone and without tools such as calculators. In the
world of work, people usually work together in agenda-setting

181

groups, using any tools they can get their hands on. (In school, that kind of problem solving is often called cheating.)

Today, however, the curriculum is changing to reflect the content and skills students need to meet new societal and intellectual demands, and good schools are recognizing that teamwork, critical thinking, problem solving, and active communication are at the heart of teaching the new mathematical understanding. This chapter examines the new methods for teaching mathematics in the light of this recognition and offers many examples of collaborative problem-solving activities.

Teaching Mathematics in the 1990s: NCTM Curriculum Standards

The emerging pattern for teaching mathematics builds content and method around the nature of learning (California State Department of Education, 1992a). Teachers are being required to shift gears from a cognitive to a metacognitive stance. Successful learning is understood to be constructive and active, with many opportunities for students to interpret mathematical ideas and construct mathematical understandings for themselves. Students need not only think skillfully but must also monitor their thinking processes as they work. Mathematics in the 1990s emphasizes connections and relationships; it is seen as a process or a journey (National Council of Teachers of Mathematics, 1991) with the student in the role of explorer. Constructing a hypothesis, engaging in problem solving, and participating in group investigations must replace the traditional chalk-talk and textbook methodology. Whereas in the past, the emphasis was on how to answer questions correctly or memorize facts, the challenge for today's teachers is how to motivate students for the lifelong learning of mathematics, awakening mathematical curiosity and encouraging creativity. Today, we want students to relate and apply math to social problems, to science, to technology, to creative innovation, and to their personal lives. To make mathematics accessible and interesting, today's best mathematics teaching derives mathematics from each learner's reality, emphasizing inquiry and valuing students' ideas. Mathematics is as much cooperative purpose and storytelling as it is formulas and calculations. When students make mathematical connections across disciplines, they demonstrate powerful tools of thinking, communicating, and a deep understanding of mathematical content (National Research Council, 1989). We want students to appreciate the beauty and fascination of mathematics; we want them to approach the mathematics they will encounter throughout their lives with an attitude of curiosity, enjoyment, and confidence.

Mathematics has a rich past and a rich present. Our goal is that all students connect their own lives to the cultural and historical settings upon which mathematics was founded and continues to develop. Students should become aware of the range of career options that depend on mathematics and the diversity of people who have played important roles in its history (DeAvila, Cohen, & Intill, 1981). But we also need to go beyond careers to look at the cultural connections of mathematics—from the Mayan calendar to Tower Bridge in London to the Towers of Hanoi. By bringing mathematics alive in our social studies and history curricula, we can learn to celebrate the contributions of diverse mathematicians from all times and places and shed light on the ways people in all cultures use mathematics every day.

A document that is having a dramatic impact on the teaching of mathematics is *Curriculum and Evaluation Standards for School Mathematics*, put out by the National Council of Teachers of Mathematics (NCTM) in the spring of 1989. This document proposes that all students meet five general goals:

1. Learn to value mathematics.
2. Become confident in their ability to do mathematics.
3. Become mathematical problem solvers.

4. Learn to communicate mathematically.

5. Learn to reason mathematically.

To meet these goals, students must be exposed to numerous and varied experiences that encourage them to value mathematics as they develop mathematical habits of mind. They must be encouraged to explore and guess, and even to make and correct errors, so they gain confidence in their ability to solve complex problems. They should read, write, and discuss mathematics, as well as conjecture, test, and build arguments about the validity of their mathematical solutions.

The new curriculum standards also include a broadened scope for mathematics. In a shift away from instruction that focuses on memorization of formulas and algorithms, more emphasis is now placed on teaching statistics and probability and showing their practical applications to the world we all live in and to situations in students' own lives, in order to promote students' willingness to persevere and work through mathematical problems to reach solutions.

Because researchers widely agree that a constructive, active view of learning must be reflected in the way that mathematics is taught (Cruikshank & Sheffield, 1992), classroom mathematics experiences should stimulate students to explore and express their own ideas and build on their past understandings. Students should have opportunities to interpret mathematical ideas, rules, and principles and to construct mathematical understandings for themselves. To do this, students need to become explorers in problem-solving investigations and projects that fully engage their thinking and reasoning skills. They will require many experiences with manipulatives, calculators, computers, and working in cooperative groups. As we will see in more detail later, working with materials in a group situation helps reinforce mathematical thinking. As students discuss their understandings of a mathematical task with their peers, they also improve their self-images and personal

confidence, and self-concept is viewed an indication of performance (Davidson, 1990).

The NCTM standards have already begun to influence curriculum writing at state and local levels and the content of both
textbooks and tests. Emphasized at each grade level are the abilities to reason mathematically, communicate mathematically in a
range of representative modes, make connections using mathematical concepts, and use mathematical applications, or tools.
These emphases and some content-specific standards are highlighted in the following activities, which were developed as illustrations and suggestions based on the NCTM standards.

- *Estimate and compare (K–4; Standard 5: estimation)*. In
grades K–4, the curriculum should include estimation, and students
should be able to explore estimation strategies; recognize when an
estimate is appropriate; determine the reasonableness of results; and
apply estimation in working with quantities, measurement, computations, and problem solving.

For example, place groups of objects in color-coded containers
(using only one kind of object in each container) and give a container to each child or place containers at several workstations. Pass
out recording sheets divided into boxes, with a container color in
each box. Have each child examine the container on her or his
desk, estimate how many objects are present, and write that guess
on the sheet, next to the color of her or his container. Next, have
the child count the objects and write the number she or he counted
next to the first number. Instruct the child to circle the greater
amount. Then have the child write a number sentence using the
greater than sign (>). Have the children switch cans, or move to
the next station, and repeat the process. Using a variety of objects
(small plastic animals, marbles, paper clips, colored shells, and so
forth) adds interest and is a real motivator.

- *Simple addition and subtraction (K–4; Standard 7: whole number operations)*. In grades K–4, the mathematics curriculum should

include concepts of addition, subtraction, multiplication, and division of whole numbers so that students can develop meaning for the operations by modeling and discussing a rich variety of problem situations; relate the mathematical language and symbolism of operations to problem situations and informal language; recognize that a wide variety of problem structures can be represented by a single operation; and develop operation sense.

For example, use manipulatives with word problems, and in each problem, have students paste counters beside the numbers. Some students need to see the whole pattern, so have them also place counters where the answer will go. Or tell stories in which the children pretend to be animals or things that must be counted. Role-playing activities that involve problem solving are highly motivational and reach multiple learning styles and interests. Here are three sample word problems:

_____, _____, and _____ are clowns at the circus. _____, _____, and _____ are more clowns who have also come to perform. How many clowns are at the circus?

_____, _____, and _____ are standing near the door. _____ and _____ sit down. How many are still standing at the door?

_____ put three books on the table. _____ put two more books on the table. How many books are there on the table altogether?

Having children use unifix cubes to represent people, objects, or animals in stories also works well. Have students do this task on construction paper or prepare counting boards on which trees, oceans, trails, houses, and so forth have been drawn.

• *Column addition (K–4; Standard 8: whole number computation)*. To meet this standard, students should be able to model, explain, and develop reasonable proficiency with basic algorithms; use a variety of mental techniques for computing and estimating; use calculators in appropriate computational situations; and select and use computational techniques appropriate to specific problems and determine if the results are reasonable.

To work with students on whole number computation, help them look for patterns within an addition problem, such as finding a ten, grouping numbers together, multiplying numbers, or rounding up or down. Ask students for other helpful ways to solve the problem. Have them work with a partner or in a small group to think of strategies for adding columns of numbers. Have group members write down all the strategies their group comes up with and then discuss the strategies with other students.

The NCTM recommendations also suggest teaching a broader mathematical curriculum that includes skills in estimating and problem solving and in using practical geometry, statistics, data analysis, calculators, probability, measurement, and patterns across all the disciplines taught in the classroom. The disconnection of mathematics from other subjects from history to sports is not a new problem, and it is now acknowledged that connecting practical mathematical applications to other disciplines adds depth and excitement to math, as well as enriching students' knowledge of the other subject areas. Teachers are now discussing civic, leisure, and cultural features of mathematics in the classroom. Instead of teaching mathematics as a separate set of skills needed primarily for the next academic level, they are positioning mathematics as an exciting and powerful way of knowing and are augmenting school learning in mathematics with museum visits, community group meetings, outdoor education programs, peer teaching, and programs for parents.

Traditional Teaching

Difficulty in learning mathematics and science is the major factor that pushes students to fail in school, but much of students' failure is due to a tradition of teaching that is inappropriate to the way students learn. As described in Chapter Two, cognitive psychologists such as Piaget and Bruner explain that students construct understandings based on their own experiences and that each individual's knowledge of mathematics and science is personal (Bruner & Haste, 1987). Yet mathematics and science lessons in which students are expected to read, listen, and memorize abstract concepts or symbolic procedures are still common, even though they are the least effective mode for mathematics and science teaching. Besides acquiring a distaste for the subjects, students simply do not retain much of what they learn from hearing lectures and completing worksheets in the classroom and as homework.

Teacher demonstrations, textbook readings, and repetition of mathematical methods may help students do well on standardized tests. But these lower-order skills are generally ineffective out of school, where students need to practice long-term higher-order thinking and problem solving. Indeed, the results are sadly disappointing when students are trained to search narrowly for limited answers or hints about how to do a page rather than to attain the true goals of mathematics education: clear thinking, conceptual understanding, and logical reasoning in applying knowledge and solving problems. Furthermore, since much on-the-job application requires a response to rapidly changing problems, specific skills training can be very limiting. Therefore, forging ahead with curriculum models without examining the future needs of students in the workplace is short-sighted and self-defeating.

To learn mathematics successfully, students must construct their own understandings, examine, represent, solve, transform, apply, prove, and communicate. This happens most effectively when students work in groups to discuss, make presentations, invent, impose their interpretation on what is presented, and create theories that make sense to them, thinking critically and in terms of relationships. How a student structures these subject matter relationships will depend on such factors as the student's maturity, physical experience, and social interactions, all of which are also enhanced by cooperative learning.

A Cooperative Learning Model for Teaching Mathematics

Small mixed-ability learning groups have proven effective in mathematics classes (Burns, 1977), and indeed, real mathematics is seldom practiced in isolation. If the task is at all difficult or requires serious thought, we collaborate with others—sharing information, opinions, and expertise and gaining the energy to persevere. As we complete the task, we try to communicate our results in a clear and convincing way. Thus, one of the central themes in the recent publications that address rethinking U.S. mathematics education (Mathematical Sciences Education Board and the National Research Council, 1990; National Council of Teachers of Mathematics, 1989; 1991) is the need for students to work together in small groups to discuss mathematical ideas and solve problems. Too often, students exhibit procedural knowledge (ability to do computational skills) but are unable to apply these procedures to real situations. We need to examine the kinds of mathematical knowledge our students possess and explore some of the ways that learners construct their understanding of mathematics, including cooperative learning.

As previously mentioned, *Curriculum and Evaluation Standards for School Mathematics* (National Council of Teachers of Mathematics, 1989) describes mathematically literate students as those who are adept in the four areas of mathematical thinking, mathematical communication, mathematical connections, and mathematical tools and techniques. The council suggests that K–4 students should use problem-solving approaches to investigate and understand mathematical content, grades 5 to 8 should discuss mathematical ideas and make conjectures and convincing arguments, and grades 9 to 12 should develop, analyze, and explain procedures for computation and techniques for estimation.

Because developing higher-order thinking is now a primary goal of mathematics education, each teacher needs a clear knowledge of what he or she want students to learn and a plan for organizing the classroom to help students to construct that knowledge. Jerome Bruner (1966) has established that a learning environment in the mathematics classroom encourages exploration, presents mathematical ideas in a concrete manner, and does not equate failure with punishment. In this learning environment, students are encouraged to explore with manipulatives—from geopieces, Cuisinaire rods, fraction pieces, and base ten blocks to plain blocks, chips, and Popsicle sticks—to find mathematical solutions. For example, fourth-grade students doing long division can use base ten blocks to find out how 426 chairs can be distributed equally among three rooms. Or students can invent their own algorithms by figuring out how to share seventeen cubes among four children. Have children describe their solutions, verify them by using the cubes, and then write out the procedures for others. There are, of course, many different ways to arrive at a solution. Ask children to find creative ways to share $.50 among four children, explain their solutions, and discuss whether the solutions are fair and whether the problem could be solved differently. Or ask them what they would get if they had $2.00 to spend at the supermarket, and how they would explain their choices.

The newest methods for teaching mathematics in active small-group learning situations include having students write about how they solved problems, keep daily logs or journals, and express mathematical attitudes through such creative endeavors as writing, building, or art. Holistic creative thinking is encouraged as well as projects and presentations that combine experiential knowledge with theoretical understandings. Emphasis is on exciting examples, investigations, and everyday applications.

Teachers can also use classroom situations to pose problems. For example, children in one classroom counted and found they had 163 sheets of construction paper. They were given the problem of figuring out how many sheets each child would receive if the sheets were divided evenly among them, and each child was directed to write her or his reasoning for the class. After the children solved the problem, they presented their results and methods to the class and discussed the different methods they had used. Finally, the children were shown the standard notation for representing division. Shortly thereafter, they began to use the standard symbol in their own writing.

When they become involved in problems and use materials at a concrete level, students will use the knowledge they currently possess to make and test their hypotheses, as long as teachers create an environment that minimizes risk and accentuates exploration and in which every mistake is an opportunity to learn. Cooperative learning fits easily into this recommended environment. To accomplish the NCTM's bold goals, students cannot work alone with most of the discussion coming from the teacher. There is simply too much material for the teacher to teach it effectively. What is needed is an active learning approach in which the mathematics teacher becomes a facilitator and a learner, and students come to share in some of the teaching chores.

There is substantial evidence that students working in groups can master science and mathematics material better than students working alone (Slavin, 1989). The more opportunities students have for social interaction, the more divergent viewpoints and perspectives can season their thinking. Through collaborative group explorations, they can be pushed to analyze what they think, discuss it, and clarify their own reasoning. Working in small groups also gives students a relatively safe environment in which to interact with concepts and verbalize their own concepts. When working together is part of the classroom culture, there is less worry about being wrong. Also, as in any other cooperative learning situation, it is important to involve students in establishing the rules for active group work, clearly defining group roles and individual responsibilities. As discussed in Chapter Three, students must have a reason to take one another's progress seriously and care about the team's success; the team must stand or fall together. If the group task is simply to complete a worksheet, the easiest approach may be to let the highest-achieving students do most of the work while suggestions or questions from low-achieving students may be pushed aside as interfering with efficiency. Active cooperation requires a different approach in which group success is based not on a single product but is the sum of the individual learning performances of all members.

Teachers in the New Mathematics Classroom

Cognitive views of learning that emphasize the importance of prior knowledge and thinking processes within the learner suggest the kinds of changes needed in the ways that educators think about learners, teaching, and organizing the school classroom (Paul, Binker, Jensen, & Kreklau, 1989). The learning environment must be built around the desire to help individuals acquire or construct knowledge. The underlying concept is that knowledge is to be shared or developed rather than held by an authority. This holds teachers to a high standard, for they must have both subject matter knowledge and pedagogical knowledge. Without the essential content base, teachers are unable to focus students' thinking and unable to provide appropriate feedback or effectively discuss the content. And without pedagogical knowledge based on an understanding of cognitive and developmental processes, it is difficult to make mathematics more personally relevant and interesting for students.

The cooperative learning model for mathematics suggested here emphasizes the benefits of learning rather than external rewards for academic performance. Lessons are introduced with statements of the reasons for engaging in the learning task, reasons such as learning to think critically or exploring the nature of an interesting topic. Students are encouraged to assume responsibility for learning and evaluating their own work and the work of others.

Whole-group mathematics learning will occur during the giving of instructions, initial brainstorming, collecting and summarizing of data, reviewing different strategies, and coming to common understandings. Whole-group learning will also frequently be used for highlighting important mathematical ideas that arise in the work. However, small-group learning should be dominant in discussions of the validity of explanations, searches for more information, tests of various explanations, and considerations of the pros and cons of specific decisions. In cooperative learning classrooms, instead of being told they need information, students learn to recognize when additional data is needed. They jointly seek it out, apply it, and see its power and value. In this way, the actual *use* of mathematical information is not an issue to be faced only in the future but is the starting point of the lesson, and the teacher facilitates the process instead of acting as a knowledge dispenser. Student success is measured on performance, work samples, application, or synthesis. Simple recall is not as important.

As teachers soon discover, teaching for understanding requires a lot of time and effort. It takes time to develop mathematical concepts, make materials, and give students opportunities for discussion, planning, experimenting, and trying out their theories. Less time will be spent on textbooks and drill sheets; more time will be given to group tasks, solving problems, writing, and discussion. But this is as it should be, since students use these components to do meaningful tasks. Moreover, as teachers channel classroom energy into productive communication and collaborative problem solving, they soon find that it is easier to interact with eight groups than with thirty individuals.

An approach that views mathematics as both an individual and a collective activity offers an account of truth, certainty, and intersubjectivity. That is, the assumption that students will inevitably construct correct internal representations from the materials presented implies that students can recognize complex mathematical relationships that are developmentally more advanced than their current level of understanding. Clearly the guidance of teachers is needed if this is to happen.

The teacher provides time for students to grapple with problems, try out strategies, discuss, experiment, explore, and evaluate. It is because the primary focus is on the students' own investigations, discussions, and group projects that teachers' role shifts become analogous to the role shifts of business supervisors who must become team coaches or expert managers. In a classroom community of learners, teachers facilitate the development of individual children's interpretations when the teachers make interventions, take advantage of learning situations, question, and probe students' understanding (Lampert, 1990). By encouraging students to talk about the mathematics they are doing, asking questions that require explanations rather than one-word answers, and reflecting on children's thinking and actions, teachers gain a wealth of knowledge about how each child is constructing the ideas presented and internalizing mathematical relationships. Teachers also need to look for evidence of misconceptions and be aware of the ideas that children have constructed incorrectly. Not all students will construct the same concept just because they have been given the same classroom experience.

Effective mathematics teachers present themselves as problem solvers and models of inquiry, letting students know that everyone is an active learner and no one knows all the answers. Teachers also need to exhibit an interest in finding solutions to problems, show confidence in trying various strategies, and risk being wrong. It is more important for them to emphasize working on the problem than getting "the answer." By creating an environment where students are encouraged and affirmed, teachers can push the boundaries of their curriculum into new spaces.

Here are some specific suggestions for the effective mathematics teacher.

- *Foster a common expectation of quality work.* Students must come to expect that large pieces of complete work are part of the program and that they are to be done well. (Complete work is work that demonstrates all the dimensions of mathematical power: thinking, communicating, drawing on mathematical ideas to make connections, and actually using tools and techniques.) This expectation can be achieved. Social studies and language arts have expected projects for decades. Students not only need to understand what teachers expect but must help set those expectations and standards, both for assignments and individual investigations.

- *Prepare students for complete work.* Students need practice in the mechanics of complete work, going beyond finding the "right answer" to demonstrating understanding and communicating their thinking. Practice in writing about mathematics will make their ideas clearer and more concise; practice with presenting will make their presentations better organized.

- *Give students the time and tools they need.* Students need a realistic chance to show what they have learned. Large pieces of work take time—time to try, to err, to get stuck, to talk to peers and restart, to consider critiques and revise, and to mull things over. Much of this time can come outside of class, with class time provided for work that should be done cooperatively. Providing tools (both literal and figurative) to students—calculators, rubberbands, and compasses; hints on model building; and help with computations—is also an important part of the process.

- *Require that mathematical work be done to a comprehensible standard.* Mathematics in student work must be clear, but evaluating mathematical thinking is more interpretative than evaluating computation. Students and teachers need a common understanding of quality standards.

- *Help students develop a habit of drafting, receiving feedback, and revising.* All students should regularly prepare drafts of major assignments, receive feedback (often from peers) that indicates what must be done to make the work better, and then revise. There must be no stigma attached to revision and no grade penalty; some work will simply need more revision before it meets quality standards.

• *Provide purposeful mathematics tasks worthy of quality, large-scale work.* It is difficult to expect students to pursue solutions to a problem if the work presented is boring, does not make sense, or does not challenge them. Because mathematical tasks are often complex and ambiguous, students may need to experiment with many different approaches to a task, learn from their mistakes, and try over and over again. All of this requires persistence and hard work. Students who approach mathematics with boredom or fear are unlikely to persist in completing complex tasks.

Mathematical power is enhanced by a positive disposition, an attitude of adventure, curiosity, and confidence. What is our goal for developing students' attitudes? How do students with positive attitudes about mathematics feel and act? Students who are positive persist in the face of frustrations, erroneous approaches, blind alleys, and difficulties. They enjoy the challenge of a tough problem and enjoy hearing other people's ideas about how to approach it. They do not want to be told the answer to the problem, and they feel a sense of accomplishment discovering something about the answer. They have an appetite for finding and explaining patterns and enjoy the power of a generalization. Finally, they are critical of teachers who give them assignments without purpose, isolate them, or tell them too many answers.

A Beginning Cooperative Activity

The pooling of tasks, exercises, and games involves students directly in cooperative experiential learning activities consisting of sequences of concrete experience, observation, generalization, reflection, concept formation, and tests or applications of the concepts or general principles to new situations (Chickering, 1977). We can see each of these stages in the following suggestion for a beginning group activity in which student groups are asked to survey the class and prepare a group poster or graph that reflects the ideas of every member of the class.

Concrete Experience. This task exposes each group to a range of cooperative procedures. The group must exchange ideas (What do we want to find out? What will it look like? What topic should we choose for the survey?) and share feelings (What are we going to do? How do we organize it?). Lack of specific instructions can lead to frustration in some individuals. Members must help each other organize, plan, and produce a product. Each group presents its work to the class and reports how the group arrived at the finished product. Hanging the graphs and posters for display creates a sense of belonging in the group.

Observation and Reflection. Learners reflect on the experience's significance for them. This is a bridge between the experience and the students' formal learning roles as observers. Students are asked to examine these follow-up questions:

- What happened in your group? Students share their perceptions of the experience with each other. This allows them to recognize that not all members perceive the event similarly.
- How did the group participants feel? Positive and negative feelings and trust and acceptance factors are revealed as well as feelings of risk and exposure.
- What does it mean? Students explore meaning, generalize, and examine group roles.

Formalization of Abstract Concepts and Generalizations. To help students interpret the knowledge gained through the experience and to guide students' applications, teachers may wish to assign follow-up readings, activities, or further tasks that use surveys, graphing, or data presentation.

Testing Applications in New Situations. Based on what they have found out, students may wish to choose a new topic to study or to create new group tasks with a real-world emphasis. The more complex the thinking and the higher-order processing of information, the greater the effect on problem solving, social skills, and attitudes.

Problem Solving in the Classroom and the World

We live in a complex time. Both personal and global problems confront us daily. Preventing a nuclear war, preserving our national resources, controlling population, resisting terrorism, and stemming drug use are only a handful of the major difficulties with elusive solutions that confront our society. Skill in cooperatively solving problems is one of the most essential and valuable tools that we can teach children. No topic presented in our schools can be more vital or pertinent. Yet despite the good intentions of school personnel, students' acquisition of problem-solving skills remains tentative at best.

Problem solving in any discipline requires a facility with language, an ability to examine and analyze, and a general understanding of the world. In the process of collaboratively solving a problem, memory and critical and creative thinking merge as students identify, analyze, and evaluate responses and products. Thinking mathematically (or scientifically) requires students to represent world phenomena and problems with mental constructs; search for the optimal solution, asking "what if" questions; and extend natural language to symbolic representation. In decision-making situations, alternatives must be weighed and the consequences of various solutions examined. Communicating with computations allows individuals to maximize the efficiency of the communication and involves inferring, reasoning from data, and analyzing and searching for explanations.

When classrooms are organized so that small mixed-ability groups resourcefully collaborate, ask questions, and explore possible answers, children can develop an energetic enthusiasm about both mathematics and science. As mathematics and science move from their computational and factual bases to a problem-solving emphasis, these subjects can come alive and stimulate students because of their real-world immediacy.

Mathematical Activities

Here are a number of activities that can use collective learning techniques and that connect experience and concrete measurement to mathematical investigations and problem solving. In many cases, they relate to the sciences or social studies, providing interdisciplinary interest.

- *Use the sun for geometry*. Have children investigate figures and their properties through shadow geometry, exploring what happens to shapes held in front of a point of light. They can also explore what happens to shapes held in the sunlight when the sun's rays are nearly parallel, and they can discover which characteristics of the shapes are maintained under varying conditions. For this activity, provide pairs of children with wooden or plastic squares (geoboards for example), and take the children to a flat-surfaced area of the playground. Have the children hold the squares so that shadows are cast on the ground, and encourage the children to move the squares so that the shadow changes. Have children talk about the shadows they find, discussing how they are able to make the shapes larger and smaller and making other observations. To make a permanent record of the shapes, have a child draw a favorite shape on a piece of paper and put the piece of paper on the ground. Let the shadow fall on the paper, and have the child draw around the outline of the shadow. This will produce a collection of interesting drawings that can serve as a source for discussion, sorting, and display. For a challenge activity, ask students to discover if they can make a triangular or pentagonal shadow using the square.

• *Make a map.* Have children use graph paper and a pencil to draw a path. Ask them label the sides of the paper for directions—north, east, south, and west. They begin the map in the middle of the graph paper. Each unit on the grid will represent one city block. Have them follow this route: walk two blocks south, turn east and walk three blocks, turn south and walk one block, turn east and walk three blocks, turn south and walk four blocks, turn east and walk one block, turn south and walk three blocks, turn west and walk half a block. Have the students compare their maps. How are they the same? How are they different? How would the maps change if the second step were a turn west?

• *Estimate and weigh different materials.* Fill several milk cartons with different materials, such as rice, beans, clay, plaster of paris, or wooden objects. Seal the cartons and label them by color or letter. Tell the children what the materials are but do not tell them which material is in which carton. Have the children guess how to order the cartons by weight, according to what they contain. Then let the children order the cartons by weight, holding them in their hands and using a pan balance to check their estimates.

• *Predict and observe melting time.* Fill one container with warm water, fill a second container with cool water, and leave a third container empty. Let the children see and feel the containers and the water. Explain to the children that an ice cube will be placed in each container and ask them which ice cube they think will melt first. Write the guesses on the board, put the cubes in the containers, and observe the results.

• *Use estimation and metric measurement on a scavenger hunt.* Divide the class into teams of three or four students each and give each team a list of challenges. For example, find how many square meters of floor space each person in the classroom has; if there are 100 students in the gym, find how many cubic meters each student has; find the number of square meters in the school playground; find the number of meters students must walk from the classroom to the principal's office and back; find two pairs of students whose combined weights in kilograms are the same; or write a problem similar to these for students to solve.

• *Use measurement in the world outside school.* Encourage children to describe what they discover as they learn about measurement and to ask if others have made the same discovery. They should compare and contrast. Encourage students talented in geometry and measurement to go further in these areas. Let them combine these skills with skills in other subjects (such as art, mechanical drawing, woodworking, metal shop, or home economics) to create new applications for their learning. For example, students who are adept at tessellating (drawing repeated patterns) may wish to extend that skill in artwork designs.

Developing Problem-Solving Power

In the 1990s, teachers are coming to recognize the goal of making students mathematically powerful (California State Department of Education, 1992a), empowered to think and communicate using mathematical ideas and drawing on the techniques and tools of mathematics. Mathematically powerful students make meaningful connections, construct mathematical models, raise questions, and test and verify them (Silver, 1985). Communication, the coherent expression of one's mathematical processes and results, during all these processes is essential.

Students should be encouraged to express their mathematical ideas orally or in writing during early conceptual development. These ideas can refer to content tools, such as adding, counting, or using proportional relationships, geometry, or limits. They may express relationships (equation, more, addition, fraction), or not (square, triangle, quantity, seven, million). But any idea that is fully understood can be extended to enable a new idea to be learned. A student who understands basic number concepts will have a much easier time mastering basic addition and subtraction facts. In geometry, the formulas for finding the areas of squares, rectangles, parallelograms, trapezoids, and triangles are interconnected by the single idea that area can be arrived at by multiplying the base times the height. That idea is built on an understanding of multiplication concepts and area units.

Students' understanding of mathematical tools and techniques must go beyond a knowledge of literal tools such as calculators and compasses to a comprehension of the procedures behind both literal and figurative tools (Burns, 1991). Students must understand the reasoning behind a rule, an algorithm, or a visual representation of data, so that they can explain not only what they are doing when they use these tools, but why. For example, many students know and can use the rule for dividing fractions (invert the divisor and multiply the numerators and denominators) but cannot explain what $1/2 \div 1/4$ *means*. They have no idea why they are doing what they are doing and are unable to make up a scenario in which the computation would be appropriate. To be mathematically powerful is to *understand* mathematical tools through understanding the procedures behind them.

Students who learn by rote—to pass a test, to please parents or teachers, or out of fear of failure—find the process of learning uncomfortable. External rewards such as extra recess time or stickers do nothing to encourage a love of the subject. When mathematics is learned in a meaningful way, the learning feels good and can often be fun. Concepts are easier to remember; new concepts and procedures are easier to understand; problem solving is enhanced and leads to self-directed and powerful learning. Studies have found that when gaining knowledge is found to be pleasurable, students who have had that experience are likely to seek new ideas on their own (Skemp, 1978).

Problem solving is a part of everyday experience. The research studies that have examined why children have difficulties solving mathematical word problems have found that, contrary to popular belief, the difficulties are not caused by poor computational skills or inadequate reading ability. When given a word problem, children often simply do not know how to choose the correct computational operation for that problem. To effectively solve word problems, students must understand what the different mathematical operations mean and how they can be connected to real situations, because mathematically powerful work is always purposeful. It may not always be practical. It may be motivated by curiosity or whimsy. But some motivation and purpose must be present.

Nearly all people enjoy learning when it takes the form of relating new ideas to past experiences in order to add to their knowledge. Thus, real situations should be the settings in which children develop mathematical understanding and apply computational skills, and teachers need to present some problems that students can discuss, and for which they can find solutions, without the distraction of numerical symbols. For example, have students draw pictures of what a problem is about or act out the problem, or have one student read the problem leaving out the numbers. Once students begin to visualize what a problem is about, they will have much less difficulty solving it. Of course, students should work in small groups when solving these problems, write out how they solved them, and discuss and check their answers with other groups.

Word problems need to be done frequently, several times a week, at all grade levels throughout the year because, in doing these problems, students must focus on the meanings of mathematical operations before they can translate the word problem into a mathematical sentence. Only then can they do the computation required in that sentence. If our students are to learn to generalize for themselves, they need many experiences of word problems in order to discover how mathematical operations are described in the language of the real world.

Using traditional word problems is not sufficient for today's curriculum, because most daily problems that adults face that require mathematics are not solved solely by translating the available information into mathematical sentences and then performing the needed calculations. In most cases, it is usually not clear at first just what information is needed to solve a given problem, nor is it usually clear where that needed information can be found. Everyday problems tend to be ill-structured, and even the criteria that will define the "right" solution may be unknown at the outset. A task such as figuring out a mortgage payment can include many ill-defined problems and many ways of finding a solution or even of deciding what constitutes a solution. On the larger scale, there are problems of energy depletion, population growth, food distribution, disease, warfare, agricultural production, transportation, space exploration, and trade, to name a few. It is not difficult to find newsworthy events that make use of a wide variety of mathematical applications. For example, we can consciously choose contexts for problems that illuminate the mathematical side of social issues. Real problems can be formulated about local communities dealing with such issues as taxes, the economy, and the environment. Here is a sample real-life problem: the 20 percent of California families with the lowest annual earnings pay an average of 14.1 percent in state and local taxes, while the 20 percent in the middle of the earnings range pay only 8.8 percent. What does that mean? Do you think it is fair? What additional questions do you have? This example requires the mathematical skill of finding percentages while it breathes new life into the discipline of mathematics by using it to shape important questions about reporting, statistics, and social justice.

When solving problems in real life and the world of work, adults call on as many resources as they can—including knowledge, past experiences, and intuition—in order to analyze, predict, make decisions, and evaluate. Forging a connection to real life and the world of work means allowing students to work in groups to achieve common goals and increase their comfort with mathematics and critical thinking. The best mathematics instruction leaves space for a child's mind to play. Powerful learning, like good teaching, is a blend of subject matter knowledge, pedagogical skill, and energetic enthusiasm. Add resourcefulness and creativity, and you have the essence of mathematical problem solving. Most students are fascinated with the mathematical unknown, genuine problems, and complex dilemmas. Yet few recognize that the probing of decision making, debating, and conflict has anything to do with mathematical problem solving. Using current issues and practical real-world examples as a focus for mathematics problems makes mathematical study multidisciplinary, better preparing students for the real world and the future and making mathematics more than a piece of information to be memorized in a textbook or captured in a procedure.

Connecting Mathematics to Technology

Many situations that arise in the classroom afford opportunities for the application of mathematical skills and the use of technological tools like calculators: collecting lunch money, planning for a class party, taking attendance, and so forth. Yet, traditionally, students have used textbook problems and have worked on them without technical aids. Stale, uninspired ritual can squash curiosity and squander a child's innate excitement for learning. We need fresh avenues for getting conceptual models across to students, and among these avenues are technologies that can breathe life into mathematical abstractions and redefine learning realities. Calculators are recommended for school mathematics programs to help develop students' number sense; skills in problem solving, mental computation, and estimation; and ability to see patterns, perform operations, and use graphics. Computers can be used to teach programming and data manipulation, to encourage drill and practice, and to present simulations, problem-solving materials, tutorials, and spacial visualizations. Both calculators and computers, of course, also relate to the world of work.

Activities Using Technology

Learning is enhanced by presenting information in multiple formats, including multisensory activities and experimental opportunities. Video and television programs as well as computer games and instructional courseware are valuable formats that aid in teaching concepts and providing practice. Here are some suggested activities using calculators and computers.

• *Addition and subtraction estimation skills.* Select two teams of students and provide a calculator for each student. As play begins, a player on the first team says a three-digit number. A player on the second team says another three-digit number. Then both players silently write an estimate of the sum of the two numbers (players are given five seconds to make the estimate). Next both players use their calculators to determine the actual sum. The player whose estimate was closest scores a point for his or her team. In the case of a tie, both teams earn a point. Then two more players take a turn, and so on. The rules for practicing subtraction are the same except that the players estimate the difference between two three-digit numbers. Students who engage in this activity for a while develop estimation strategies that benefit them in and out of the classroom.

• *Multiplication estimation skills.* Give students calculators and a series of multiplication problems in which one multiplicand is missing. For each problem, have students find the missing number by using the calculator and the problem-solving strategy of guessing and checking, recording all of their guesses. They should not solve the problems by dividing but instead should see how many guesses each problem takes.

For example, given the problem 4 x _____ = 87, a student might start with 23, and 10 adjust. The solution might look like this:

4 x 23 = 92
4 x 22 = 88
4 x 21 = 84
4 x 21.5 = 86
4 x 21.6 = 86.4
4 x 21.7 = 86.8
4 x 21.8 = 87.2
4 x 21.74 = 86.96
4 x 21.75 = 87

The goals is eventually to reduce the number of guesses that need to be made to arrive at the answer.

• *How much is a billion?* Ask students to guess how long (in hours, days, months, or years) it would take them to count up to a billion if they counted one number per second. Have them write their guesses down and then use a calculator to find out the actual answer, which will surprise them.

• *Counting skills and related concepts.* The calculator is a powerful counting tool. Important concepts of sequencing, place value, and one-to-one correspondence are learned when a child interacts with this almost magical counting device. To make a calculator count, enter the number 1 (or any other number) and press the + key twice. Next, press the = key. As you continue to press =, the calculator will begin counting in increments of the number you selected. (If this set of instructions does not work with your calculator, check the directions to find out how to get a constant function, and any of the following counting activities will then work for you) (Reys, Suydam, & Lindquist, 1989).

For another exercise using this technique, have each student choose and enter a number from 2 to 12, press the + key twice, and then the = key. Each time the = key is pressed, have the student write down the new number displayed, continuing until there are at least twelve numbers on his or her list. Have the student describe the patterns he or she notices in this list (Burns, 1991, p. 200).

• *Count backwards.* A calculator can also be programmed to count backwards and is a great way to introduce children to this idea. Enter the number by which you want to count backwards, push the - key twice, push the = key once and enter the number from which you want to start counting backwards. For example, if you want to count backwards from 100 by 1s, enter 1 - - = 100. Then press =. The calculator should show 99. Continue to press =. With each press, the next number in the reverse sequence appears.

• *Skip count.* A calculator can skip count also. Encourage students to count by 100s and 1000s, or by 3s, 5s, 7s, 9s, and so on. They can begin with any number and count by any number. Have students try the following skip counting exercises and then make up their own. Encourage speculation about what the next number will be. Can they find a pattern?

$$5 + + 10 = = =$$
$$3 + + = = =$$
$$100 - - = 1000 = = =$$

Hold a counting race. How long does it take counting by 1s to count to 1000? How long would it take counting by 100s to count to 1,000,000?

• *Logo programming for young children.* Seymour Papert developed the Logo language to teach children geometric concepts. He believes children can learn mathematical relationships more efficiently if they can project themselves into the world of mathematics. To program a computer to draw a square or circle, a child must understand the nature of a square or circle well enough to teach the computer, but young children are just becoming familiar with geometric shapes and the vocabulary. Using a Logo program, such as LogoWriter, a teacher can develop short procedures and program the computer so that young students can see the shape immediately when they type in the correct word. Because children delight in watching the figure drawn on the screen at their command, a wait command can be added, so that the shape remains on the screen for a certain amount of time and then disappears so the next child can try it, or the first child can try it again. Simple procedures like these can be modified by changing the color and shape of the geometric drawing.

• *Video segments.* For K–6 students, tape selected segments from the "Square One Television" program, choosing those that deal with concepts you will teach throughout the year. The program features five-minute segments on specific topics, using music video techniques to give basic facts, game show quizzes to present fractions, soap opera dramas to present problem solving, and so forth. Show one of these segments during your math lesson and support it with relevant activities, manipulatives, or props.

It is difficult to listen to the news on television or pick up a newspaper without noticing the extensive use of charts, graphs, probability, and statistics. Following are a few activity suggestions for teaching some elementary concepts about probability and graphing.

• *Define the terms "certain," "uncertain," "impossible," "likely," and "unlikely."* Give students a list of statements and ask them to sort them into three piles labeled certain, uncertain, and impossible. Use statements such as these:

Tomorrow, it will rain.

Joan will be here every day next week.

I will get 100 percent on my next spelling test.

Tomorrow, we will all visit Mars.

If I flip a coin, it will land either heads or tails.

As the children classify the statements, discuss with them the reasons for their classifications. When they have finished, ask them to further classify the uncertain statements as either likely or unlikely. Let students turn to activities and experiments to clarify their thinking. As a follow-up activity, have students come up with their own list of statements to classify into categories (Cruikshank & Sheffield, 1992).

   • *Predict.* Ask students to predict whether a coin will land heads or tails. Flip the coin and show the result. Ask students to predict the outcome of several flips of the coin. Discuss whether one flip seems to have an influence on the next flip, and describe how events are called independent if one event has no effect on another. Give each child a penny and ask him or her to flip it ten times and tally the heads and tails. Talk about such terms as equally likely, random, and unbiased.

   Show the children a spinner with three colors (say, red, yellow, and blue). Spin it a few times to show that it is a fair spinner, then ask students to predict the number of times they could expect to get yellow if they spin the spinner thirty times. Can they find a formula for predicting the number of times a color will come up? If the probability of landing on each color is equally likely, they can write the probability of landing on one color as:

$$\frac{\text{the number of favorable outcomes}}{\text{the total number of outcomes}}$$

In the example of the spinner, the total number of outcomes is three because there are three colored sections altogether. Therefore, the probability of getting yellow is $^1/_3$. Ask the children to predict the number of times they could expect to get yellow if they spun the spinner 30 times. Have them do the experiment using different colors and different numbers of spins. Can students find a formula for predicting the number of times a color will come up?

• *Find a random sample.* Discuss with students how they might take a random sample of marbles. (A random sample is selected in such a way that every member of the source group has an equal chance of being chosen for the sample.) Put five red and forty-five blue marbles in a bag. Tell students to take a random sample of ten marbles and then to predict the total number of marbles in the bag. Next, let them know there are fifty marbles altogether and discuss their predictions, asking, for example, Would you trust your prediction based on the results of only ten draws? What if you repeated the ten draws several times? Create as many interesting probability activities as time permits.

• *Explore statistics.* For example, have students work on this problem about athletes' salaries: the following are the salaries of five professional basketball players—$80,000, $80,000, 100,000, $120,000, and $620,000. The players are complaining about their salaries. They say that the mode of the salaries is $80,000 and that they deserve more money for all the games they play. The owners claim that the mean of the salaries is $200,000 and that this is plenty for any team. Which side is correct? Is anyone lying? How can you explain the difference in the reports?

Ask students to look in newspapers and magazines for reported averages in any area. Are there any discrepancies in the reports? Ask them to bring in reports for discussion in class and encourage them to read any reported statistics carefully.

• *Graph with young children.* The concepts of graphing can be learned as early as kindergarten, and children should graph data frequently in the early grades, since graphs, tables, and charts are often used to display data and communicate findings in the real world. The teacher might instruct students to bring their favorite stuffed bears to school. As a class, the students can sort the bears in various ways (size, color, or type) and graph the results of their examinations. Students can also paste paper counters or stickers on paper to make personal graphs.

- *Survey, collect data, and graph.* Divide the class into small groups of four or five. Have the students brainstorm what they would like to find out from the other class members (favorite hobbies or television shows, kinds of pets, and so forth). Once a topic is agreed upon and approved, have the groups organize and take their surveys of the class members. After the statistics are gathered and compiled, each group must make a clear descriptive graph, which can be posted in the classroom. Encourage originality and creativity.

- *Graph data from the world of work.* Have students gather information about mathematics in the workplace and careers that spark their interest. Draw up a simple survey form that lists occupations students are interested in, with spaces to gather data about ways mathematical ability is used on the job. Have students interview workers, parents, community members, professionals, and friends to find out how they use mathematics and mathematical tools in their work. Have students assemble and display the data in charts and graphs and then look for patterns and comparisons. Are there generalizations that can be made? Conclusions that can be drawn?

Using Problems and Investigations

When we ask students to calculate a formula we give them or solve a textbook exercise, they are required only to follow a procedure correctly to complete the problem. They do not have to define the problem, select a technique for solving it, or communicate any thinking. Even in more sophisticated exercises, such as solving verbal puzzles in order to decide what calculation to do, the expectations for students are still rather limited. Of course, students should be able to obtain correct results in exercises like these, but to demonstrate mathematical power, students will have to do much more.

Here is a sample problem that asks students to do more: take six Cuisinaire rods: one black (length 7), one purple (length 4), and four light green (length 3). Make a three-dimensional object using all six rods. Find the object's surface area. Compare your results with other students' results. What are the minimum and maximum possible surface areas for objects built with all six rods? In this problem, students must do much more than demonstrate an ability to multiply and add. They must think, visualize, and explain their reasoning clearly (Schoenfeld, 1985). Problems like this one focus the direction of student thinking and students' communications about their work, even though the teacher has preorganized some of the information and formulated the mathematics with a solution in mind.

Here is a related task (California State Department of Education, 1992a) that calls on students to perform an investigation rather than solve a given problem. They must formulate the problem themselves and plan how they will communicate their work. An investigation is far more demanding than an exercise. This particular investigation challenges students to go to the heart of the mathematical idea of proportionality in similar shapes. It also challenges students to generalize the results of their mathematical exploration.

Have each child sketch the house (or apartment) he or she lives in. Each child then measure the dimensions of the house and builds it with paper and tape, making it about the same shape as the house in the drawing, but not necessarily the same size. Then have each child build two more houses, each similar to the first house. That is, they are exactly the same shape but different sizes. Finally, each child prepares a report, describing how he or she made the houses similar and answering the question, "What can you say, in general, about the relationships among the dimensions, areas, and volumes of similar houses?" The three houses are glued to a piece of paper and turned in with the written report.

Students are told that their reports will be graded on the basis of these questions:

1. How well did you explore the relationships among the three houses? How well did you formulate your generalizations?

2. How do we know your houses are similar? Was your approach to making the houses similar a sound one?

3. How well did you present your thinking? Are your ideas understandable to the reader? Did you use mathematical representations such as graphs, formulas, diagrams, and tables effectively?

4. Are your measurements and calculations appropriate and correct?

Investigations can be culminating activities that help students integrate what they are learning; they can also introduce and motivate bodies of mathematical ideas. While exercises might require only a minute or two and a problem perhaps a class period, an investigation might take more than a week, using some class time and time out of class. At the end, each student presents an analysis and a conclusion rather than a solution. Like a problem, an investigation lets students use several different approaches; however, it also requires students to do more of the problem formulation and creates a context that invites more sustained work.

In these examples, the problem and investigation both give directions to the students to get them started on the right track: the problem has the students build, measure, and compare first; the investigation suggests an approach. Eventually, students will be able to handle more challenging investigations in which they formulate the issues and problems entirely on their own. For example, students could try this more advanced investigation: have students select several different objects of their choice and find the relationships among the objects (for instance, relationships in linear size, surface area, and volume). Ask students to make some guesses and support them with sound mathematical reasoning and concrete examples.

When students work on investigations and good problems, we learn about their mathematical power. We look to see if their work demonstrates all four of these dimensions of mathematical power: thinking, communicating, connecting, and using tools and techniques (including mathematical ideas). The real-world and multi-disciplinary connections that teachers can encourage students to see have been discussed in detail earlier. Here is a summing up of the remaining three dimensions.

Mathematical Thinking

Mathematical thinking grows out of the kinds of thinking that are naturally part of everyone's repertoire. Many of the words we use to describe mathematical thinking—such as classify, plan, analyze, conjecture, design, evaluate, formulate, investigate, model, and verify—have meaning for kinds of thinking other than mathematical thinking (Van de Walle, 1990). Other varieties of mathematical thinking are less frequently found in everyday life. These thinking skills include deducing, inferring, making hypotheses, and synthesizing. As a group, these skills are often referred to as higher-order thinking skills. They are used for reasoning, problem solving, and making connections and have specific characteristics (Resnick, 1987).

- Higher-order thinking tends to be complex. The total solution is not clear from any single direction.

- The path of action in higher-order thinking is not known in advance.
- Higher-order thinking often has many solutions, rather than single solutions, each with costs and benefits.
- Higher-order thinking involves nuances, judgment, and different interpretations.
- Higher-order thinking involves applying many varied criteria, which sometimes conflict with one another.
- Higher-order thinking often involves uncertainty. Not all information that pertains to the problem at hand is known.
- Higher-order thinking involves self-discipline and self-regulation of the thinking process. No one calls the plays at every step.
- Higher-order thinking involves imposing meaning, finding structure in apparent disorder.
- Higher-order thinking is effortful. There is considerable mental work involved in the kinds of elaborations and judgments required.

The young child does not have to be motivated to learn. Learning takes place naturally. By grappling with the unknown, exploring, discovering, and investigating, children learn new ways of understanding their world, and during the first years of life, children are able to master complex language and behavior structures (Gardner, 1991). They become proficient at speaking and understanding language, singing songs, catching balls, riding tricycles, thinking, and remembering. They are able to deceive someone else in a game and can even recognize when someone else is playing a trick on them. As discussed earlier, they begin to develop powerful theories of how the world works and are able to make predictions of what will happen in given situations. Lauren Resnick (1987) argues that it is a mistake to believe that children must master lower-order thinking skills before being presented with higher ones. When children do not exhibit higher-order thinking in mathematics, it is not that they are incapable of engaging in this thinking but that they have seldom encountered this thinking in the process of learning and understanding mathematical ideas. It is not a part of the well-developed but informal sets of ideas about mathematics that children bring to school with them as part of their rich knowledge base about the world around them.

Students formulate their ideas, build internal mental concepts, and construct their understandings by interpreting experiences and assigning meaning. This is an active process. The mental representations that a child arrives at are tied to meaningful interpretations made, and the human drives to make sense and achieve purpose are among the strongest organizers of all individuals' thinking. It is this view of learning that has forced teachers to examine the consequences of some of the views currently held about teaching and communicating and to view the teaching of mathematics as both an individual and a collective activity, one that should help students make sense of their own experiences and achieve meaningful purposes.

Mathematical Communication

As students do mathematics, they must communicate their thinking and understanding to themselves, to peers, and to parents, teachers, and other adults. Students can communicate in many ways, through informal conversations, verbal presentations, written texts, diagrams, symbols, numbers, graphs, tables, models, and algebraic expressions. Whatever form it takes, this communication makes students clarify their thinking, while the feedback from this communication gives them useful information for revision, which in turn makes it possible for all students to improve the quality of their work. Frequent and varied communication also helps both students and teachers assess where students are in their understanding of mathematical ideas.

Mathematical Tools and Techniques

Students must come to recognize the unifying ideas that bridge the dimensions of mathematics and reach out to explain problems in other disciplines as well. The most important ideas of mathematics, such as patterns and proportional relationships, have a simplicity that makes sense to the youngest thinkers but also a depth and power that students can appreciate only over time (Trafton, 1989). To help students see these ideas as unifying tools, teachers should use them to knit the curriculum together and provide continuity throughout the mathematical experience. The collection of units that makes up a year's work should develop all the unifying ideas of mathematics at the appropriate grade level.

To do thorough mathematical work, students must put their mathematical thinking to use. Typically, this step will involve using intellectual tools and techniques as well as specific problem-solving tools, including technology. Mathematical tools and techniques make it possible for students to use their hands and eyes to experiment and explore relationships in the world, extending their thinking power and translating ideas into action (Leitzel, 1991).

Students should use tools and techniques

- To see patterns and relationships (using pictures, tables, graphs, blocks, algebraic formulas, or spreadsheet software)

- To create models (using drawings, computer software, concrete materials)

- To extend memory, so that many things can be worked on at once (using graphs, tables, paper and pencil, manipulatives, and calculators)

The Relevance of Mathematics

Our effort to restructure our schools is driven not only by our new understanding of the ways learning occurs but by our need to restructure our workplaces. No longer an industrial economy, our society today is driven by information and services, and that societal shift must have a great influence on what is taught in our schools. In order to survive the globally competitive climate and rapid changes in the specific skills needed by our industries, the U.S. workplace is rethinking its structure and recognizing the need for a better-educated work force. It is requiring a much higher percentage of well-trained workers who have teamwork skills and can engage in critical thinking and lifelong learning. It requires personnel who can learn to adapt to new and changing situations and who will be able to learn the jobs that may be in existence ten years from today.

Mathematics provides the language and computational techniques necessary for the changing face of science and technology in our society. People with mathematical ability and sound mathematical preparation are in demand in almost all fields, not just the traditionally scientific ones. Advances in business, social science, industrial manufacturing, economics, and statistics make preparation in mathematics essential to an adequately prepared work force. U.S. citizens of the future will be called upon to approach and solve problems not even envisioned today. Understanding the conceptual bases of mathematics, having the ability to communicate mathematical ideas to others, and being able to reason and use technological tools are more important than ever. Approaching mathematics through cooperative learning and critical thinking will help students to learn new ways of interacting and thinking, to recognize the relationship of mathematics to other aspects of their lives, to feel confident in their ability to do mathematics, and to have an appreciation of the power, beauty, and fascination of mathematics.

Chapter Eight

Scientific Literacy

> As humans, we were evolved over millennia to find
> meaning not only in language mediated ideology
> but in the affordance of our human world, in such
> things as stones, water, weather, the loving work of
> human hands, the expressive sounds of human
> voices, the immense, mysterious, and eternal. It is
> not too late to return with conscious sophistication
> to these concerns, because they have been the
> unconscious tides of scientific and artistic practice
> all along.
>
> —*Ellen Dissanayake (1992)*

Scientific literacy has long been associated with a knowledge of mathematics and technology as well as the axioms of science. It includes knowing elements of our cultural and intellectual history, and it cuts across subject areas. Thus, many of the best models in science education involve students in working in cross-subject and mixed-ability teams. The action learning of science is in the hands of teachers, and effective science teachers begin by making connections between science and other disciplines and real-world concerns. This chapter describes the critical and creative scientific thinking that needs to be taught to our students in collaborative learning environments and through activities based in reality if these students are to develop the level of scientific literacy the future will demand of them. (Science teachers focusing on this chapter are also asked to read Chapter Six, since much of the material and many of the activities in that chapter apply specifically to science as well as mathematics teaching.)

To be scientifically literate today requires an awareness of what the scientific endeavor is and how it relates to our culture and our lives. It involves having a broad familiarity with today's scientific issues and the key concepts that underlie them. The National Council on Science and Technology Education (American Association for the Advancement of Science, 1990) identifies scientific literacy as:

- Being familiar with the natural world and recognizing its diversity and unity
- Understanding important concepts and principles of science
- Understanding some of the important ways science, mathematics, and technology depend on each other
- Knowing that science, mathematics, and technology are human enterprises (creations) and what this implies about their strengths and weaknesses
- Having a capacity (ability) for scientific ways of thinking
- Applying scientific knowledge and ways of thinking to achieve personal and social purposes

Teaching this kind of literacy means organizing science-based learning around real-life problems.

The recognized importance of a scientifically literate citizenry has resulted in national efforts to reform K–12 science education in the United States, and scientific literacy for all students has emerged as a central goal of U.S. education. New instructional strategies include concrete, physical experiences; opportunities for students to explore science in their lives; and an emphasis on ideas and thinking skills. They require teachers to sequence instruction from the concrete to the abstract. Students are to be actively involved in the learning process, developing effective oral and written communication skills and the ability to participate skillfully in frequent cooperative learning, which is to be the primary grouping strategy in the classroom. They are to be given many opportunities to question data, design and conduct real experiments, and carry their thinking beyond the classroom experience. They are to be encouraged to raise questions that are appealing and familiar to them and to participate in activities that improve reasoning and decision making.

Science can be thought of as a way of thinking and asking questions. One of the important new goals of U.S. education, as articulated in *America 2000*, the Department of Education's statement of goals for the year 2000, is not only to prepare students who can make use of scientific knowledge and connect the implications and techniques of science and its thinking and questioning styles to their personal lives and to society but also to produce graduates who are the most accomplished in the world in science and technology (Alexander, 1991).

Yet, currently, this is an elusive goal. In its *1990 Science Report Card*, the National Assessment of Educational Progress (1992) found that fewer than half of graduating high school seniors could interpret tables and graphs, make judgments about experiments, or demonstrate knowledge of scientific information. In addition, the growing number of African-American and Hispanic students, often coming from the poorest schools, performed much worse than white students in advantaged schools. Inner-city schools were found to be in especially poor shape in terms of resources, teachers able to teach science well, students' home environments, and overall academic outcomes (Prothrow-Stith, 1991).

People in the United States have always been concerned about science education and the importance of transmitting scientific attitudes, shared values, and ways of thinking to the next generation. Today, our concern about the level of scientific literacy is more critical than ever because of two trends: U.S. students' knowledge of science is *down*, relative to our industrial competitors, while the potential impact of that knowledge is *up*, as every part of contemporary life is reshaped, some feel bombarded, by science and its offspring, technology. Part of the essence of scientific literacy is an accompanying ability tc clarify attitudes, possess certain scientific values, and make informed judgments about science-based changes in our lives. To acquire this ability, students need to cultivate scientific patterns of thinking, logical reasoning, curiosity, an openness to new ideas, and skepticism in evaluating claims and arguments (Aronowitz, 1990).

Being able to understand the basic principles of science, being numerate, thinking critically, measuring accurately, using such scientific tools as mathematics, calculators, and computers are all part of the scientific literacy equation. It is also important for teachers to inculcate positive attitudes toward learning science in students if students are to be creative critical thinkers, capable of solving problems with others in the sciences as well as in other disciplines. Building positive attitudes requires that students be allowed to manipulate the materials of science and to communicate scientific understandings both orally and in writing (American Association for the Advancement of Science, 1990).

Traditional Teaching and Misconceptions About Science

Students' anxiety about taking science courses and teachers' anxiety about teaching science have long been of concern. Despite their critical role in disseminating scientific ideas and helping students acquire learning skills in science, many teachers are poorly prepared for the science curriculum and spend little time teaching it (Hand & Treagust, 1991). As mentioned earlier, problems in learning science and mathematics are major causes why many students do poorly in school, and traditionally, school programs have produced students with increasingly negative attitudes about science as they progress through the grades (Hazen, 1991). As in mathematics, much of this student failure is due to a tradition of teaching that does not match the way students learn.

Current science teaching is frequently inconsistent with what is known about how students construct meaning and develop scientific understandings (Bruner & Haste, 1987), and researchers have found that students often exhibit only superficial understandings of what they have been taught in science (Perkins & Simmons, 1988). Studies of college students have found that even those who have had formal instruction in physics, for example, frequently do not understand what Newton's laws really say about the way objects move (McCloskey, 1983; Clement, 1982, 1983). Recent studies conducted at prominent universities found that college graduates had difficulty in defining simple concepts about the phases of the moon, the reason for the seasons, and the causes of the apparent motion of the planets and stars (Schneps, 1988; Gardner, 1991). This material is supposedly covered in the elementary grades. These results revealed deep disparities between teaching, testing, and the reality of student understandings, from the elementary school to the college campus (Tinker, 1991).

Teachers can fool themselves into thinking that effective instruction has taken place when students successfully answer problems on tests. But it turns out that developing real understanding of science is much more than filling in bubbles or blanks. The breadth of the misconceptions about elementary astronomy, for example, is rooted in students' trying to make sense of real phenomena they do not understand by *inventing* private, nonscientific theories to explain coincidence and luck in relation to such things as horoscopes and lotteries.

How is it possible to teach for understanding in science? Piaget's suggestions that learners must construct their own knowledge and assimilate new experiences in ways that make sense to them was brought home in the area of science education to one of the authors of this book when she had the opportunity to invite Leonard Grzhonko, a physicist and science educator from Russia, to her science education class at San Francisco State University. Grzhonko had written a new children's book entitled *Jeff and Magic*

Molecule Land (1993). The book consists of a discussion between father and son and the son's dream fantasy about molecules, and it is illustrated to show how molecules are connected to each other and the effect of temperature change on molecules.

After a graduate education student read the book aloud to the class, Grzhonko discussed and demonstrated the book's concepts with the class, illustrating ways to bring the concepts to life for young students. The story answered the questions children naturally ask, such as, Why does ice cream melt? Why does the tea kettle burn my hand? Where does steam come from? Why is it so difficult to break rocks? Grzhonko first explained that molecules and atoms are the building blocks of matter. Heat energy and cold can change molecular form. He then went on to ask questions based on the book to assess students' understanding of the concepts. The class of prospective teachers especially enjoyed participating in the demonstration of how molecules work. Before beginning the demonstration, Grzhonko explained that matter and energy exist and can be changed but not created or destroyed. He then asked for student volunteers to role-play the parts of molecules, directing the volunteers to join hands to show how molecules are connected to each other and explaining that the role-players represented matter in a solid form. Next he asked the volunteers to show what happens when a solid becomes a liquid and heat causes the molecules to move more rapidly and be less tightly bound together. Students dropped hands and started to wiggle and move around. To deal with the question, How do you think molecules act when they become a gas? Grzhonko carefully moved students to the generalization that heat transforms solids into liquids and then into gases. The class enjoyed watching the role-players zip around as they assumed the role of molecules turning into a gas. The last part of the demonstration illustrated how molecules stop moving altogether in a frozen object. The demonstration and follow-up questions sparked a lot of discussion and more questions. This simple demonstration shows how connecting physics principles with active learning works. This is the kind of teaching that involves students in discovery, gives them premises and lets them figure out results, and helps them visualize and physically experience a version of what actually happens.

Benchmarks for Science Learning

Education reform is needed because our nation has not acted decisively enough in preparing young people, especially minority children, on whom the nation's future depends. But reform will take a unified vision of what we want schools to achieve. *Science for All Americans*, a 1990 report from the American Association for the Advancement of Science (AAAS) initiative called Project 2061, is a start on formulating that vision for science teachers. The report defines scientific literacy, as described earlier, and presents a basic premise of Project 2061, which is that schools do not need to teach more but to teach less, so that what they teach can be taught better.

The association's recommendations cover a broad array of topics common in school curricula; however, the treatment of these topics differs from traditional ways of teaching. Boundaries between traditional subject matter categories are softened and connections strengthened. Students are expected to retain considerably less detail than in traditional science, mathematics, and technology courses. Ideas and thinking skills are emphasized rather than the memorization of specialized vocabulary and procedures. Concepts are taught at a simplified level, which then provides a solid foundation for learning more complex interpretations. Details are treated as enhancing understanding not as just adding more facts to the knowledge base. In the new curriculum, time is devoted to understanding what the scientific enterprise is and how science, mathematics, and technology relate to each other and the social system. This instruction includes important historical data. Although modern science is only a few centuries old, its roots (especially in mathematics and astronomy) can be traced to early Egyptian, Greek, Chinese, and Arabic cultures. Finally, the concepts that form the foundation of today's science curriculum are the major conceptual themes that span all scientific thinking. Integrating those themes is the exhilarating challenge faced by educators today.

Project 2061 has suggested grade-level standards for students' scientific literacy (American Association for the Advancement of Science, 1990). Here are some examples of what students should know by the end of selected school years:

Second Grade

- When a scientific investigation is done the way it was done before, we expect to get a very similar result.
- Scientific investigations generally work the same way in different places.

Fifth Grade

- Results of similar scientific investigations seldom turn out exactly the same.

Eighth Grade

- When similar investigations give different results, the scientific challenge is to judge whether the differences are trivial or significant, and it often takes further studies to decide.
- Scientific knowledge is subject to modification as new information challenges prevailing theories.
- Some scientific knowledge is very old and yet is still applicable today.

- Some matters cannot be examined usefully in a scientific way, such as matters of morality.

Twelfth Grade

- Scientists assume that the universe is a vast single system in which the basic rules are the same everywhere.
- From time to time, major shifts occur in the scientific view of how the world works.
- No matter how well one theory fits observations, a new theory might fit them just as well or better.

Project 2061's approach of developing a curriculum that helps children make connections among disciplines and real-life experiences and that emphasizes ideas and critical thinking, rather than preservation of the traditional boundaries between disciplines and of the need to learn a specialized vocabulary and memorize data, can also be applied to other subjects that are undergoing systemic change.

Organizing the Science Classroom

Often teachers fall into familiar patterns that end up becoming reasons for avoiding science teaching. Many of these patterns relate to classroom management. Hands-on science learning calls for a readjustment of teachers' thinking so that teachers become engaged in helping students find out concepts rather than "right answers." In the new science classroom, activities stimulate teachers and learners mutually. Here are some initial suggestions—some logistical, some methodological—that can help teachers succeed with the cooperative, constructivist, and thematic activities suggested later in this chapter.

- *Organize materials in various locations and give more responsibility to students for these materials.* Having students help plan, set up, put away, and maintain materials facilitates science learning on the most simple logistical level. Students no longer push and pull each other as they reach or grab for materials. More importantly, by sharing responsibility for class activities and materials, students develop a sense of responsibility and respect for themselves and their classmates. They have an investment in the lesson. They also come to have a greater appreciation for classroom materials and the classroom materials manager, the student who supervises these procedures. This responsibility can lead to such activities as compiling a classroom inventory or listing of science supplies and materials, which can be entered on the computer.

- *Spend a few minutes introducing the activity or mini-lesson.* Stimulate interest in the topic to be taught. Avoid long explanations but do demonstrate or model important activities. Provide clear goals and directions.

- *Start the groups on their tasks.* Group activity periods should take up most of the science time (twenty to forty-five minutes). Once group members have the materials in their hands, they do not want to listen to the teacher. Instead, teachers should move from group to group, providing needed information, discussing ideas, and monitoring progress. This teacher involvement cuts down on discipline problems, makes it easier to straighten out group glitches and equipment problems, and minimizes safety concerns.

- *Avoid asking "why" questions.* During the process of discovering, trying out ideas, talking in groups, and discussing results, it is natural and appropriate for students to ask why, as they try to figure things out for themselves. It is usually inappropriate for a science teacher to ask why because students frequently do not have the scientific knowledge or experience to respond. Instead, it is more important to ask students to describe what happened or to suggest what might account for what happened.

- *Use technology.* Calculators, videodiscs, computers, and multimedia have changed the way science is taught and learned. New models of instruction that encourage using technology and collaborative learning have sprung up to deal with this new reality. We are now at a stage where teachers and students must move from treating technology as a source of knowledge (a means of practice and drill) to engaging with it as a forum for communication and intelligent adventure. Teachers should help students make intelligent use of technological innovations that require the students to do additional thinking, problem formulating, and interpersonal communicating (Forman & Pufall, 1988).

- *Provide closure.* Closure is usually a short sharing period (five to ten minutes) that allows the class to come together in order to express thoughts and ideas and that gives the teacher a chance to record students' thinking. It also provides opportunities for dialogues between students and teacher about science content. The goal is to develop opinions of science based on informed reality, not prejudice or ignorance.

Teaching Strategies in the Science Classroom

As the benchmarks cited earlier show, the purpose of scientific inquiry is not to compile an inventory of factual information. We should think of the result of this quest, rather, as a logically articulated structure of justifiable beliefs about a possible world, a story which we invent and criticize and modify as we go along, so that it ends by being, as nearly as we can make it, a story about real life (Medawar, 1987).

What is the essence of science? Most scientists would agree that it is the excitement of exploring the unknown, of discovering something new, of adding to the realm of knowledge, creating, and inventing (Rouse, 1988). Given the level of agreement, it seems reasonable to expect that exploration and discovery would play a large role in science education classrooms. Yet from kindergarten through college, students rarely actively participate in this journey. Few students have the opportunity to *do* science. Instead, they learn what others have done, and if they are lucky, follow directions for lab experiments where all the methods have been worked out. They memorize information from textbooks but seldom experience firsthand the excitement of discovery. Rarely do they try to create, dare to question, or attempt new understandings. To advance science education, students need to engage in collaborative projects where they can construct their own knowledge and understandings, just as they must do in every other discipline. How can we expect the next generation of practitioners to learn without practicing?—to say nothing of preparing the next generation of voters, who will live in a technological society. Without an appreciation of scientific knowledge, it will be difficult for them to assume the responsibilities of responsible citizenship (Kitcher, 1993).

But this kind of learning will require changes in teaching. Many new elementary science programs were initiated in the decades from 1960 to 1980, and the impact of federally funded science programs on elementary education has been greater than their actual use in classrooms would imply. The past century has been one of unprecedented social, economic, scientific, and technological change. The elementary schools are, to a large degree, a mirror of the surrounding culture, and they are probably more sensitive to social change than any other educational level. They are in harmony with the prevailing philosophies and state of knowledge in existence at any particular time. Fundamental changes in philosophy, in theories of child rearing and educability, and in the need for universal and extended training for all children and adolescents of our society with capacity to learn have been accepted within this century. And science has progressed from the superficial activity of the leisured intellectual to the basic and fundamental activity of a substantial percentage of all Americans.

Nevertheless, many educators today are hesitant to tackle yet again another curriculum innovation. In the 1960s, the National

Science Foundation–sponsored projects were launched. Science kits were given to teachers, but few were trained in how to use these materials. In the 1970s, the popularity of the original science projects waned. Schools found it difficult to adapt the prepackaged material to local curricula. School finances diminished as a long inflationary period steadily eroded school budgets. For many teachers, the activities were too complex and required too much preparation time in an already busy school day. So the trend, again, was for schools to develop their own science programs (usually from a textbook). In the late 1970s and into the 1980s, science teaching stressed the acquisition of knowledge, with little or no attention given to application or the reforms offered in the 1960s. Today, science teaching may not be all that it could be, but renewed interest in science is growing.

Moreover, the blueprints for reform related to the education of teachers, the materials and technologies for teaching, the testing that should be used, and the organization of schooling are underway, along with the new educational policies and more educational research. National endeavors, like Project 2061, are trying to significantly enlarge the nation's pool of experts in school science and curriculum reform and are publicizing the need for nationwide scientific literacy.

Here are steps that can be taken by individual teachers:

• *Improve the teaching of science.* Effective teaching must be based on principles of learning. These principles include providing students with active hands-on experience, placing emphasis on students' curiosity and creativity, and frequently using a student team approach to learning. Learning is enhanced by presenting information in multiple formats, including multisensory activities and experimental opportunities.

• *Attend to the importance of students in the learning process.* Students need to be placed in situations where they develop and create their own science understandings, connect concepts with personal meanings, and put ideas together for themselves. For students to connect in a meaningful way with science, it is important for scientific concepts to be derived by the students themselves at all grade levels, using their problem-solving and research skills. Researching *their* questions, experimenting, observing, discussing, and then asking new questions are some examples of ways students take responsibility for their science learning.

• *Incorporate innovative and alternative teaching and learning strategies*. Classrooms organized so that small mixed-ability groups are a forum for collaborative mathematical/scientific discussions, discovery, creativity, and connections to other subjects help students develop an energetic enthusiasm about science from their resourceful collaboration. As classroom science moves from its computational and factual base to a problem-solving emphasis, it comes alive and stimulates students because of its immediacy. Learning strategies to be used include investigations, interviews, questioning techniques, and journal writing. New assessment techniques can include performance assessment, portfolios, and use of multimedia. A substantive knowledge base now exists regarding the social and psychological characteristics of children's learning about science. Yet studies indicate that even experienced teachers are not familiar with this knowledge (Carey, Mittman, & Darling-Hammond, 1989). One of the most important conclusions of the current research on higher-order thinking skills is that transfer of skills from one area to another does not occur automatically (Peterson, 1988). Some students intuitively see connections between science, critical thinking, and problem solving; others do not. For many, generalizations must be planned, or they do not occur. The research suggests that, if teachers are aware of and actively promote generalizations, transfer of scientific thinking to real-world situations will be more likely (Hendricksen & Morgan, 1990). Learning moves along a path from concrete experiences to abstract manipulations. This supports the instructional principle that chil-

dren learn science more effectively when they can concretely connect experiences with principles (Langbort & Thompson, 1985).
In addition, the success factor is strongly related to the amount of
learning that takes place in studying science. Even if students are
actively engaged, they learn most effectively only when they are
performing mental activities with reasonable rates of success
(Chickering, 1977). In science classrooms, students' efficiency of
learning is also related to the extent to which their class and study
time is turned into academic learning time. This means the longer
students actively attend to a task the higher the rate of success
(Champagne & Klopfer, 1988).

•   *Develop new curriculum models.* To achieve the goals of scientific literacy, the science curriculum must be changed to reduce
the amount of material covered and to emphasize a thematic
approach. It must focus on the connections among the various disciplines of science, mathematics, and technology and build integrated understandings through cooperative learning practices that
link mathematics, science, and technology in students' projects.
The scientific endeavor must be presented as a social phenomenon
that influences human thought and action.

•   *Extend learning beyond the classroom.* Students need opportunities to assume autonomy in their learning, to use their scientific literacy to improve their own lives, and to experience
responsible roles as citizens. To meet this challenge, encourage students to identify with problems of local interest and to actively use
resources to locate information for solving real-life problems.

•   *Provide students equal access to knowledge.* A central role of
scientific literacy is promoting intellectual processes through
encounters with knowledge. The richer an individual's experiences
with the tools of science, mathematics, and technology the greater
her or his prospects for living a rich life. Unfortunately, rather than
being the essence of a literate human dialogue, scientific and technological knowledge is often translated into and taught as frag-

mented bits and pieces. In addition, access to the most generally useful knowledge is too frequently limited by misguided decisions about grouping and tracking, maldistributed to poor and minority children and youth, and overlooked by poorly prepared teachers. Finally, teachers must emphasize career opportunities in science, mathematics, and technology.

All the strategies described here for classroom organization and for teaching can be a part of the constructivist, cooperative, and thematic activities described in the remainder of this chapter.

Applying a Constructivist View of Science

As we have seen, the constructivist view of learning rests on the premise that the way we learn anything is by integrating observations and experiences into our personal frameworks (memories, associations, feelings, sounds, rules, and so forth). If our learning framework is rich, we will have the ability to explain, predict, analogize, connect, and possibly, discover new perspectives. In the constructivist view, the true goals of science education are to help students learn how to apply knowledge, solve problems, and promote conceptual understanding. Thus, because students should learn science by doing science, rather than reading about it, *realia* and such visual aids as pictures, models, and actual objects should enhance verbal instruction and effectively reinforce the presented concepts. Students should be able to use scientific processes to change their own theories and beliefs in ways that are personally meaningful and consistent with scientific explanations, that is, they should be able to integrate scientific knowledge into their personal conceptions.

The constructivist view also encourages applying other disciplines to science learning. Writing, reading, and speaking skills can be developed through the use of cooperative learning groups, oral reporting, and active note taking, all of which assist students to process information about science. For example, one particular way to promote language development within the science curriculum is to have students paraphrase what is said and/or what they are supposed to know.

Constructivist Perspective on Activities

Although our constructed understandings are resistant to change, they can change as a result of disequilibration. Activities that provide experience offer that disequilibration. Some of the activities suggested in Chapter Six are useful in the science classroom, also: for example, have students generate their own problems to discuss, based on survey data, newspaper stories, or current information from educational television. The exercises in which students perform surveys and graph the results are also valuable. In addition, science teachers can bring a variety of graphic organizers (such as webs, maps, and Venn diagrams) into play to help students grasp important concepts. For instance, concept circles (see Exhibit 8.1) are useful graphic organizers for demonstrating meaning, developing visual thinking, predicting, and summarizing. Teachers can have groups of students construct concept circles to represent their understanding of science concepts.

Such televised science programs as "Nova," "Wild Kingdom," "Science and Technology Week," "3–2–1 Contact," or even the Weather Channel and the evening news offer a wealth of material for activities. Teachers can tape short segments and design short projects around them: for example, an endangered species mural, a chart of weather patterns for the country, a computer newsletter, an audiotaped radio news release, and so on. Student teams are great at coming up with their own projects, especially once the teacher has sparked their interest in a topic.

Exhibit 8.1. How to Construct Concept Circles.

- Let a circle represent any concept (plant, weather, bird, and so on).

- Print the name of the selected concept inside the circle.

- To show that one concept is included within another concept (or to indicate relative amounts), draw a smaller circle within a larger circle. For example, a large circle might indicate planets, a smaller circle might indicate the earth.

- To demonstrate that some elements of one concept are part of another concept (for example, that water contains some minerals), draw and label partially overlapping circles.

- To show that two concepts are not related, draw and label two unconnected circles (for example, one circle to indicate bryophytes—mosses without true leaves—and another circle to indicate tracheophytes—vascular plants with leaves, stems, and roots).

Using Collaboration to Enhance Thinking and Learning

Even teachers who are well prepared to teach mathematics and science content can make predictable mistakes in instructional approaches (Shulman & Colbert, 1987). Without a knowledge of pedagogy, it is difficult for teachers to manage a class or make mathematics and science meaningful and interesting for students through meeting students' interests and giving them the experiences that foster the development of the core thinking skills outlined in Chapter Two: focusing, information gathering, remembering, organizing, analyzing, generating, integrating, and evaluating.

To learn science concepts, students must experience a cluster of related ideas and reflect upon the applications of these ideas in solving problems, discovering relationships, analyzing patterns, and generalizing concepts. As in other fields, this learning happens most effectively when students work together in groups to examine ideas, present their understandings, solve problems, transform ideas, apply and confirm their thinking with others, and create their own theories. A collaborative science learning environment encourages students to engage in a great deal of invention as they impose their interpretation on what is presented and create theories that make sense to them. When teachers incorporate applications of ideas with supportive collaborative strategies, they assist students in taking responsibility for their thoughts while using higher-level thinking skills and building inner confidence, and they enhance students' scientific literacy over the long haul, not just in the classroom.

Cooperative Activities

The following cooperative activities have proven highly motivational and effective at reaching multiple learning styles.

Mathematics/Science Nature Search (Elementary Grades)

Science and mathematics applications are all around us. Mathematical patterns and symmetrical geometric forms abound in nature, architecture, art. This activity is designed to help students see and apply real-world connections to concepts in science and mathematics by making them more aware of the mathematical/scientific relationships all around them and having them use technology to report their findings. To begin the activity, divide the class into four groups. Group members are directed to find and bring back as many objects as they can that meet the requirements on the list that each group has been given. Objects that are too difficult to bring back to the classroom are to be sketched out on paper, but encourage students to bring back as many objects as possible. Each group engages in a different kind of search and has a different list.

Group One: Measurement Search. Find and bring back as many objects as you can that are:

> As wide as your hand
> A foot long
> Further away than you can throw
> Waist high
> Half the size of a baseball
> As long as your arm
> Smaller than your little finger
> Wider than four people
> Thinner than a shoelace
> As wide as your nose

Group Two: Shape Search. Find and bring back as many objects as you can that have these shapes:

> Triangle
> Circle
> Square
> Diamond
> Oval
> Rectangle
> Hexagon
> Other geometric shapes

Group Three: Number Pattern Search. Find and bring back as many objects as you can that show number patterns. For example, a three-leaf clover matches the number pattern three.

Group Four: Texture Search. Find and bring back as many objects as you can that have the following textures or physical qualities:

> Smooth
> Rough
> Soft
> Grooved/with ridges
> Hard
> Bumpy
> Furry
> Sharp
> Wet
> Grainy

When students return from their searches, have them order or classify their objects. Then have them use a graphing program on the computer (or colored paper, scissors, and markers) to visually represent their results—in a bar graph, for example. The teacher brings closure by having the groups share what they found.

Cooperative Construction: Building Bridges

This activity is interdisciplinary and reinforces skills of communication and group process and ideas from social studies, language arts, mathematics, science, and technology. While originally designed for grades 4 and 5, it has been successfully adapted for lower grades by some teachers. Bridges are a tribute to technological efforts, and they require community planning, engineering efficiency, mathematical precision, aesthetic considerations, group effort, and construction expertise.

Materials. This activity requires masking tape; one large, heavy rock; and one cardboard box. Also, have students bring in stacks of newspaper. You need approximately one one-foot stack of newspaper per person.

Procedure Steps.

1.   Divide students into three groups. Each group will be responsible for investigating one aspect of bridge building.

- *Group one: research.* This group is responsible for going to the library and looking up facts about bridges, collecting pictures of kinds of bridges, and bringing back information to be shared with the class.
- *Group two: aesthetics, art, and literature.* This group must discover songs and books about bridges and paintings, artworks, and so forth that deal with bridges.
- *Group three: measurement and engineering.* This group must discover design techniques, blueprints, angles, and measurements of actual bridges. If possible, visit a local bridge to look at the structural design.

Each group presents its findings to the class.

2.   Assemble the collected stacks of newspaper, tape, the rock and the box at the front of the room for the actual building of the bridge. Divide the class into groups of four or five students. Each group should have at least one member from each of the three investigative groups. Instruct each group to take an even portion of newspaper and one or two rolls of masking tape and explain that each group will be responsible for building a stand-alone bridge

using only the newspapers and tape. The bridge is to be constructed so that it will support the large rock and so that the box can pass underneath.

3.   Give the groups three to five minutes of planning time in which group members are allowed to talk and plan together. During the planning time, they are not allowed to touch the newspapers and tape, but they are encouraged to pick up the rock and make estimates of the box's height.

4.   At the end of the planning time, give the groups ten to twelve minutes to build their bridges. During this time, there is no talking among the group members. They may not handle the rock or the box, only the newspapers and tape.

Evaluation.   Stop all groups after the allotted time. Survey the bridges with the class and allow each group to try to pass the two tests for its bridge: Does the bridge support the rock? Does the box fit underneath? Discuss the design of each bridge and how these bridges compare to the bridges researched earlier.

Follow-Up/Enrichment.   Have each group measure its bridge and design a blueprint (include angles and the length and width of the bridge), so that another group could build the bridge by following this blueprint.

Environmental Relationships Activity: Quick Frozen Critters

In this activity to introduce the concepts of adaptation and limiting factors in biological populations, students play an active version of freeze tag while role-playing animal predators and prey.

Students are given the following information to ground the activity. A *predator* is an animal that kills and eats other animals for food. *Prey* describes an animal that is killed and eaten by other animals for food.

Animal populations are subject to limiting factors, and there are many of these influences in the life history of any animal. When one of these factors (for example, disease, climate, pollution, accidents, or food shortages) exceeds an animal's limits of tolerance, it becomes a limiting factor for that animal. It then drastically affects the well-being of the animal. Predators are limiting factors for prey. Prey are limiting factors for predators.

Animals display a variety of behaviors in predator/prey relationships. These are adaptations to survive. Some prey behaviors are signaling to others, flight, scrambling for cover, and freezing on the spot to escape detection or capture. The behavior selected depends partly on how close the predator is when detected by the prey. For example, if the predator is far enough away for the prey to feel some safety, the prey may signal to others.

After this activity, students should be able to discuss predator/prey relationships, including adaptations; describe the importance of adaptations in predator/prey relationships; and recognize that limiting factors—including predator/prey relationships—affect wildlife populations.

Materials. You will need food tokens (pieces of cut-up colored paper or cardboard), enough for three per student; gym vests or labeling devices to mark predators; four or five hula hoops or pieces of string or rope to serve as cover or shelter markers; and pencil and paper to record number of captures, if desired. You will also need a large open area—a gymnasium or playing field.

Procedure Steps.

1.　Identify students as either "predators" or "prey" for this version of freeze tag, with approximately one predator for every four to six students acting as prey. Predators should wear something that clearly identifies them as predators.

2.　Identify one end of the gymnasium or playing field as the "food source" and the other end as the "shelter."

3.   Place four to five hula hoops or circles of rope in the open area between the shelter and the food. These represent additional shelter, or cover, for the prey.

4.   Food tokens are placed on the ground in the food source zone. Allow three food tokens for each prey animal.

5.   Use a whistle or other prearranged signal to start each round. When a round begins, prey set out from the primary shelter at the end of the field. Their task is to move from the primary shelter to the food source, collect one food token, and return to the primary shelter. To "survive," prey have to make three trips and obtain three food tokens. Their travel is hazardous, however. They need to be alert to possible predators. If they spot a predator, they can use various appropriate prey behaviors—including warning others. Prey have two ways to prevent themselves from being caught by predators: they may freeze anytime a predator is within five feet of them, or they may run to cover (they are "safe" if they have at least one foot within one of the hula hoops or rope circles). Frozen prey may blink but otherwise should be still, without talking.

6.   Predators start the game anywhere in the open area between ends of the field, and thus are randomly distributed between the prey's food and primary shelter. Predators attempt to capture prey to survive. Capturing is done by tagging the prey, and predators may tag only moving (not frozen) prey. Each predator must capture two prey animals in order to survive. Captured prey are taken to the sidelines by the predators who capture them.

7.   Play four rounds, allowing each student to be both prey and predator. Limit each round to five to seven minutes.

Follow-Up/Evaluation. Discuss with students the ways they escaped capture when they were prey. Ask such questions as, Which ways were easiest? Which ways were most effective? What means did they use as predators to capture prey? Which ways were best? What did predators do in response to a prey animal who froze? In what ways are adaptations important to both predator and prey?

Ask students to summarize what they have learned about predator/prey relationships, discussing how predator/prey relationships serve as natural limiting factors affecting wildlife. Students can also be asked to pick any animal predator and its prey and describe each animal's adaptations.

Variations and Extensions. Have prey who are captured become predators and each predator not getting enough food become prey in the succeeding round. This quickly illustrates the concept of a dynamic balance as prey and predator populations fluctuate in response to each other. Or allow students to move only by walking, or assign different locomotive forms to each animal.

Thematic Integrations

Exploration, discovery, and connection are born in the science classroom any time a learner uses her or his higher cognitive skills to find new relationships or meanings in a given situation. Discovery takes place when a kindergarten teacher permits students to discover which objects will sink or float in a pan of water. Discovery takes places when students create graphs to show the distance metal objects travel when sliding down an inclined plane at various angles. Fifth-grade students may discover on their own the relationship between the angle of the incline and the distance the metal object slides across the table. An in-depth study of almost any subject can connect science to another part of human experience—to history, art, technological tools, environment, music, medicine, sports, artifacts, cars, *anything*. Conceptual motivational teaching provides opportunities for learners to experience for themselves the phenomena or materials under study. Conceptual teaching is focused on the big ideas, helping children learn concepts in stages of increased complexity, with the highest level enabling them to make predictions about similar or related phenomena and to generalize based on the learned concepts.

For example, students may have a preconceived idea that metal objects sink in water. In their sinking and floating exercises, however, they may discover that a dish- or boat-shaped metal object floats. Conceptual teaching uses the students' experiential discovery to tackle their preconceptions, asking such questions as, What do the metal objects that float have in common? or instructing students to explain their thinking about the metal ship and share their ideas with members of their group. Through formulating answers to appropriate questions about their experiences, students learn to reshape their own conceptual framework.

It is, of course, the *depth* of the *investigation* of the floating objects, not the immediate topic of calculating displacement and buoyancy, that makes this example good science and good education. The idea is for both teacher and student to focus on themes, integrating the overarching concepts of science through the strategies of problem solving, reasoning, and making connections in small groups.

Recent efforts to integrate scientific themes into the classroom have experienced surprising success. The Voyage of the Mimi is a well-publicized example of a highly successful, elementary science curriculum. Using television, computer programs, and print media, it organizes an entire school year around the theme of whales. The broad focus of this program extends from topics such as the songs of whales and routes of whale migration to the study of mammals, navigation, ocean temperatures, and communication. In the course of their study, students explore biology, physics, ecology, political issues, literature, art, and other fields. They may also discover that science, like art, can appeal to all the sensory modalities.

Science modules, multimedia technologies, hands-on science experiments, and science kits are all needed to redesign our beleaguered science programs, so that realistic science experiences will foster the teaching of scientific thinking. And new and innovative science materials *are* appearing. Many school districts have developed science resource centers and are providing the all-important in-service training for teachers (Hassard, 1990). Science progresses through the application of the scientific method and through communicating ideas that can, eventually at least, be tested. Improved science teaching will take more than new textbooks or new topics of study. It will require our transition to classrooms where students are active learners and generators of their own knowledge, progressing through theory to investigation as science itself does.

Activities for Thematic Learning

A carefully balanced combination of direct instruction, self-monitoring, and active group work can meet diverse student needs. The activities suggested here are designed to encourage higher-order thinking and provide collaborative vehicles for thematic integration of the curriculum.

Guided Imagery

Guided imagery, or creative visualization, is much like telling a story. The teacher guides students through an imaginary journey with a scientific purpose, encouraging them to create mental pictures and ideas. This kind of activity should be done in a quiet, relaxed atmosphere. You may wish to dim the lights or have students rest at their desks while the visualization is read. After the visualization, have students follow up with some kind of creative activity: discussing their experiences with other members of their small group, writing in their science logs, or creating artistic expressions of some kind.

The following example contains the instructions for a guided imagery experience that makes a good introduction to a unit on rocks. Have each student bring a rock to class. Each student gets to know his or her rock by describing it to someone else and by touching it. Collect the rocks in a box, then tell the students you will pass the rocks back. Have the students get in a circle, put their hands behind their backs, and start passing the rocks along behind their backs. They cannot look at the rocks, but when they think a rock is theirs, they can take a peek. When they are successful, they take their rock and sit down. The process continues until each student has found his or her rock. Next, students perform this visualization:

> Close your eyes and imagine that you are walking in a lush green forest along a trail. As you are walking, you notice a rock along the trail. Pick up the rock. Now make yourself very very tiny, so tiny that you become smaller than the rock. Imagine yourself crawling around on the rock. Use your hands and feet to hold onto the rock as you scale up its surface. Feel the rock. Is it rough or smooth? Can you climb it easily? Put your face down on the rock. What do you feel? Smell the rock. What does it smell like? Look around. What does the rock look like? What colors do you see? Is there anything unusual about your rock? Lie on your back on the rock and look at the sky. How do you feel. Talk to the rock. Ask it how it got there, ask how it feels to be a rock. What kind of problems does it have? Is there anything else you want to ask the rock or talk to the rock about? Take a few minutes to talk to the rock and listen to its answers. When you are done talking, thank the rock for allowing you to climb and rest on it. Then, carefully climb down off the rock. When you reach the ground, gradually make yourself larger until you are yourself again. When you are ready, come back to the classroom, open your eyes, and share your experience.

After the visualization, students write, share ideas about their rock, and then do some scientific investigations, testing to find out how hard the rock is and answering such questions as, What type of rock do you think your rock is? What is its history?

Elementary Lessons Through Experimentation

Students can perform a number of simple demonstrations of physical, chemical, or biological processes to have real experiences of scientific concepts that they can then discuss and think and write about. For example, students can give themselves elementary lessons in chromatography. Chemists use paper chromatography to separate mixtures of pigments or other substances. It is a simple process, but it often involves chemicals such as ether and acetone, making it unsuitable for elementary students. Luckily, students can perform a version of paper chromatography that illustrates several concepts of physics and chemistry and requires only inexpensive readily available materials.

Materials.   For a class of twenty-five, you will need a large roll of white paper towels; 75 to 100 water-soluble markers; five rectangular baking pans, each larger than the paper towel; and ten plastic clothespins.

Procedure Steps.
    1.   Distribute several markers of different colors to each student. Have the students apply small concentrated dots (less than 0.5 cm. in diameter) of each color on a paper towel, about 3 cm. apart and 3 cm. from the towel's bottom edge, forming a line of dots.
    2.   Fill a baking pan with water to within 1 cm. of the top, and set the pan near the edge of a counter. Fold the paper towel on the line of dots, so that it can hang down over the edge of the pan. The dots should be outside the pan just below the edge, and the bottom edge of the towel should be touching the surface of the water inside the pan. To ensure that the towel stays in place, clip it to the edge of the pan with clothespins or large paper clips. The paper towel absorbs water, which, when it reaches the dots of color, carries the dyes along, much as bright fabrics bleed in the wash. Each color is

made up of a mixture of dyes, so the children will observe that some dyes continue to move with the water, while others do not. (This occurs because highly water-soluble dyes move swiftly with water, while less water-soluble dyes move more slowly. Dyes that consist of positive and negative particles—molecules with unequal charge distribution, called polar molecules—dissolve most readily in water. This is because water molecules are polar, so their positive and negative regions attract the charged particles of the dyes). Students will see several areas of color develop from each of many of the original dots. Often the dullest colors form the most colorful chromatography.

3.   Have students experiment. Hang one towel over the pan and suspend another from the paper towel roll so that the end just touches the surface. After five minutes, ask the students to measure the distances the colors traveled on each towel and compare results.

Projects That Sum Up Multidisciplinary Connections

Students may participate in projects that bring together various kinds of specific knowledge and of general understanding around a theme. These projects may take forms that are more common in other disciplines than they are in science classes.

The example given here illustrates a culminating activity to a primary grade (first to third) social studies/science unit about the civilizations of the Americas and the development of maize agriculture around 2000 B.C. Students have had opportunities to explore historical literature and look at the ethical, cultural, and geographical meanings of maize for the Incan, Mayan, and Aztec societies. They have written stories, made collages, developed maps and timelines, mapped the location of the development of maize on the globe, and created calendars based on archaeological records. They have become archaelogists and gone on a dig (obtain five ceramic vessels—stoneware is recommended—from a second-hand store, break them, and bury the pieces in sand). Now, they participate in a final experiment and a readers theater activity with poetry and creative movement, in order to reinforce the concepts they have learned, connecting ideas and techniques from science and children's literature. Students really enjoy this fun math, science, and readers theater activity (and they can eat the popcorn from the experiment when they are done). Note that the readers theater script suggested here is just one possibility. The students' small groups can write stories from anything that they are reading, or they can use other prepared scripts. (Follow the general guidelines in Chapter Six for readers theater presentations.)

Experiment. Put out a large piece of butcher paper for each small group of students and give each group an air popper and some popcorn. Have the students:

1.   Estimate how far kernels will go.
2.   Pop popcorn (with top off) and observe the trajectories of the kernels. Have students draw the arcs of the kernels.
3.   Discuss the physics behind this phenomena.
4.   Measure the actual distances the kernels traveled.
5.   Eat.

Readers Theater. Give the students these directions: Kneel down. When your turn to read comes *hop up* and *read* your part. When not reading, kneel back down.

The Song of the Popcorn

EVERYONE: Pop, pop, pop!
1ST CHILD: Says the popcorn in the pan!
EVERYONE: Pop, pop, pop!
2ND CHILD: You may catch me if you can!
EVERYONE: Pop, pop, pop!

3RD CHILD: Says each kernel hard and yellow!
EVERYONE: Pop, pop, pop!
4TH CHILD: I'm a dancing little fellow!
EVERYONE: Pop, pop, pop!
5TH CHILD: How I scamper through the heat!
EVERYONE: Pop, pop, pop!
6TH CHILD: You will find me good to eat!
EVERYONE: Pop, pop, pop!
7TH CHILD: I can whirl and skip and hop!
EVERYONE: Pop, pop, pop, pop!
Pop, pop, pop!

Organizing an interdisciplinary lesson around a theme can excite and motivate all students to actively carry out projects and tasks in their group. In this final activity for a thematic unit on the three great civilizations of Middle and South America, social studies, science, movement, and language arts curricula merge in an interesting way.

Arctic Survival Problem-Solving Exercise

This exercise is adapted from instructions from survival experts. It is presented in the form of a scenario and requires students to perform extensive problem solving and to use many critical thinking skills as well as display a body of scientific knowledge.

Scenario and Instructions.

Your small plane carrying five passengers was forced to crash land in an isolated region in the Canadian north, killing the pilot and damaging the aircraft beyond use. It is mid January and the temperature is -30° Fahrenheit. The last reading taken by the pilot puts your position at about twenty miles from the nearest town. Your small party was able to salvage the following articles from the plane:

Ball of steel wool

Compass

Hatchet

Plastic sectional air map

Can of shortening

Twenty-foot by twenty-foot piece of heavy canvas

Five newspapers

Loaded .45 caliber pistol

Cigarette lighter (without fluid)

Five large chocolate bars

Quart of 100 proof whiskey

Extra shirt and pair of pants for each person

As a team, you must decide on a plan for survival. Next, rank order the items in the list in terms of their priority in your survival plan (number one will be the highest priority and number twelve the lowest). Base your plan rankings on team consensus. When disputes occur, use strategies of compromise and group discussions moving toward agreement, not a simple point averaging system. When you are done, check your responses with those of the survival experts.

Experts' Survival Plan and Answer Key.

To survive, the team must plan to stay at the site. Most rescue attempts are made within twenty-four to forty-eight hours. Any attempt to walk out would almost certainly doom the team to death. The most pressing needs of the survivors are staying calm, warm, and sheltered. Once the survivors have found ways to keep warm, their immediate problem is to attract the attention of the search

parties. All of the items the team has salvaged should be assessed
for their value in meeting these priorities. The items are ranked here
in order of their importance.

1. *Cigarette lighter (without fluid)*. The greatest danger is exposure
to the cold. The greatest need is for warmth. The second greatest
need is for a signalling device. Building a fire should be the first
priority. The cigarette lighter, even without fuel, will produce
sparks to start a fire.

2. *Ball of steel wool*. Steel wool provides the best substance for
catching the sparks made by the cigarette lighter and supporting a
flame.

3. *Extra shirt and pair of pants for each person*. Besides adding
warmth to people's bodies, these versatile items can be used for
shelter, signaling, bedding, bandages, string, and tinder (for fires).

4. *Can of shortening*. Both the can and its contents have many
uses. Mirror-like signaling devices can be made from the lid. Once
the lid is polished with steel wool, it can be used to reflect sunlight. A simple mirror can generate five to seven million units of
candlepower. The reflected beam can be seen across the horizon.
Getting on high ground and signaling will greatly enhance the
team's chances of being rescued within twenty-four hours. In
addition, the shortening itself can be rubbed on exposed skin for
protection against the cold or eaten in small amounts. When
melted, it is useful for starting fires. Shortening-soaked cloth
makes an effective candlewick. The can also has many uses, such
as a container for melting snow for drinking.

5. *Twenty-foot by twenty-foot piece of heavy canvas*. Canvas can be
used for shelter from wind and snow. It also makes a good signaling device.

6. *Hatchet*. This tool's many uses include chopping wood, clearing the campsite, cutting boughs for ground insulation, and constructing a frame for a shelter.

7. *Five large chocolate bars*. Chocolate is a quick energy source that does not require a lot of energy to digest.

8. *Five newspapers*. Newspapers can be used for starting fires or rolled and placed under clothing to serve as insulation from the cold (by providing dead air space). They can also be read for recreation, spread out for visual signaling, and rolled into a cone for voice signaling.

9. *Loaded .45 caliber pistol*. The gun can be used as a signaling device (three shots is the international distress signal) and may be especially important as survivors get weaker and unable to made loud responses. The butt can be used as a hammer and the shell powder in starting fires. Unfortunately, the pistol's disadvantages counter its advantages. Survivors' possible anger, lapses of rationality, and frustration make a lethal weapon especially dangerous. Individuals could waste too much energy trying to hunt with this weapon. It takes a skilled marksman to kill an animal and too much energy would be used transporting the carcass back to the camp.

10. *Quart of 100 proof whiskey*. The only productive uses for the alcohol are in fire building and as a fuel. Alcohol remains fluid even at very low temperatures, but drinking it at -20° Fahrenheit poses a serious danger to the mouth, while drinking it warmer causes dehydration. Drinking alcohol results in a rapid loss of body heat.

11. *Compass*. This is a dangerous item because it may encourage some survivors to attempt to walk to the nearest town. The glass may be used as a sun reflector and signaling device, but it is the least effective of the team's potential devices.

12. *Plastic sectional air map*. This item is dangerous because it will encourage survivors to walk to the nearest town, thereby condemning them to almost certain death.

Cooperation Across the Dimensions of Learning

Some things are becoming clear. Significant efforts and a change in thinking will be needed if we are going to create a citizenry that is scientifically literate. Science skills taught in isolation lead to isolated thinking and an infrequent use of these skills in real-world situations. Failure to grasp scientific concepts "is the cause of a host of dim-witted decisions" (Paulos, 1991, p. 113). If we are to enter a more advanced period in U.S. education, it is important for all children to talk, collaborate, think, and act scientifically.

It is equally important to unleash the power of knowledgeable teachers, letting them use their informal ideas and judgments to invent the science classrooms of the future, letting them involve themselves actively in the learning process, and letting them shift the focus to instruction, making instruction more important than curriculum. There is a need for teachers to experience the kind of instruction they are being asked to provide. They must have opportunities to be actively engaged in using science, so they can watch themselves as learners, play with ideas, see their own minds getting involved with the topic, and experience the confusion, hesitancies, and excitement that come from growth and from collective learning. In addition, the new research-based knowledge about the ways children learn must be made accessible to both practicing teachers and college students in teacher education programs.

For the science teacher, progress will involve cooperation, introspection, reflection, and critical thinking. For the science student, progress will frequently involve problem finding and evaluating the benefits of various problem solutions, acts that require critical thinking skills for looking beyond information given in order to make connections and create personal meaning.

Curiosity about the nature of scientific knowledge is an integral part of designing thoughtful lessons. The idea must be to break down some of the more traditional ways of working with science and, using the ideas and kinds of activities described here, to encourage students to use their small-group opportunities to expand their thinking, becoming not only scientifically literate but expanding the influence of scientific literacy itself to other subjects. The scientific method, for example, is the intellectual tool that helps students collaboratively answer "what if" and "why not" questions in many subjects. And even if all the answers are not available, knowing enough to formulate the questions enriches our understanding of the present and encourages us to anticipate answers in the future. Eleanor Duckworth (1987, p. 25) expresses our goal wisely.

> The nature of creative intellectual acts remains the same, whether it is an infant who for the first time makes the connection between seeing things and reaching for them, or a musician who invents a harmonic sequence, or an astronomer who develops a new theory of the creation of the universe. In each case, new connections are being made among things already mastered. The more we help children to have their wonderful ideas and to feel good about themselves for having them, the more likely it is that they will some day happen upon wonderful ideas that no one else has happened upon before.

Chapter Nine

The Arts

Imagination is to break through the limits.

—*Henry David Thoreau*

Arts education has always taught that no part of a composition, whether that composition is a painting or a curriculum, is independent of the whole in which it participates. As teachers work with models that explore connections within and across disciplines, they can also explore learning strengths within learners. In this way, arts education acts as a prism, allowing students to connect multiple dimensions and directions of focus (Miller & Drake, 1990). Visual arts, dance, music, or theater can provide active entry points to other subject matter and critical thinking. This chapter describes why arts education must be retained in our schools, in opposition to those who consider it as nice to have but not essential, and how arts education can inform every other discipline in the school curriculum, teaching students new ways to see, news ways to make connections, new topics on which to collaborate, and key ways to engage in critical thinking.

Arts education is moving away from the current emphasis on performing or doing to a more balanced curriculum that includes instruction in culture, aesthetics, criticism, and the ways the arts relate to or illuminate other subjects. Taking a discipline-based approach to the arts, plus integrating them into the overall curriculum, will help our students become better consumers of the arts and more understanding of diversity (Viadero, 1993). Besides enriching the study of other cultures and nonartistic subjects, the arts raise students' awareness of the aesthetic qualities of their sur-roundings. As teachers try to plug critical thinking and coopera-tive learning into subject matter, the arts can be the pathways along which that thinking and learning travel to synthesize and inter-connect topics and generate a sense of community.

Arts Education in School Reform

Although most states today require some form of arts education, the current quality and emphasis vary greatly. However, arts edu-cators have developed new standards for national student assess-ment. When the *Goals 2000: Educate America Act* was passed in 1994, the arts were recognized as one of the core content areas in which students should show competency at grades 4, 8, and 12. The governing board of the National Assessment of Educational Progress plans to begin testing students' grasp of the arts in its 1996 national assessment. This represents the federal governments' first prescription for reversing the decline of instruction in the visual arts, dance, drama, and music. As the United States goes ahead with the concept of national assessment, new standards for a disci-pline-based arts education will bring a higher level of quality to the field.

As part of the effort to include arts education in national cur-riculum reform, a series of reports entitled *Discipline Based Art Edu-cation* has been put forward by the Getty Foundation (Getty Center for Education in the Arts, 1990). These reports encourage schools to help students go beyond art as classroom crafts to the study of art criticism, history, and aesthetics. In other small-scale projects, art educators and historians, philosophy professors, and local teachers have gathered to collaborate in making aes-thetics less mysterious for children and young adults, feeling that, even at early levels, students need to be grounded in the ability to reflect on art, study its disciplines, and test out skills involved in production.

The 1994 standards are even more specific in stating that every student should:

1. Be able to communicate in four arts disciplines: music, visual arts, theater, and dance.
2. Be able to communicate proficiently in at least one art form.
3. Be able to present basic analysis of works of art.
4. Have an informed acquaintance with exemplary works of art from a variety of world cultures and historical periods.
5. Be able to relate various types of arts knowledge and skills across the arts disciplines.

In 1992, the National Endowment for the Arts (NEA) entered into an agreement with the U.S. Department of Education to create an "in-depth arts-in-education program" that could be part of the national effort to "reinvent" U.S. schools. In this agreement, the arts were recognized to represent a body of knowledge as well as a practical study of technique. Isolated school experiments are proving that there are a number of ways to integrate arts content and provide in-depth arts programs beautifully on a small scale. Among the excellent models or prototypes of art education are a discipline-based arts program in Minneapolis and an exemplary arts education model in Augusta, Georgia, supported by the NEA. The latter program uses the arts to improve the general learning environment and social equity among students and to improve students' academic achievement, self-esteem, attendance, and creative thinking.

The question is whether the call for "world-class standards" in the arts will mean real change for a significant numbers of schools (National Art Education Associates, 1992, p. 18). Moreover, although continuing our rich artistic tradition by producing artists is important, no response to arts education should be considered the only right one. In fact, seeking the objective of what some adults see as good creative products often makes the appearance of these outstanding products less likely. Instead, teachers can mix the modeling of intellectual stimulation with the natural rapport and creative production that is such an important part of the mysterious art of good teaching (Fowler, 1992).

Art criticism, history, and aesthetics contribute both to the production of artworks and artistic performance and to a child's ability to draw inferences and interpret powerful ideas. Art (like television, writing, or mathematics) makes use of certain conventions and symbol systems to express figurative meaning. In the visual arts, for example, this may include symbols embedded in style (the fine detail) or in composition (arrangement of elements), creating the possibility for multiple meanings. Reading an artist's symbols is as much a skill as reading print or video images.

Arts education must go beyond transient messages that are often overvalued by a culture. In a multicultural society like that in the United States, arts education also means weaving artistic expressions from other cultures into the curriculum, enabling diverse students to creatively confirm the truth and beauty of their heritage. Art is not limited to specific times or cultures. Greek art learned from Egyptian art. Christian art was shaped by ideas from Greece and the East. African, Chinese, Egyptian, and Mexican art have influenced Modernism. Eurocentric art borrows from other cultures and from the geopolitical circumstances of its time. Influences fly in every direction. A high-quality national culture can, in actuality, be a unifying frame for a rich multiplicity of cultural influences.

Exposing children to a variety of artistic forms and materials will make it easier to locate their areas of strength and weakness. All students will then have a similar range of choices, but it is how they make their choices that will count. Allowing children to choose from a variety of artistic and intellectual possibilities is beneficial for building both their creative strength and their basic skills. Children can also be involved in artistic interdisciplinary projects—ranging from illustrating their own books to choreographing movement to writing poetry to producing videos. Process, production, and critical dimensions are all important; however, to understand any art form, children must have some experiences as critics of examples of that art form.

Questioning, challenging, and aesthetic reflection all contribute to creative habits of mind and set up possibilities for action. Students must see how the arts set up possibilities for positive action and take on our world concerns. In the Los Angeles riots of 1992, for example, one of the first requests from the headquarters of Rebuild Los Angeles (a nonprofit group established to tackle the problems of inner-city life) was to the Design Arts Institute. The institute was asked to provide design concepts and tools to help solve such problems as the lack of affordable housing, attractive parks, and small shopping centers and to make the community more aesthetically pleasing.

Providing a Sense of Opening

When students learn how visual art, dance, music, and theater interconnect with each other and other subjects, they take a step toward becoming powerfully engaged in these interconnections. Since the beginnings of civilization, the arts have had a central place in ceremonies or as artifacts (such as cave paintings) that connected ritual, religion, and daily life. The visual arts, dance, poetry, plays, and music have long been organizers or points of integration for a whole range of human activities. Indeed, their probable original purpose—which to some extent still obtains—was to enshrine a reproduction of experience, in order to gain some control over that kind of experience and influence the future. Encounters with the arts also have a unique capacity to provide openings for imaginative breaks from the expected. The arts continue the universal human practice of making *special* certain objects, sounds, movements, or representations that have been linked with human survival for countless generations.

Thus, the arts have always provided a sense of opening things up, a loving of questions about the nature of things, and a unique communal resource. This sense of opening up frees students from following only in the tracks of the predicted and the expected. It results in what Emily Dickinson called "a slow fire lit by the imagination" (1924), and as the United States moves toward the new millennium, we need all the imagination we can get.

Today's school reform process should not push aside such a basic aspect of social consciousness and interdisciplinary knowing. When there are no arts in a school, there are fewer alternatives for exploring subjects. There are fewer ways to open doors of the mind and provide new spaces for the active construction of knowledge. What a powerful tool arts education is for countering the tendency towards standardization! The notion that the arts can encourage wonder, inquiry, speculation, and technological literacy has for too long been lost in a morass of indifference, nostalgia, crafts, didacticism, and an already overcrowded curriculum. To rescue this notion will require a greater emphasis on professional development that increases teachers' familiarity with the arts and discipline-based arts education, because it will take the skill of teachers to keep light from the arts shining at the center of the human spirit and to use the arts in fostering an interconnected exuberance of learning. Performance and creation will continue to be important. However, as arts education becomes more focused on analysis, history, and culture, study of the arts will depend more than ever on the intellectual preparation and commitment of the teacher. Specialists can help, but it is the regular classroom teacher who will continue to be the primary source for arts instruction.

Could We Lose Arts Education?

Ellen Dissanayake (1992, p. 42) observes that "social systems that disdain or discount beauty, form, mystery, meaning, value, and quality—whether in art or in life, are depriving their members of human requirements as fundamental as those for food, warmth and shelter." This deprivation is what we will face if arts education cannot gain a firm footing in our schools.

In *Candide*, Voltaire defined blind optimism as a "mania for maintaining that all is well when things are going badly." The ability to think that things are going well when they are not has not been lost. A number of futurists, for example, predict that our culture will soon be as filled with the arts as it is with television and sports (see, for example, Nesbitt, 1986). They see the arts as being central to the curriculum in the new millennium (Eisner, 1991). But that centrality is unlikely to come about as automatically as they seem to think it will.

People are taking a stand, however. Educators and artists are arguing that children without knowledge of the arts are as ignorant as children without knowledge of literature or math. (Alexis de Tocqueville predicted that American democracy would diminish the character of art. It has taken seventy years for educators to take a position that proves him wrong—at least for a while.) And some artists are trying to break down the disconnection between the nation's establishment (including the arts, academia, and the press) and the majority of the nation's citizens, hoping to show people that art is indeed central to their lives. Some of this disconnection results from learned behaviors among those in the arts, academia, and the press who do view, value, and appreciate the arts and express themselves in the arts, but popular and traditional media also play a role. Many citizens get most of their information from television, newspapers, movies, and videos, and have little exposure to the arts. If children and adults from all cultures and linguistic groups can use the arts to enhance their joy, spontaneity, and satisfaction in learning then we all will be richer.

Many people think of the arts as elitist, therapeutic, frivolous, or impractical or as mindless entertainment. But the process of understanding or creating art is more than unguided play, self-expression, or a tonic for contentment. Advancing culture, art, creativity, and human values has everything to do with the life and quality of this nation. The arts can be tools for shattering stereotypes, changing behavior, building a sense of community, and delivering sociopolitical commentary. In the visual arts, for example, Barbara Kruger develops popular imagery that merges words and concepts from other disciplines. Along with other post-modernist artists like Keith Haring and Jenny Holtzman, she works outside the artistic and the aesthetic frame to harness the formative power of images and affect deep structures of personal and social belief. In a similar manner, Alexis Smith combines quotations and flotsam and jetsam to speak to the artifices and pitfalls of a belief in a mythical America. When the right object is connected to the perfect quotation, the result can range from the humorous to a tough and intriguing social observation. If we look toward music, storytelling and dance, we see Lori Anderson extending the edges of experience with performance art by combining nearly every basic art form with literary references and video imagery. Like many modern artists, she releases possibilities by making use of collaborators across time and various media and subject matters.

But whether visual, musical, or theatrical, the arts have the potential to help us be receptive to new thinking and generous toward the production of something fresh. They proffer important intellectual tools for understanding many subjects. They also build on qualities that are essential to revitalizing U.S. schooling: teamwork, analytical thinking, motivation, and self-discipline. The arts provide cultural resources that people can draw on for the rest of their lives. They are even an important part of the U.S. economy. U.S. films and music are among our most successful exports.

Nevertheless, educational decision makers in the United States have generally not paid much attention to the value of arts education. The arts are most often found on the fringes of the U.S. school curriculum, owing in part to our lacking a long tradition of prizing artistic expression that ranges beyond the cute and the comfortable. Little is expected of either our leaders or our citizens when it comes to knowledge about artistic forms. The United States spends nearly $50 billion a year on science and much less than $1 billion on all the humanities put together. In contrast, in recent years, the West Germans spent more than ten times as much on the arts as the United States (*The New York Times*, August 2, 1992).

The arts can open new horizons, enrich the spirit, and educate students to expand an American cultural vision. But when the arts are viewed as a personal luxury and not associated with "real" wage-earning occupations, developing or maintaining a good arts education program is more difficult. This is a disappointing portrait of ourselves, a reflection not of human strength and aesthetic vision, but of its absence. Building a faith in the arts and arts education will help us build our faith in ourselves as a nation.

Human societies have always depended on the arts to give insight into truths, however painful or unpopular they may be. Today, in many countries, there is wide agreement that the arts can aid children in developing creativity, becoming good citizens, and being productive workers. The basic notion is that the person and the world is poorer without the arts and the enlightenment and thoughtfulness they foster. From Asia to Europe, serious arts education is one of the integrating features of the school curriculum. Such an investment in the arts is seen as an investment in the community, and vice versa. Americans are beginning to take notice.

Inventing the future of arts education means expanding the links among the arts, the community, and the schools. There is a world out there that students must explore with the arts if they are to be broadly educated, to say nothing of developing their self-examination, critical-thinking, and problem-solving skills. All these skills can be taught and reinforced through the arts. But without our continued attention to the substance inherent in the arts and without concerted educator action, the arts run the risk of being dismissed as expendable in an era of curriculum gridlock and financial difficulties.

Reinvigorating U.S. schools will depend not only on schools' and teachers' skills but also on the perspectives rendered by the arts to show what thinking, learning, and life can be. The increasing influence of the discipline-based art education movement is deepening and broadening the arts curriculum, connecting it through artistic expression and aesthetic criticism to cultural, historical, and social contexts. In the new literature-based reading curriculum, for example, students are expected to develop the thinking skills necessary for literary criticism. Should we expect less when it comes to the arts? A renewed emphasis on artists, criticism, aesthetic discourse, and the importance of discipline-based arts education must accompany education into the next century.

Establishing a Collaborative Arts Community

Valuing a range of contributions within a supportive and collaborative learning community can make the difference between a student's having a competent self-image and having the devastating belief that nothing can be done right. Recasting the teacher's role from authority figure dispensing knowledge to that of collaborative team leader (coaching mixed-ability teams) is a major ingredient of cooperative learning in the arts. This supportive process is particularly important when children are creating works with new media, such as videotapes, because it takes a small group, not just an individual, to do much of the production.

Active collaboration around a thematic or interdisciplinary approach also requires depth of planning, redefinition of testing, and cooperative classroom management skills (Albert, 1990). In a collaborative setting, the teacher helps students gain confidence in their ability and the group's ability to work through problems; consequently, they rely less on the teacher for validating their thinking. However, such teaching requires a conceptual reexamination of today's student population, the learning process–decision making relationships, and classroom organizational structures. Making students active participants in deciding what and how they should learn does not diminish the need for informed decision makers. But without this—and other—changes in the power relationships within schools and within the schoolroom, educational reform will be stymied. Challenges for the professional teacher in this new environment include:

- Taking a more active role in serving students of multicultural backgrounds and at-risk students. In many cases, this means addressing non-Western artistic formats.
- Focusing and taking advantage of cooperative learning teams to foster students' thinking, reasoning, and problem-solving abilities.
- Making use of cooperative learning strategies, peer tutoring, and new technology to reach a range of learners and learning styles.
- Working to professionalize arts education and legitimize the arts in the schools. This includes acquiring the ability to assess student knowledge, ability, and performance.
- Developing exemplary materials supportive of cooperative learning. This development must pay particular attention to the promotion of thinking skills; the needs of at-risk students; the needs of teacher professionalism, assessment, and accountability; and the advent of new technologies.

Although children are capable of both imitating structure and figuring it out on their own, they can use mechanisms for thinking and digging deeply into subject matter and themselves. Through collaborative learning, they can acquire the structures they need for analyzing works of art, music, dance, and drama—frameworks for sorting out what is real in the environment. To their collaborative groups, they bring widely divergent talents and interpretations that they derive from their own perceptions and the ways they filter the world. For those who believe in educating as many "intelligences" as possible (to use Howard Gardner's 1987 term), the arts are a vital educational tool, one that gains power as it is used collaboratively.

John Dewey (1958, p. 27) tells us that "communication is a process of sharing experience till it becomes a common possession. It modifies the disposition of both parties who partake in it." Good exercises in art education require students to communicate and then alter familiar or unfamiliar images along lines they feel are promising, while effective teachers strive to ensure that what is being learned is a center of interest for students. This often means walking a fine line, engaging students as active thinkers without interfering when they are working well on their own. Students' creative experiences in the arts are a blend of informed adult encouragement and opportunities for creative exploration. A flexible arts curriculum requires not only knowledge about each child but judgment about when to intervene, recognizing (like Emerson, 1990, p. 214) that sometimes it is best to "let the bird sing without deciphering the song."

A collaborative arts curriculum that engages students' interests and encourages the reflection and experience students need to be creative rests on the same ideas that we have seen before in relation to other disciplines.

- *Active learning.* Students exchange ideas when they are involved in well-organized tasks with materials they can manipulate. Active learning is enhanced when students can collaboratively make predictions, find patterns, and explore and construct ideas, models, and stories.
- *Interesting activities.* Lessons should include activities designed to develop higher thinking skills rather than stimulate quick

right answers. Problems on diverse topics that encourage speculation or estimation are most likely to motivate and encourage students to work together on the lesson.

- *Chances for student interaction.* Students need to develop the ability to work together, and they must become sensitive and responsive to group members and group needs. There is a need for activities that involve all group members as well as a need to sensitize the group to include all members in active involvement.

- *Opportunities for thinking.* Students should be given opportunities to explore diverse ideas emphasizing concepts and relationships. Challenging tasks and opportunities for interaction with peers can lead to more advanced thinking and creative discussions.

- *Teachers as advisors and curriculum developers.* Textbooks and teacher's manuals need to be altered or replaced by teacher ideas, materials, and activities that arouse student interest and encourage cooperation. The teacher's role becomes that of a consultant, advisor, and learner who interacts with teaching peers.

- *Lesson structure and accountability.* Opportunities should be provided for group- or teacher-led summaries of important aspects of the tasks. Students need to discuss what they have learned with the teacher and other students in order to understand and explain the activities they have worked on.

Students are also to be encouraged to take an active role in planning what they will study and how they will do it. One way to divide a class into small groups is to have students self-select into cooperative groups based on common interests in a topic. Students decide specifically what they wish to find out, divide up the work among themselves, perform it, summarize it, and present their findings to the class. There is much freer communication and greater involvement when students share in the planning and decision making and carry out *their* plan.

The broad perspective of the cooperative learning model amplifies basic subject matter and guides students and teachers toward becoming better cooperative thinkers and decision makers, and the integration of diverse subjects has advantages sufficient to encourage further examination of what content best lends itself to this approach. Also, like any concept for organizing learning, the interdisciplinary curriculum is valuable to the extent that it is well implemented. Effectiveness of any approach always comes back to teachers and their knowledge of their discipline. Like E. B. White, who wrote that he wanted to keep the notes of his own meeting, teachers must learn to script their own lesson plans.

Collaborative and Interdisciplinary Activities

The following activities illustrate ways to apply the ideas just described and to connect arts education to other disciplines.

Listening to Stories Rich in Imagery

Teachers can read students stories that contain a great deal of visual imagery, stopping every so often to permit students to share the mental images they have as the story comes to life in their minds.

Teachers can also do "mental adventure" exercises frequently. Ask the children to close their eyes while you read a guided imagery exercise. Here, for example, is a guided imagery exercise of taking a walk in a wooded forest.

> Picture yourself in a forest. You are walking along a path among the trees. What is the weather like? [*Pause to let the students imagine the situation*.] As you walk along, you see a person running in the other direction. Why? [*Pause*.] You continue strolling on and soon come to a body of water. What is it? How deep, how wide, how cold? [*Pause*.] You cross it. How? [*Pause*.] You find the path again on the other side and continue walking. Soon you spot a cup in the mid-

dle of the path. You bend down to pick it up and examine it carefully. What does it look like? [*Pause*.] You put it down. Why? [*Pause*.] You keep walking until the path leads you to a house. What does the house look like [*Pause*.] You enter the house and find yourself in the kitchen. What is the kitchen like? [*Pause*.] You sit at the kitchen table and see something interesting on the table. What is it [*Pause*.] While you are looking at it, the person you saw in the forest walks into the kitchen. Describe that person.

Ask students to orally retrace their individual journeys for the class, or at later stages, ask them write about their journeys. Students may also wish to act out their journeys for the rest of the class or to draw their journeys sequentially.

Using Mind Pictures to Determine What Comes Next

Spontaneous storytelling techniques can be the bridge that connects a child's pictorial imagination with oral language and writing. These techniques work at all grade levels, but they require practice and the initial enthusiastic participation of the teacher as storyteller. (Also, when a child working on an oral or written creation tells the teacher that he or she does not know what comes next, instead of responding, the teacher may distract the child from the task by instigating a very brief chat about something totally unrelated to the task. Allowing the child to get away from the intensity of creating for a few seconds often allows the child to return to the task with fresh ideas and immediate inspiration. This technique is often used by professional writers.)

Singing Activities in the Primary Grades

In the following four-step exercise, teachers can connect singing with linguistic and musical literacy learning.

- Select a song that is one of the children's favorites and that contains simple words and rhyme, rhythm, and repetition.

- Link the words of the song to print by writing the lyrics on a song chart. Lead the group in singing the song one phrase at a time and model strategies for sounding out words by thinking out loud as the words are written down.

- Invite the children to sing along once the chart is completed. Use instruments to accentuate the rhythm. (Students may want to make some of their own instruments.)

- Encourage the creation of new lyrics, matching new words that have the appropriate number of syllables to the rhythmic structure of the song.

Singing Activities in the Intermediate Grades

In grades 3 to 6, some students are ready to build on the strong foundations formed by their positive dispositions toward music, and they may wish to engage in concentrated skill development. For these students, focused practice through participation in orchestra, band, or other instrumental or vocal music programs is a viable option. However, all students should have frequent opportunities to sing, play instruments, engage in choral rhythmic readings, harmonize with others, create their own songs, make up rhythms, and write lyrics, so that music can continue to be a joyous, integral part of their curriculum. For example, teach a song that is currently popular to intermediate-grade children. Ask them to improvise some simple actions to go with it. Afterwards, survey the students. Did they enjoy the song? What did they learn by putting actions to music?

Learning About Artists Through Literature

Through reading literature that allows them to readily identify with lifelike characters who are artists, students become more open to various art forms and begin to experience the creative forces felt by real-life artists. For example, Tomie De Paola's *The Art Lesson* (1989) and Cynthia Rylant's *All I See* (1988), two picture story-books designed for young students, are both about children and their experiences with art. Both books have as major characters artists for whom creative expression is a driving force in their lives. The reader gains access to the minds of the artists and their unique artistic visions. Each vision has the capacity to stimulate young readers and make them eager to reflect on how *they* see people and the world.

After reading these books, students in one class, on their own, spent their recess sketching other children on the playground and jotting down some metaphors that the children's movements brought to mind. Back in class, the students enthusiastically shared their sketches with their classmates, struggling to articulate exactly what it was that inspired their sketches.

Loving and Living Poetry

We have often heard that children are natural poets. We need to broaden our definition of poetry, expanding it to encompass all that children can hope to think or imagine. The following exercise helps children turn their own thoughts into poetry.

First, ask children to read this poem (Hughes, 1990):

The Meaning Makers

Bring all of your dreams,
you dreamers,
Bring me all of your
Heart melodies
That I may wrap them
In a blue cloudcloth
Away from the too rough
fingers of the world.

by Langston Hughes

Next, ask students to describe the best dream they ever had. This can be a daydream as well as a dream they had when they were asleep. Then ask them to rewrite their dreams as poetry, reminding them that the way their ideas are expressed should cause the reader to look at the subject in a fresh way. This assignment can be designed to be completed *in school*. Poetry writing makes a refreshing change from the classroom routine, and students can share their creative excitement with other "poets." Allow students to walk around the class as they are creating. That way they can become inspired by other students' ideas and word choices. They may even wish to borrow other students' thoughts. This is perfectly acceptable.

Connecting Subject Matter with Themes in the Arts

Wlodkowski and Jaynes (1990, p. 46) call the result of integrating various subjects around a theme and thus enhancing thinking and learning skills "the metacurriculum." The arts are especially useful in developing these metacurricula and starting dialogues between disciplines that often ignore each other. When bodies of knowledge from diverse subject matter areas are brought together so that diverse intellectual tools can be applied to a common theme, issue, or problem, the result can be a new and valuable way of looking at the world. Subjects from the Greek classics to radiation theory need the historical, philosophical, and aesthetic perspective afforded by a conscious application of language and methods from one or more disciplines to a central theme, issue, topic, or experience in another discipline. Thus, the arts and humanities have proven useful tools for integrating curricular areas and helping students transcend narrow subject matter concerns (The College Board, 1985). Teachers at many levels use intellectual tools from the fine arts as thematic lenses for examining diverse subjects, and some schools have even worked out an integrated school day, in which interdisciplinary themes based on the fine arts add interest, meaning, and function to collaboration.

Mathematics, writing, science, and reading (and studies of each of the arts themselves) can all be wrapped around central themes in the arts, so that rich connections stimulate children's minds and senses.

The research suggests that using an interdisciplinary thematic approach improves students' knowledge of subject matter and helps them transfer the skills learned to domains outside the school. An additional finding is that good units organized around themes can improve students' abilities to apply their knowledge to new subjects (Sharan, 1990). For example, language development flourishes when children are encouraged to discuss the arts materials they are using and to reflect on the nature of their art work through writing.

Before we can deal with teaching the thinking skills that are vital for today's students, we must give children some solid content to think about. Interdisciplinary studies often bring content and skills together in ways that stimulate learning, allow students to practice the skills they have learned from many subjects, and help students make sense of the world (Maeroff, 1988). This is a holistic approach that focuses on themes and problems and deals with them in depth, rather than asking student simply to memorize facts and go through the text from cover to cover.

In addition, interdisciplinary studies imply cooperation among people as well as disciplines, and the notion that students of different abilities and backgrounds can learn from each other can be a natural outgrowth of the collaborative tendency inherent in the interdisciplinary approach. Students' collaborative involvement not only allows student input into the planning process but also develops student self-responsibility and long-term commitment to learning (Fraser, 1990). When parts of the curriculum are organized around themes, they become mutually reinforcing and this linkage can stimulate lifelong learning.

There is always the danger that teachers will water down content in an attempt to cover all areas. But good teachers can, for example, effectively teach the work of Newton on one hand, while clearly placing that work in a historical context on the other. They can show how the history of ideas, political movements, and changing relationships among people are part of the fabric of our world. And they do this because they know that we cannot narrowly train people in specialist areas and expect them to be able to deal with multifaceted twenty-first century jobs.

Thematic Strategies for Connecting Subjects and People

The different ways of knowing represented by the arts and the sciences do not need to grow farther apart. The underlying unity of all cultural and scientific effort was the unwritten rule until the eighteenth century. However, as art and science have progressed over the last two hundred years, both have become more extensive within themselves while simultaneously becoming more narrowly specialized from the viewpoint of the outsider. Now, artists are once again proclaiming the relevance of their work to the totality of our lives and to our ability to see things in new ways.

For example, in his seventh-grade Vermont classroom, teacher Trevor Tebbs has worked with another teacher to build students' learning around a black history theme. The two teachers assembled a list of significant events, terms, literature, and questions, and students worked in partnerships to research, discuss, and create a timeline collage of visual images depicting the theme. They were also responsible for written pieces, maps, and creative journal writing. Partners had to work cooperatively to complete the assignments, which were presented to their colleagues and their parents. The goal was to examine both their ethnic and human heritages while searching for the proper balance between the two.

In one of the collaborative projects drawing on the arts that surrounded this theme, a small group of students was given the total responsibility of completing an audio slide presentation based on the timeline and then giving the presentation to others. In this kind of project, the arts connect the mind and the senses, uniting the cognitive and affective dimensions of learning. In Tebbs's words (1991), "The whole enterprise was a superb success. I am of the opinion that collaborative art offers the opportunity for a really powerful and beneficial experience for our students."

Thematic units direct the design of classroom activities, providing them with a logical sequence and a scope of instruction that values depth over breadth of coverage. Content should be chosen by how well it represents what is currently known in the field and its potential for making dynamic connections (Rogoff, 1990). Thematic units can last an hour, a day, a few weeks, or a semester. Of course, shorter, flexible units of study are easier to set up than semester or yearlong thematic units. No matter what their length, they are not intended to replace a discipline-based approach but to act as supportive structures that foster the comprehensive study of a topic as teachers plan interdisciplinary work around issues and themes that emerge from the ongoing curriculum. Deliberate steps should be taken to create a meaningful and carefully orchestrated program that is stimulating and motivating for both students and teachers.

How are themes found? By asking, What if? These are magic words. They add exciting new possibilities to our world and the world of the child. What if I drop a rock into this tub of water? What if I make a ship for the rock out of tin foil—would the rock float instead of sink? Since the beginning of time people have grappled with similar types of questions. An Italian sailor asked his colleagues what would happen if he sailed west across the unknown ocean? That sailor discovered America. A sixteen-year-old German schoolboy asked himself what would happen if he sent out a beam of light and could keep up with it? That boy was Albert Einstein. Ten years later, his "what if" led him to create the theory of relativity.

In music, a frequent way of creating new possibilities is to invent variations on a theme. A melody may be speeded up or

slowed down. Musicians may shift keys, change notes, or add harmony. Jazz performances, for example, are often based on musicians'
variations on a theme. Music is not the only endeavor in which
variations are invented. To open doors for students, teachers can
start anywhere with anything. They can vary a theme in a science,
math, literature, history, social studies, or of course, music class.
The way to find variations is easy, and is much the same whether
you are working with music, poetry, or mathematical equations.
You experimentally rearrange the parts of what you began with,
looking for new arrangements that afford new possibilities.

For example, the theme of comparing paintings can integrate
arts, mathematics, language arts, social studies, and science activities. For an arts activity, ask each student to select a painting and
reflect upon his or her feelings and reactions to it. For the language
arts activity, each student chooses a partner who has reflected upon
a very different painting, and each pair of students sits down
together and forms lists of words and phrases to describe the two
chosen paintings. For a mathematics activity, the teacher can
instruct students how to make a Venn diagram to graphically illustrate what is alike about the two paintings and what is different
about them, based on the word lists. When students discuss where
the artworks were painted and are asked what they can infer about
the countries or settings of the paintings, they are dealing with
social studies questions. Finally, for a science activity, they can learn
about the medium used to create the paintings and experiment
with it.

Many middle schools have already incorporated the idea of curriculum blocks or cores, in which the teaching of language arts,
reading, and social studies is combined. Math-science blocks and
humanities cores are other examples. Teachers who are discipline
specialists team together to teach these blocks. However these collaborative interdisciplinary curriculum models come about, they
require a change in how teachers go about their work. It takes extra

planning and energy to create effective integrated lessons, and teachers often need more time for subject matter research because they frequently find themselves exploring and teaching new material. The matic teaching also means planning lessons that use nontraditional approaches, field trips, guest speakers, and other special events, and it takes additional teacher time and planning to contact parents, staff members, and community resources who can help expand the students' learning environment. Schools and teachers need to plan professional development that will help teachers perform long-range planning and other important elements of the process.

The arts have a power beyond aesthetics. They can help us view ourselves, our environment, and our future differently—even challenging our certainties about the arts themselves. In connecting the basic concerns of history, civilization, thought, and culture, the arts provide spatial, kinesthetic, and aesthetic skills and understandings that are the foundation of what it means to be an educated person. Such understandings do not occur spontaneously. They have to be taught.

There is a connection between productive citizenship, academics, and the arts, but for students to make the connection, it will take more than a specialist in the art class for one hour a week or an inspirational theater troupe visiting the school once a year. These brief experiences can inspire—but it takes more sustained work in the arts to make a real difference. Quick "drive-by teaching" in the arts is the equivalent of driving a motorcycle through an art gallery; you will get some blurred notion of color but not much else. Schools that cheat on daily arts education deny students a vital quality of life experience—expression, discovery, and an understanding of the chances for human achievement (Schubert & Willis, 1991).

The arts can open up a sense of wonder and provide students with intellectual tools for engaging in a shared search. This cannot occur, however, if children are having fewer experiences with the arts at school and in their daily lives. They at least have to know enough to recognize what to notice and what to ignore.

Discipline-Based Arts Education Activities

The following examples of discipline-based art activities are organized around an interdisciplinary unit entitled You and Your World, a theme selected to show how critical thinking skills and interdisciplinary content can be made an integral part of classroom life. In any interdisciplinary study, it is important that children learn to be more flexible and to move freely among different communication media. To accomplish this, children need exposure to many different communication forms. Therefore, before beginning this kind of unit, teachers should discuss with children the need all people have to communicate ideas and how there are many ways to carry out this communication. Encourage the children to brainstorm all the ways people communicate. List the suggestions on the board or a chart. Young children may wish to find or draw pictures, which can be placed on a bulletin board that becomes an ongoing resource for students as additions are incorporated throughout the year.

Introduction to You and Your World

Give the students the following background information and initial concepts.

> When you think of how you are related to others, the people that you are most likely to talk about are family members. But even if you had no family at all and were alone in the world, you would not be unrelated. The fact that you have read these words relates you to all English-speaking people. As a student, you have a relationship with those who attend your school and with those who

work there. The music you listen to and enjoy is enjoyed by others. Your relationships with your fellow humans are marked by the foods you think are good, the clothes you think are fashionable, the jokes you tell.

Ralph Waldo Emerson, a nineteenth-century American writer, saw in our relationships a basic theme of imaginative thinking. He felt that people depend on their relationships in order to understand what they read. Emerson thought, because each person is related not only to a few others but to all people, that each of us has within ourselves the sum of human history. Perhaps you have never read yourself into history. But chances are you have watched characters in movies or on television and sensed that they felt as you have felt and acted as you would have acted, that they were, in a sense, related to you.

Relationship Activities

The following instructions will guide children through activities that help them understand themselves in relation to their world.

• Make a map of significant relationships in your life. Put your name in the center of a sheet of paper. Then begin thinking of the important people in your life and write their names on the paper. Organize or group the names that belong together. You may wish to connect the names with lines to show the relationships.

• Make a list of ten words you chose at random from the dictionary. Next write or make up something about yourself that uses all the words you have listed. It could be a paragraph in the form of a news report, a story, a creative drama, whatever works with the words you have. (Make sure you *use* the words, not just mention them. For example, the word "hare" is just *mentioned* in the sentence, "Hare is another word for a rabbit." It is *used* in the sentence, "I saw a hare, chewing on a carrot in my garden." Let the words guide what you write.)

• Suppose there is a lottery in your state. A three-digit number is picked at random. For $1.00, you can buy a ticket, picking any number from 000 to 999. If the number on your ticket matches the number on the ticket drawn, you win $500. Is that a good payoff? Why or why not? How much of the money the state takes in does it keep?

• Reflect on and then describe an episode from a television series that you regularly watch. Here are some questions (adapted from Dalton, 1991) that may help you think about the program. Jot down your answers. Then write a paragraph or two about what you have learned.

1. For what sorts of people is the program produced?

2. Are the main characters people like yourself? Are they people you want to be like?

3. Are the main characters unusual in some way? If so, in what way? Are they unusually attractive? Do they have special skills?

4. If the program is a comedy, what are the jokes about? Is there a laugh track? Do you laugh as often as you hear people in the audience laughing?

5. What kinds of problems do the characters in the program have? Are they the same sorts of problems you have?

6. Are the characters in the program richer or poorer than you are?

7. Describe the plot. Does it make sense? Do the characters in the program act the way real people act?

8. Does the program use background music? What sort of music? What does the music contribute to the mood of the program?

9. Try looking at the program without listening to the sound. What do you notice? Try listening to the program without watching the picture. What do you notice?

10. Do you know what is going to happen before it happens or are you surprised? How do you feel when the program ends?

Choosing Art That Defines, Challenges, and Explores

Octavio Paz (1986, p. 42) has observed that "every Latin American work is a prolongation and a transgression of the Western tradition," meaning that the arts challenge the very traditions upon which they rest. As they simultaneously recall what exists and question it, the arts have the power to define us, challenge us, and help us explore the frontiers of human existence. Their effect goes well beyond the art classroom, gallery, or performance space to connect to other domains.

But if the arts are to achieve this effect, the teacher has to examine his or her own thinking about which of the arts is worthy of attention. A teacher might not like rap music, for example, and yet that music might be very useful in the classroom to connect the arts and other disciplines. This teacher is advised to ask why he or she dislikes most rap music. Is it owing to the teacher's age, class, race, sex, educational level, or cultural background, or the limitations of spoken "music," or some other issue or belief? Is rap racist, sexist, divisive, or therapeutic? Is that a topic that should be discussed in class? The lyrics of rap artists characterize America's failed dream as a nightmare, sending confidences to those living in the inner city and opening windows on that environment for others.

Rap music captures the experience of a generation of youths who feel shut out of mainstream culture, trapped in an environment that forces them to seek other routes to success. While some rappers are known primarily for the swearing and violence that mark their lyrics, the art form can be used to express political messages that go much deeper, presenting a point of view that is at odds with middle-class U.S. society. Young white fans usually focus more on the music than the message. But with white youngsters making up much of the audience at some concerts, their elders are getting concerned, much as *their* elders became concerned with rock music in the 1950s and 1960s. Like reggae and some other forms of black music, the theme of black anger has, until recently, gone largely unnoticed by much of white society. Rap may generate and channel the energy of a mass of people much as rock music did in the late 1960s or as opera helped generate Italian nationalism in the 1860s. By its very nature, art is critical, and nothing is more deadly dull than the sanitized art that governments tend to approve. Teachers should be wary that they do not dismiss art simply because it appears unruly.

Herbert Read (1992) once said that the goal of education is the creation of artists, defined as people who can creatively make things with potential social impact. Exposure to good art shapes these artists. Good art also participates in the creation of culture. Malcolm Muggeridge (1989, p. 36) recently suggested that culture is formed in "a natural cafe of the mind, in which we are all the clientele; a meeting place which can be raucous at times, both political assembly and place of entertainment, dance floor and theater with all kinds of rooms off it."

Once we understand how the arts cause us to explore and challenge ourselves and develop a culture, we can use that understanding to look across disciplines and to see that they have similar functions, providing openings to the untried and sharpening our imaginations. Jerry King (1993), for example, has concluded that, in its purest form, mathematics produces an aesthetic experience. He proposes a "math-world" (comparable to the art world) that would comprise mathematicians' works and a public prepared to at least partially understand the ideas presented to them and to learn to view the world in new ways. In King's math world, good teachers play a key role in preparing the public to assimilate difficult concepts, in much the same way art critics prepared the public to view and interpret nonrealistic art. To generate ideas, perhaps we do need a rowdy natural cafe of the mind, one where we can find every discipline, a band, and a dance floor.

Using the Arts to Teach Diversity

Because the arts open children's imaginations to new areas of understanding, they fit naturally into the whole language (literature-based) movement in reading. The study of literature has always connected directly to the arts. So have social studies and the drive to help children understand and respect cultural differences. Ethnic background images must be available in schools even when good choices require some effort to obtain. The typical painting of Native Americans, for example, represents a romantic vision of Indian life that obscures the damage done to Native Americans and the hard realities of their lives. If teachers are not careful in choosing examples, they will simply add to the mound of sentimental clichés that relegate the arts and philosophies of non-European cultures to the cutesy and marginal in U.S. life.

The arts can motivate the social, civic, and cognitive development of students as well as students' aesthetic development. They can provide evidence of a shared U.S. perspective while also celebrating multicultural diversity. In spite of our differences derived from our respective European, Asian, Native American, or African traditions, we share certain common cultural values and a uniquely American multicultural perspective built upon the premise that human lives are fully real and valuable no matter how far from the engines of power and celebrity they are lived. And the arts that teach us such lessons are now available in many U.S. communities. (As just one example, to see a really good play thirty years ago, you had to go to New York. Now, thanks to public support and NEA, we can see high-quality theatrical productions all over the country.)

Many of the poorest areas in the United States share one characteristic: swift and overwhelming demographic change. Today's teachers are responsible for classrooms that represent a rainbow of colors, languages, backgrounds, and learning styles. Data indicate that by the year 2010, nearly 40 percent of school-age children will be persons of color. In the states of California, Texas, Arizona, New Mexico, and Florida, "minority" students will be the majority (Hodgkinson, 1989). "Minority" students already constitute a majority in twenty-three of the twenty-five largest school districts (Gay, 1989). Schools *must* take seriously their role as multicultural communities; they are the one place young people from all our different backgrounds come together. There must be an open dialogue to honor what this cross-section of students finds in schools today. This means, for example, exhibiting student artistic expressions so that students' thinking is made public. Many local papers will devote an occasional section to projects designed by students— what an opportunity for artistic design connected to the mass media and communication! Using a camcorder to create a spin-off of thirty- or sixty-second television commercials creates a similar opportunity. Many cable television systems are required to run these or other student videos as part of their community access agreements.

Placing the arts closer to the heart of school reform is important to maintaining our civic values and the full functioning of our minds. Students learning from the arts can discover that we are all one human world and that the arts cannot be separated from thinking, dreaming, and social change. There is danger in the belief that the isolated self is the center of the universe and that getting in touch with one's feelings is more important than rational discourse. When it becomes more important to focus on your own problems than on larger social issues, bad things start to happen. Art can make the interdisciplinary connections that challenge the self-centered view.

Collaborative art projects are particularly effective in reducing students' insecurity. Students working on these projects not only come to share a commitment to each other and to honor what each individual brings to the process, but they also discover many access points to the arts, other subjects, and the world, many ways they can reach understandings. Finally, solid intercultural friendships and a broad consensus in the classroom that bigotry is not acceptable can reduce the social display of both intentional bias and inadvertent discriminatory behavior. Arts programs, encouraging the early formation of strong multicultural relationships, can make a major contribution to intergroup understanding.

Making Connections to Models Outside School

Fostering creativity in the arts means encouraging students to think for themselves, coming up with different solutions to problems by linking arts education to their personal experiences. Both in and out of school, creativity produces innovative answers to questions, answers that sometimes change the very nature of the questions themselves.

To make a connection between the arts in education and in personal life, some schools are experimenting with residencies by area artists. Others have connected to adult models by sponsoring projects on-site—in an art gallery, a symphony hall, a ballet company's theater. In-depth thematic units can be developed that allow students to work on-site to solve complex real-world problems, understand subject matter in depth, and make connections across disciplines. Recently, expeditionary learning schools have been established in Portland, Maine; Boston; Decatur, Georgia; and Douglas County, Colorado. In these model schools, expedition advisors, teachers, and principals work on school-initiated curricula in teams. The lesson is that creating an educational renaissance will require all the community resources educators can connect with.

All social and educational institutions convey messages that can affect creativity and artistic development. Deep questions of value are involved in the kind of models we set and our methods for evaluating artistic products. Art may belong to everyone, but being literate in the subject means being able to understand, critique, and create in a whole array of symbol systems. It is best to get high-quality instructional experiences and training early on, and good models from outside the classroom are critical.

Activities That Encourage Reflection

Making all the kinds of connections discussed so far in this chapter require children to use many thinking skills, skills that we might sum up for the moment as the ability to reflect. Reflecting is a special kind of thinking. It is both active and controlled. When ideas pass aimlessly through a person's mind, or someone tells a story that triggers a memory, that is not reflecting. Reflecting means focusing one's attention. It means weighing, considering, choosing. Suppose you want get into your car to drive home. You get your car key out of your pocket, put it in the car door, and open the door. Getting into your car does not require reflection. But suppose you reached in your pocket and could not find the key. Then getting into your car would require reflection. You would have to think about what you were going to do, considering possibilities and imagining alternatives.

A carefully balanced combination of direct instruction, self-monitoring, and reflective thinking helps meet diverse student needs. The design of the following suggested activities encourages higher-order thinking and learning, and of course, the activities also function as collaborative vehicles for arts education.

• *Look at the familiar differently.* Students are asked to empty their purses and pockets on a white sheet of paper and to create a face using as few of the items as possible. For example, a pair of sunglasses might suggest a face, a single earring might represent a mouth, or a necklace could form a profile, outlining forehead, nose, and chin. This activity gives students experience in consciously working to see things differently; it is a form of aesthetic education. As students reflect on their work in this kind of activity, they can be learning to cast off preconceptions and cease evaluating abstract forms in traditional terms. They can be preparing to look at the varied aspects and intentions of artists and to have the heady experience of viewing contemporary art.

• *Create collage photo art.* Students at all levels can become producers as well as consumers of art. For this activity, the authors of this book have used a videotape of David Hockney's work from the series "Art in America." Students watch the video and hear and see Hockney, one of today's important artists, speaking about his work and explaining his technique. The students then use cameras to explore Hockney's photo collage technique in their own environment. Student groups can use several sets of the same photos in order to tell several different stories with different compositions of the same pictures. They might add brief captions or poems to make connections to the language arts, social studies, science, or music. Photographers know the meanings of their pictures can depend to a large extent on the words that go with them. Students can describe the images in the photos and learn to talk about art in descriptive terms and to avoid editorializing. They can discover it is not necessary to like a photo to discuss it intelligently. If students have a grasp of the principles of art, they can develop an understanding of how an artwork's elements are manipulated by a trained artist. As part of this activity, students can express their own ideas of what a photo means to them, they can share personal feelings and experiences with their classmates, and they can produce a written critique. (As mentioned in Chapter Four, teachers should always preview videos to make sure they contain nothing inappropriate for the grade level.)

• *Paint with watercolors and straws.* Have students simply apply a little suction to a straw dipped in tempera. Working in pairs, students then gently blow the paint out on a sheet of blank paper to create interesting abstract designs. This activity can be used, for example, to introduce children to Cubism. The Cubists looked for reality in space, reality in a moment of time, and reality in life. In the later stages of Cubism, artists included actual everyday materials in their paintings, finding this more realistic than painting those materials. To help students reflect on this activity, teachers may want students to write down their feelings about the reality expressed in their paintings.

• *Paint with oil-based paints floating on water.* Have students working in groups of three float different colored oil-based paints on a flat dish of water. Have them apply paper, watch it soak up the paint and water, and then pull the paper out and let it dry. As students reflect on and discuss their paintings, they can learn that art history involves the investigation and interpretation of works of art. The teacher can guide them in relating concepts about art to the forms and images in the paintings they have produced.

• *Form thoughtful writing partnerships.* Divide a two-person writing partnership into a "thinker" and a "writer." The thinker reads a short concept or question out loud and tells what he or she thinks the answer should be. The writer writes it down if he or she agrees. If the writer does not agree, he or she tries to convince the thinker that there is a better answer. If they cannot reach agreement orally, the partners write two answers and initial the one they agree on.

• *Combine literature and movement.* Some poems, stories, myths, and ballads are particularly suited to interpretation through movement. Choose one or two students to read while the others respond to the reading with creative movements. Part of the group can even sing or hum while moving. Create a magical atmosphere with poetry. As suggested in Chapter Six, have children use penlights in a darkened classroom or colorful ribbons for creative movement that requires group effort and harmony. Try one or both of the following poems (Corrin & Corrin, 1982; Millay, 1981) in a creative movement exercise that will require children to think about the meaning of what they are hearing.

Fireworks

They rise like sudden fiery flowers
That burst upon the night,
Then fall to earth in burning showers
Of crimson, blue, and white.
Like buds too wonderful to name,
Each miracle unfolds,
and catherine-wheels begin to flame
Like whirling marigolds.

by James Reeves

Eel-Grass

No matter what I say,
 All that I really love
Is the rain that flattens on the bay,
 And the eel-grass in the cove;
The jingle-shells that lie and bleach
 At the tide-line, and the trace
Of higher tides along the beach:
 Nothing in this place.

by Edna St. Vincent Millay

* *Improvise short original music pieces.* Students can improvise music pieces and variations on existing pieces of music (traditional, nontraditional, jazz, or rock), using voices or instruments (acoustic or electronic). Joyful singers of songs (or players of instruments) learn much more than "just singing." The whole child is involved.

With reflection and the appropriate guidance from the teacher, children grow socially by collaborating in the production of a song. They grow emotionally through expressing their feelings in a powerful mode. They develop coordination and control by responding physically to music through such simple experiences as clapping to rhythms and moving to a beat.

• *Visit the art museum with a partner.* In a trip to an art museum, students might focus on a few paintings or pieces of sculpture. Have students make up a question or two about a particular artwork that they wish to explore further, and also have them reflect upon and respond (in a notebook or writing pad they take with them) to five or six questions from the following list.

- How would you compare and contrast technology and art as ways for viewing the past, present, or future?

- How are pictures, pottery, and music used to communicate?

- Visuals are authored in much the way print communication is authored. How does the author of a picture or piece of sculpture guide the viewer through such techniques as point of view, size, distortion, or lighting?

- How do combinations or organizations of things work to make you feel?

- How is the artwork you selected put together?

- How did the creator of the artwork expect the viewer to react or respond? Is the content or subject of the artwork the most important part of it? What else might the artist have wished to produce?

- How does your background affect how you view the message?

- What are the largest or smallest artistic designs of the artwork?

- What is the main idea, mood, or feeling of the work?

- When you close your eyes and think about the artwork, what pictures do you see? What sounds do you hear? Does it remind you of anything—a book, a dream, television, something from your life?
- How successful is the sculpture or artwork? What is your response to it?
- Where did the artist place important ideas?
- Does the artwork tell us about big ideas, such as courage, freedom, war, and so forth?
- How does the artwork fit in with the history of art?
- What does the artwork say about present conflicts concerning art standards, multiculturalism, and American culture?
- How did the artwork make you feel inside?
- Was the artwork easy or hard to understand?
- Why do you think the artwork was made? What would you like to change about it?

Teaching and Learning Productive Creativity

Even though the focus of the new arts education is on ways arts education enhances other disciplines and teaches skills and understandings that are useful across all disciplines, there is still much room for teaching and learning aesthetic creativity. Such creativity seems to be deeply rooted, manifesting itself in very early symbolic products that convey the meaning of the child's world. Even very young children can describe, interpret, and evaluate their visual and auditory perceptions, and adult creative effort often draws on the creator's early efforts in the arts.

Creativity in any realm rarely occurs from scratch. Most often a creative product is the result of a combination of choices made from a particular area. There is an aesthetic world out there that youngsters must explore if they are to be truly educated in any subject. Thus, imaginative insight and artistic expression in children should be prized and viewed as essential to cognitive competence and effective citizenship. Creativity is also more than originality. There is a strong connection between creativity (including originality and novelty) and basic academic skills. The two feed on each other. Developing a unique clarity, style, and focus is as essential as acquiring any skill or body of knowledge. The rote drill approaches of educational fundamentalists represent narrow thinking patterns that hinder comprehension and creativity. Dry facts must be fleshed out with substance, basic skills must open up into a multiplicity of images that can be creatively tapped and explored.

Not too long ago, the notion of educators was that if fluency, flexibility, and originality were systematically taught, true creativity would follow. Unfortunately, it was not that simple. To begin with, teachers did not know how to teach or model these concepts. Fluency does not count for much if all the ideas generated are simply novel or trivial. Worse yet, if flexibility, instead of offering freedom, clouds issues or discourages student decision making, it can impede learning. Even originality has sometimes been understood in educational contexts as simple social accommodation rather than either intuitive boundary pushing or barrier breaking. This is an outgrowth of the view that the arts are only extensions of emotions rather than a discipline with a knowledge base and social, historical, and philosophical roots.

Traditionally, common school practice encouraged children to be plodders who saw rules as conduits for action rather than as springboards for changing realities. In the real world, however, we learn a lot about creativity from our failures, accidents, and personal restructurings of our reality in the face of uncertainty. Taking risks, dealing with failures, admitting a desire to be surprised, and enjoying ambiguity are all essential elements in creative behavior. All are difficult for teachers to teach and model *and* for many students to accept. However, both students and teachers profit from undergoing the welcome fatigue of having to figure things out for themselves.

Seeking the rewards of what adults see as good creative products makes their appearance less likely. No student response should
be considered the only right one. The mix of modeling intellectual
stimulation and building natural rapport is part of the mysterious
art of good teaching. The research, too, suggests that one way to
fuse creative thinking to basic skills is to provide a rich arts environment and enough structure for a student to search out interesting material. Skillful teachers, then, examine the quality of the
thought that has gone into student productions and help students
with critical analysis and self-cultivation. Some U.S. educational
institutions have proven that they can design learning experiences
in the arts that are optimal for a diversity of learning styles and student dispositions. They have succeeded by assisting students in
developing *both* disciplined basic skills and genuine creativity, thus
providing multiple paths for student development (Gardner, 1990).
Gaining creative observational skills, in particular, seems to help
students develop distinctive styles and gain familiarity with a wide
range of artistic approaches.

Children frequently have the innate ability to do creative work
in the arts. What they frequently lack are basic artistic understandings and opportunities for expression and analysis. The challenge to teachers is to provide the necessary background and open
the right doors so that meaningful concepts and images will emerge
when students do have the chance to express themselves, experiencing the excitement of producing in their own ways and conveying their personal aesthetic experience through the use of such
figurative language as metaphors and similes in their writing and
symbolism in their painting. As students paint their own paintings,
compose their own music, and collaborate in arranging their own
dances, they come to experience the inner nature of aesthetic creativity.

Without arts education, students would be denied the opportunity to develop the mental skills that make art possible. As this
chapter has argued throughout, art is more than some abstract
notion of beauty. Good art helps us rethink our conception of real-

ity and alters our perspective. The creativity engendered in students can be a catalyst for information gathering, change, and the enrichment of their intellectual, cultural, and civic lives. Even at early levels, students need to be grounded in the ability to reflect on their own and others' art and to think about the thinking skills involved. The playful invention of a young child may be closer to the way an innovative scientist or an artist works than is the "sophisticated" invention of the older student. Both good artists and good scientists have a highly developed sense of wonder and skepticism. They share a world of complex options and multiple paths that require flexibility and energy to negotiate. And neither the art nor the science world is well understood by many Americans. Even the well-educated have barely enough understanding of art, science, or politics to act effectively on aesthetic, scientific, or political matters that they encounter in their personal, professional, or civic lives. This situation is one that education reformers believe should and can be changed.

Teachers of the Arts

With dozens of other subjects to be taught at the elementary level, our schools are fortunate to have teachers who also have enough artistic knowledge and skill to teach painting, pottery, music, movement, and video production. Exploring the broad philosophical dimensions of art will have to be teachers' next step. Teaching expanded lists of facts and bits of knowledge is of little use unless this material is integrated into a larger whole. In this integration, it is just as important to understand concepts about the arts as to worry about performance or the end product.

Interesting students in a topic or problem and in interacting with others within an environment that allows thoughtful and creative expression is an objective with which few educators will disagree. Yet how, with today's already cluttered curriculum, testing requirements, and red tape, does a teacher find time to unearth art topics of interdisciplinary interest? Team training can help teachers share the load and community resources can free up some teacher time. But to keep reform going, we are going to have to change organizational structures and protect teachers from bureaucratic requirements.

Most teachers can supply classroom vignettes about effective teaching: the butterfly that hatched from a chrysalis in their classroom, students' creative language stories, and children's experiences with movement and dance, creative dramatics, and painting murals. Some teachers might recall the newscast of the whale trapped in the ice that spawned an array of activities: research on whales, letters to elected representatives, a bulletin board charting bird migration patterns, and an attitude survey graph. Good teachers know that to be really excited about a subject they and their students must really care about it.

Their students need the chance to try things out and the interest and excitement to persevere by reflecting on what they have done and trying again. Most teachers know how to encourage or reorient students if they are getting nowhere. They also believe all children will learn, and they recognize the need for high expectations as they strive to reach every individual. Good teachers are also able to facilitate, probe, and draw on additional information, examples, and alternative approaches for those students who are unable to connect with the information initially. To achieve level of performance, however, it is important for teachers to know the subject well enough to feel comfortable with it.

Children possess an innate capacity to absorb knowledge—but it takes intelligent teaching to help them use that knowledge to reason effectively. Curriculum development in arts education requires staff development, for it is often family support and adult models, such as teachers, that make the difference between a student's commitment to the arts and his or her dismissal of aesthetics as irrelevant. The arts are natural to the way children learn. With inspired teaching and hard work in the arts, students can develop the artistic sensitivity and the reasoning and problem-solving skills that will touch other subjects. The distinctive modes of human intelligence will then manifest themselves in surprising circumstances. Making schools responsive to the uses of the arts and the other ways students learn will involve changing institutional structures, increasing school autonomy, for instance, and moving away from bureaucratic and other outside interference. School reform requires a change in the power relationships at all levels. To produce graduates who are confident and competent, schools should give every child access to a rigorous arts curriculum in a climate of reasoned thoughtfulness and high expectations where teachers and students cultivate, and shape, students' interests. The arts also offer insights into the educational process itself, helping us, as Martin Heidegger suggests, see beyond what *is*, to open spaces. This clearing can help us reach beyond the mundane to something new (Rogoff, 1990).

As an agent of social change in general and education in particular, arts education has a role in creating an educational renaissance. If artwork, music, dance, and drama are not found in the public schools, then everyone's chances for thoughtfulness, self-expression, and aesthetic appreciation are bound to be diminished, along with the schools' chances to counter the tendency for standardization in the school reform process. "Art," says Alfred North Whitehead (1933), "flourishes where there is a sense of adventure." The possibilities the arts offer for a unique opening up of new spaces in the curriculum will be sorely missed if the arts are relegated to the margins of the educational restructuring debate.

Chapter Ten

Social Responsibility

> To educate a person in mind and not in morals is to
> educate a menace to society.
>
> —*Theodore Roosevelt*

Socially responsible action and moral purpose should guide our school restructuring efforts. In practice, this means we should have schools look at themselves through a moral lens, and we should consider how what goes on in school affects students' values. As we move through a difficult social and economic time, educating for moral character is increasingly tied up with the future of our children and our society. Today's concern over what might be called the moral condition of U.S. society argues for including values generally across the curriculum, in addition to their place as a natural part of social studies instruction.

Social studies can be defined as the study of how humans think, feel, and act. It is important in teaching cooperative learning and critical thinking skills, and it has a special ability to reach across and integrate the curriculum. In this book, we have already seen how social studies concepts, activities involving a range of the world's cultural heritages, and oral history activities can provide subject matter for other disciplines to work with and how the understanding of others that social studies tries to inculcate is manifested in the social responsibility and participation in group activities that cooperative learning encourages: Chapter One examined how diverse cultures might live together; Chapter Two provided a number of teaching strategies for stimulating and encouraging collaboration, divergent thinking, and discussion; Chapter Three delved further into cooperative group learning; and Chapters Six through Nine approached social science concepts as strands within language arts, mathematics, science, and arts education.

These chapters also suggested connecting basic subject matter to an appreciation of our democratic heritage, since, as Gutmann (1987, p. 23) reminds us, "the development of deliberative character is essential to realizing the ideal of a democratically sovereign society." However, once citizens realize this, they then "have good reason to wonder how deliberative or democratic character can be developed in children, and who can develop it." It was Thomas Jefferson's view, to which the authors of this book subscribe, that developing this deliberative character was the job of education; indeed, that the central purpose of education was to help students be productive citizens in a democracy (Michaelis, 1992). However, that still leaves the question of how this character can be developed. This book has suggested that cooperative learning and critical thinking are important tools for inculcating and practicing a deliberative character. Social studies is content that can reinforce this character. This chapter takes a broad view of social studies, addressing the democratic aims of education and the effective teaching of social concepts in order to show how we can reach those aims as well as instill a base of knowledge about various cultures.

Teaching Democratic Values in an Age of Distraction

Of course Americans cannot be expected to vote simply because they like the exercise of walking to the polling place. The process has to be seen to make a difference. Our politics, at its best, has always dealt with real possibilities, from the bottom up. Town meetings really did get things discussed *and* done. Then, over the years, we delegated much of our obligation to be informed and to make decisions to the various, often elected representatives to whom we had already delegated our individual authority. Delegating authority was efficient; delegating our need to be informed and make decisions was an abdication of responsibility. Now all of us (the media, schools, leadership, and citizens together) must struggle to reappropriate our civic heritage of discussion and decision and create conditions for productive citizenship. Two basic requirements for a successful outcome to this struggle are media that deal with the world of ideas and, the issue this book addresses, a pedagogy that is meaningful for today's civic reality.

On a whole range of issues, children and young adults seem to be more susceptible to change than are adults. Therefore, the structure of classroom interaction and the timing of educational efforts have important consequences for the development of democratic values and attitudes toward citizenship (Krosnick & Alwin, 1989). Attitudes, opinions, and degrees of openness to ideas are concepts forged in the classroom that tend to be held for most of an individual's life span (Hechinger, 1992). Research also suggests that if the school environment allows children to avoid social and academic interaction with peers, and thus avoid learning to have their ideas tested and challenged, it is difficult for them to develop such civic skills later on (Harman, 1986).

An important part of the test for the quality of our schools should be whether they help children develop a civic consciousness. Specifically, this consciousness includes analytical abilities, group work skills, a concern for others, and communicative competence across disciplines. Successful schools must go beyond the basics to help all their students develop civic understandings and intellectual talents, including the ability to think critically and comprehensively. Innovative approaches (such as using cooperative learning and peer tutoring, teaching critical thinking, and developing a curriculum that links subject matter to real-life problems) *can* amplify the learning of democratic processes for all students (Baron, 1988).

Developing a Common Identity

Our government, our business, and our schools are already struggling to take the necessary steps that will result in a cooperative fusion of the increasingly diverse social elements within our society. Individuals may differ over the reasons this fusion is essential, some citing moral imperatives, some global competitiveness, and some enlightened self-interest, but what is clear is that what traditionally held Americans together was not a common ethnic origin but a belief in the ideals of democracy and the possibility of advancement through education. The practice of these ideals was far from perfect, but individuals' learning about democratic traditions made transgressions more obvious and narrowed the gap between reality and principle. Education *is* the key to helping people from diverse cultures work well together (Beane, 1990).

A powerful civic consciousness has allowed Americans to forge a nation from culturally diverse peoples. By having these peoples come together in common spaces (like schools), the nation has traditionally nourished the collective spirit. Nevertheless, one of the central questions for Americans today is how to live in relationship with others, a goal made increasingly difficult by a hardening class structure, narrow cultural experiences, stereotypical thinking, ineffective leaders, crumbling schools, and many elements of popular culture. It is hard to calculate or fathom the forces currently being unleashed. Take one "entertainment" industry example: some popular rap music mixes tolerance of drug use and negative attitudes toward women with a glorification of gunplay. And children from many different backgrounds are listening. From the lyrics in music videos to the stereotypes of television comedy, cultural misunderstandings increasingly filter into U.S. consciousness.

Responsibility for what young adults learn must be shared. The schools alone cannot effectively counter media messages exalting the immediate gratification of sexual desire, remorseless violence, and the "gangsta" values of self-interest and materialism. If we are to unify a society increasingly divided along racial, cultural, and class lines, we will require structures that accommodate the best group and personal realities under one roof. Instead of rejecting differences, the schools and society must reach out and include the positive elements of diversity.

Education is entrusted with the role of imparting society's best and deepest meanings to a new generation. To fill this role, schools must open their doors to fundamental change, transforming their own consciousness and society's support mechanisms and paying attention to the hidden curricula, values, attitudes, assumptions toward learning, and human relationships that are reflected in their current policies, practices, and public support.

The good news is that there are some small, but tested, possibilities out there, successful models for developing citizenship skills and academics. The Memphis 2000 project, for example, formed a broad-based coalition that successfully campaigned for more money when the schools adopted some of the changes suggested by teachers and the community. When it comes to raising money for schools, communities are most successful when new taxes go hand in hand with convincing school reform plans. In several schools designed by Outward Bound, students learn by going on expeditions not only to wilderness areas but also to museums, factories, libraries, hospitals, and industry sites. No one has flunked museums yet, and there has been a positive effect on character. Many of these small-scale programs have also had success with a character-building curriculum (Elmore, 1990). Programs that work best are usually based on a thorough knowledge of what students need. They are comprehensive, accessible, and accountable. They make student life more pleasant, interesting, varied, and productive.

If we in the United States are going to learn to swim in the knowledge of the twenty-first century, we need big themes *and* big dreams that address our issues in a bold way. With today's incessant electronic clutter, sorting through the information din and thinking critically and acting responsibly is more important than ever.

Like other aspects of the national goals for education, citizenship education must be broadly conceived and developed as a cooperative educational venture. Students need to be more familiar with their own rich heritage and the heritage of other cultures as they prepare, as Americans, to take their places in a world of diversity. The mass media, the schools, the family, and the society are all responsible for making this happen.

Social Responsibility and a Community of Learners

New blueprints for reintroducing civics and social responsibility and duty into schoolwork will require a curriculum that helps students develop the knowledge and skills needed to participate in a civil society: open-mindedness, willingness to compromise, a tolerance for diversity, and a general civility. Democracy is not shouting each other down or political mud wrestling. As this book has stressed throughout, teachers contribute to social responsibility when they teach important social skills like cooperation, effective group communication, and a sense of responsibility toward living in a community with others. Citizenship skills include knowing steps for social problem solving, handling conflict, and saying no to negative influences. Social and civic responsibility means going beyond self to taking a degree of responsibility for the various groups that one is part of. As the framework for national civic education points out, a major goal is to encourage students to "participate in all elements of a civil society" (National Council for the Social Studies, 1991).

The teaching of civics and social responsibility can begin by providing classroom practice in using social skills while establishing a classroom community of learners. Teachers and students should create ground rules that emphasize caring and respect for others in the classroom. Students should learn that, when they are socially responsible in their immediate groups, it is easier to deal with knowledge regarding social issues, institutions, and policies.

They should learn what it means to be a citizen in a democracy. Social responsibility is also fostered by having students explore issues of importance to them and their various groups, or "communities." Ideally, they can become active participants in planning and carrying out social service projects. Elementary school classes could, for example, create a wall mural for the larger community. This approach, which emphasizes *practicing* social responsibility, actively engages students and teaches them about taking action to make things happen. Developing a sense of responsibility for the world around them while they are in school adds to students' capacity to make a difference to the world throughout their lives. The merger of public issues with citizenship education and personal development helps young people recognize the importance of a life of contribution to the public good (Snauwaert, 1993). Being informed *and* active in the community is part of civic competence.

When students must balance intellectual challenges with deep personal involvement and open expression of ideas and feelings, teachers must help them create a strong sense of community and trust in their groups, because it is in this supportive environment that students will best learn how to exchange ideas with people who have different personalities, interests, and backgrounds. Small collaborative groups can then connect students to large concepts, engaging students in deliberations concerning public problems and controversies. For example, have students perform such tasks as selecting a controversy from the television news or a newspaper and writing an analysis of it, presenting arguments for and against the issue and drawing on history to show similarities and differences. Looking critically at social issues (like economic systems in turmoil) and environmental issues (like destruction of the rain forests) can help students recognize that many of our actions are globally interdependent.

Implicit in the idea of civic education is the privilege to criticize, oppose, or support different public policies. Individual responsibility, by itself, is simply not enough. Social responsibility, that is, a personal investment in the well-being of others and of the planet, is needed, but that responsibility does not just happen. To play their role in building a society with a stronger moral foundation, schools must contribute to improving the social ethic as well as individual moral behavior. Students who have feelings of powerlessness must be helped to develop a sense of community and confidence about the possibility that they can make a difference in the world. Their right to be involved in social issues that affect them can be implicit in a social studies curriculum. Deliberation on public issues cannot be put on hold until adulthood. Students need to make sense of community concerns and take some kind of action on authentic problems now.

To develop the skills for informed democratic participation, students require a civic education, an understanding of how to act on ethical issues. This civic education comprises several skills or behavioral habits (Boyer, 1990).

- *Communication*. Democracy is built on thoughtful discourse. This means teaching students to think critically, listen, and communicate effectively.

- *Active Participation*. Students need to be actively involved in learning and in the decision-making process. Rather than working in textbooks and filling out worksheets, students need to work on group projects, write about issues and ideas important in their lives, discuss, research important questions, debate, and work cooperatively.

- *Thoughtful debate*. Students must be able to deal with sensitive, often controversial social issues, conflict, and consensus concerning the common good. They must be given opportunities to think carefully about life's most important concerns.

- *Responsible school and community behavior*. Students need to recognize their role as part of the school community and work on and participate in decisions that affect their lives.

- *Connections between learning and life*. Too many students feel disconnected and rejected. Students need to understand that learning is connected to living. This means developing decision-making skills, forming convictions, and acting boldly on values held.

These skills must rest upon a core of basic knowledge that reflects the democratic perspective. This core should include a knowledge of history and government as well as social issues and problems.

Some of the social teaching schools are asked to do today stems from the schools' traditional responsibility for inculcating values in the young, but the new emphasis on these school responsibilities also results from the breakdown of institutions that helped hold the United States together in the past but that have been damaged. Grim social realities often overpower the best of educational intentions. What do teachers need to know to meet these new demands for civic and moral education? Today, there are fewer points of common knowledge that can serve to inform individuals and small groups than in the past. Many teachers are afraid to teach values, not knowing whose values they should teach. But there are still common values. James Q. Wilson (1993) suggests that "four innate sentiments dispose people to a universal moral sense. These are sympathy, fairness, self-control, and duty. The human species could not have evolved without them." To these traits could be added caring, honesty, and respect for others. There may be cultural variations in how the values attached to these traits are applied, but they can be found across cultures, and most Americans think they should be taught. When it comes to U.S. civic values, we can be even more specific: a democracy functions by the sustained involvement of its people; the ideas of intellectual freedom, tolerance, equity, and due process are all important for students to understand.

In addition, teaching a balance between participation, knowledge, and moral development is key to establishing students' social consciousness. Schools should both focus on the appropriate cognitive skills and knowledge *and* arrange for students to learn participative skills through community service projects or internships.

Focal Points for Collaborative Learning

The focal points suggested in the following pages are meant to invite ideas for activities in social studies classrooms. They involve the enhancement of reasoning ability, cooperation, and active communication. The results of activities based on these viewpoints might serve as moral and intellectual frameworks for exploring other problems, literature, and current events.

- *Focus on inquiry skills.* Classroom emphasis on inquiry skills and the processes of science makes a significant difference to student knowledge, skills mastery, and attitudes. Problem solving and critical thinking can be taught throughout the social studies curriculum, helping students acquire the skills of testing hypotheses, collecting data, reporting, generalizing conclusions, and communicating results that will be important intellectual tools in their lifelong learning.
- *Give students practice in brainstorming skills.* Have students pair off to brainstorm a topic in any discipline. (You may wish to set a time limit for brainstorming activities.)
- *Generate ideas using convergent thinking.* Teachers can take a situation in current events or from literature and have students in small groups generate ideas about it for ten minutes, using brainstorming techniques and deferring any judgment about the value of the ideas. Groups are then given ten minutes to evaluate their ideas. Following this, they make lists of their five best and five silliest ideas to share with the class. (The teacher explains that the most unlikely ideas frequently result in the best solutions.) For example, taking a situation from literature, students might put themselves in the situation of Daniel Defoe's Robinson Crusoe. If

they were washed ashore on a desert island with nothing but a large belt and a belt buckle, how would they use these tools to survive? Give them ten minutes to brainstorm as many ideas as possible in their small groups and another ten minutes to evaluate their ideas, and then ask them to present the best and the funniest ideas to the whole class.

• *Focus on students' strengths*. Generally the school focuses on a child's weaknesses rather than her or his strengths, and places the child accordingly. We do students a disservice when we emphasize learning difficulties and group by ability. When it comes to tracking needs, the varying needs of culturally different students may illustrate the less obvious needs of all students. It is just as important to emphasize student strengths and group students on the basis of diversity, not confusing differences with defects. A diverse student population presents a classroom of students with many possibilities for learning about a wide range of cultures as they work with each other.

• *Become aware of students' diverse interests*. Teachers can channel the understanding of differences into a framework of cultural unity. It may seem easier for students to attack enemies than to solve common problems; activities should strive for the interdependence that reflects our increasing global interdependence. This late twentieth–century form of "integration" can serve everybody.

• *Provide opportunities for excellence for all*. Most parents, teachers, and concerned citizens realize they cannot ignore their responsibility for promoting social justice. Traditionally, people's taking on this responsibility has resulted in equity programs, such as multicultural education, many of which have been helpful. Teachers should continue to devise challenging content and effective methods for teaching *all* students and avoid programs that are superficial gestures designed to quiet calls for fundamental change.

• *Use group evaluations*. For example, count fluency scores by giving one point for a common response and three points for a creative one. Teachers can also ask each group to choose one creative response and expand on it by writing a paragraph. Groups then share paragraphs and include them in a class book for others to read. These activities develop students' ability to think divergently, a skill that many academically gifted students do not have.

• *Teach about demographic change*. It is important for children to understand that U.S. identity is changing at an ever-increasing rate. It is projected that by the year 2050 the United States will have nearly 130 million more people than it does today. This future America will not only be more crowded but much more ethnically diverse. One in five citizens will be Hispanic, the Asian population will increase at least five-fold, and whites will represent roughly half of the population. Students can learn that respecting the diverse cultural elements within U.S society does not require abandoning the idea of national identity. Instead, it means thinking about national identity as something that is changing and fluid as well as connected to the past. Visions from both particular and common cultures interact and shape one another in a constant process of change, and ethnic and national identities do not have to be viewed as antithetical.

• *Meaningfully engage students in language learning*. One obvious arena in which students benefit from a multicultural approach is the study of foreign languages. Students have traditionally learned about the culture in which the target language is spoken and the grammar and literature in an isolated context, from the instructor and from textbooks. When students discover the differences between the culture of the target language and their own through cooperative learning and authentic texts, they become more meaningfully engaged in the material, and their newly acquired knowledge, discovered by active discussions of their own experience, gains a relevance that is lacking in traditional passive learning. The use of authentic texts (newspapers, magazine articles, short stories, essays, television news clips, and so forth, written or spoken in the target language and intended for native speakers), rather than simplified and sanitized excerpts in textbooks, also allows students to examine a foreign culture and compare it to their own. Students actively participate in the reading process when they employ the decoding processes used to read authentic texts (Applebee, 1991). Authentic texts also bring the readers closer to native speakers' points of view, not only through exposure to colloquial expressions but also through the speakers' diversity of opinion, a diversity generally absent in textbooks. Teachers can also have students read versions of a significant event (the opening of the Berlin Wall, for example) in both the target language and the students' native language, thus enabling students to learn about drawing comparisons and observing differences. Or students can read several articles on the same topic in the target language.

- *Present the historical view.* To keep children from concluding that everything worth knowing has already been discovered, present a historical view, not only in social studies but in mathematics, astronomy, literature, and art.

- *Connect areas of learning with practical applications.* Concepts make sense to students when they are applied to real situations. Therefore, teachers should guide students to demonstrate democratic behavior in group activities, and encourage students to observe examples of democratic behavior in school and community activities, find examples in books and other materials, and to brainstorm other examples within their small groups. The kinds of democratic behavior they should look for include cooperation, responsibility, open-mindedness, concern for others, creativity, respect for others, and civic behavior. Students can be asked to record on a chart which kinds of democratic behavior they perform themselves, which ones they observe, and which ones they brainstorm.

- *Examine similarities in folklore and literature.* Student groups can explore myths, folk tales, legends, and fairy tales to look for similarities and differences between peoples, times, and cultures. They can also construct group lists, concept maps, collages, visual images, or writings that show the group findings. (For the collage, students might take photocopies of printed texts, paste them down on a large piece of tagboard, and paint on top of them.)

• *Make use of biographies and historical fiction.* Biographies can describe selected individuals' values, motives, and accomplishments, so that these individuals can be role models for students. Historical fiction enables students to gain an appreciation of various authors' works while it shows literature is not written in isolation but based on culture. Particular themes, such as those in the myths of Faust and Prometheus, can lead to discussions of major themes among humanity.

• *Develop communication skills through oral history.* Oral history is a systematic way to obtain from the lips of living Americans a record of their participation in the political, economic, and cultural affairs of the nation. Students collect historically significant reminiscences, accounts, and interpretations of events from people who grew up in a different time and manner. They use the whole range of language skills by collecting, compiling, selecting, and organizing the data obtained. This activity connects generations and really makes history come alive for students. Students can construct and compare the experiences of older Americans from different cultural, ethnic, or racial backgrounds. The local newspaper might be willing to come in and cover the event. In a small community, the newspaper might even carry the final "book" for others to read. Exploring how community or historical figures developed their ability to read, write, and think imaginatively can also be informative. Teachers can follow these steps for an oral history project:

1. Prior to the interviews, students identify topics of interest, and do some preliminary research on the topic they are going to discuss.

2. Students identify several individuals to interview and contact these individuals to arrange an interview time, giving the purpose, time, and place.

3. Working in groups, students prepare some questions for the interviews and review with the class the questions they have chosen. Questions should be simple, relevant, and varied. A more direct connection can be made with social studies by asking social focus questions about specific events or periods (World War II for example).

4. Students and the teacher prepare for the interviews by reviewing procedures for interviewing (let the respondent do the talking, do not interrupt a story, and so on).

5. During the interviews, students take notes or audiotape or videotape the data.

6. Following the interviews, students transcribe their notes or recorded data to prepare material for publication or oral presentation.

7. Students interpret and edit materials, verify dates and obtain written releases from the respondents so they can "publish" the material for the whole class.

Multicultural Education Activities

Multicultural education, as it is used here, includes multiethnic and ethnic heritage studies in a comparative culture context. The idea is to encourage teachers to place the study of ethnic groups within the entire human experience and to emphasize students' developing an appreciation of their own and others' cultures. In this learning, students should examine various groups' value systems, life styles, cultural heritages, and current conditions, as well as their cultural contributions. Understandings of each student's own culture and the cultures of others in the student's group are brought together to help students answer such questions as, Who am I? Who are we? Who are they? What is special about each individual? Students learn about their root culture, their family's historical culture, and the common culture all of us share. The activities that follow build on these themes.

- *Create a personal ethnography.* Have students research their family history, including dates, events, and anecdotal accounts, by interviewing family members and writing their personal histories.

- *Study yourself.* This activity might be called About Me. Have each student create a collage or picture about herself or himself. Students should include their strengths, what they are good at, and what they like. They may wish to write a story or poem or, perhaps, create a coat of arms. To create coats of arms, students think of three things they are good at, their family's greatest success, and a personal failure. They answer the question, If you were guaranteed success what would you do? They then express all their responses with cutouts or drawings to form coats of arms. When they finish their projects, they should come up with a family motto and paste it at the bottom of the coat of arms. These projects can be placed on a class bulletin board.

- *Explore the customs of several groups of first Americans.* Ask students to tell who they think the first Americans were. Then instruct students to read a short passage about the first Americans and to discuss these questions: Where did the first Americans come from? What groups are described? What area of the country did each group settle? What ways of living are described for each group? After the discussion, have students write reports focusing on the location of each group; each group's ways of obtaining food, clothing and shelter; the roles of men, women, and children; and the unique contributions of each group. Finally, have individuals or small groups investigate and research other groups of the first Americans: What are they doing today? Where are they living?

- *Explore the plight of immigrants* (Michaelis, 1992). Show a filmstrip or video on immigrants, such as "Immigrants: The Dream and the Reality." Or use a television news clip or a newspaper article that presents at least two sides of the immigration issue. Ask questions such as these about the immigrants: What dream did they have? What problems did they have? How did they solve the problems? Why do countries need some control over immigration? To what extent did the immigrants accomplish their dreams? What still needs to be done?

Activities to renew the idea of a shared American culture can be combined with an examination of the diversity of present-day Americans. As students examine their backgrounds, and the backgrounds of friends, they can develop a worldview that connects planetary perspectives to our national uniqueness, and they can ponder how we think about ourselves, who we are, and where we want to go.

Influencing Social and Educational Policy

Central to a vigorous campaign against ineffective education is a change of orientation in our nation, toward the common good and away from egocentrism and an overly rigid focus on special interests. Sociologist and communitarian Amitai Etzioni (1993) argues that restoring civility and improving the condition of U.S. society requires emphasizing responsibilities over rights, stressing the community over the individual, reinvigorating spiritual and moral values, and building on the pillars of U.S. society—the family, the school, and the community. The basic notion of the communitarian movement is that restoring the moral, social, educational, and political foundations of the country is a precondition to successfully meeting the demands of the twenty-first century. Communitarian proposals lack real teeth, fail to challenge economic unfairness, and occasionally suggest intervening in private lives. Still, in spite of the controversiality of communitarianism, it is influencing individuals as diverse as U.S. President Bill Clinton and former secretary of the Department of Housing and Urban Development Jack Kemp (Etzioni, 1993). Others of note who are investigating and thinking about our civic needs and future include social scientist Charles Murray, who has researched the issues involved in the soaring number of babies born to single mothers;

sociologist William Julius Wilson, who has dissected the downfall of inner cities; and Michael Lerner, whose "politics of meaning" has caught the attention of national policymakers.

Whatever its philosophical associations, mental and moral reform is as important today as political and educational reform, and students must be helped to understand how a democratic society works and what might be done to make it better. They must also be taught to use change as an ally. In the 1990s, we will see schools continue to emphasize the development of democratic citizenship among students as a basic goal of the social studies curriculum. That curriculum is a central place for learning about history, geography, and civics, and other social sciences and literature can also be integrated into it. Continued attention should be given to global multicultural unity, the influence of religions on human affairs, and the impact of science and technology on ways of life.

Good schools teach children how to acquire *and* enact culture. As important as collaboration and thinking skills are, integrating the teaching of socially responsible values into the larger curriculum may prove even more important when it comes to inventing our civic future. And teachers *can* educate for character, showing students how to learn and act cooperatively, while also respecting each student as an active, responsible learner. However, creating a context in which this teaching is encouraged will require sustained economic, political, and public support for extending the best U.S. education into all of our schools, so that all students can learn in a climate that fosters good character and the skills of ethical decision making.

Out of necessity, schools are taking on responsibilities that go well beyond their traditional educational mission. One of the major challenges of the 1990s is how to organize an environment that deals with everything from feeding children who come to school hungry to teaching ethics. Developing character in young people is a difficult and subtle process. For it to work, both the home and the school environment must be places where ethical issues are taken seriously. Creating a caring culture for learning provides a springboard for this to happen.

An inevitable, intimate relationship exists between education and other social institutions. Failure to provide our students with a vigorous civic education will diminish U.S. democracy and put decision making into the hands of a few. Unless citizens are truly educated, the United States could drift into a new dark age, with the flickering light of the video screen in the background.

Chapter Eleven

Conclusion: A Bottom-Up Approach to Reform

This book has urged educators to design effective classroom programs that involve collaborative learning and critical thinking and that get children actively and physically involved in learning that connects with the real world, with technology, and with children's interests. The goal is for teachers to teach learning and thinking skills that students will use all their lives to gather information, reflect on it, and make decisions, and to be responsible citizens and community members in a strong and healthy society and a fast-changing world. This book has also focused on the content areas of U.S. education, showing how active learning and thoughtfulness can be taught in conjunction with the content of language arts, mathematics, science, arts, and social studies, and offering a variety of instructional strategies and learning opportunities.

In conclusion, let us look at the realities that must be faced as we work for education reform and the instructional methods that will produce successful students today and successful workers and citizens in a democracy tomorrow.

Taking a Bottom-Up Approach to School Improvement

As we have all seen, the schooling of U.S. children has increasingly become an area of national distress. There is growing agreement that business as usual is no longer adequate in education. The degree of change demanded requires experimentation within the schools to provide reformers with valid information about what actually works in education. Some of that experimentation has been cited in this book. With help from other institutions, the public schools are trying to redesign themselves—while continuing to deliver a program. There are millions of professionally trained teachers working in the schools, and they are going to have to carry much of the load of education reform. Teachers may be part of the problem, but without them there can be no solution. They are tired of being given less money, more orders, and no voice in change efforts. When teachers see the goal and are given the resources, they can internalize and implement valid possibilities for instructional success.

School reform requires that educators everywhere be involved in developing a school environment and classroom methods that can tap into the gifts present in each child. Elliot Eisner (1990, p. 36) is right when he suggests that the schools need a climate in which professionals are encouraged to work at the "edge of their competence." Change is unsettling and risky, but it is better to try to understand the process, to take the risk and do something, than to fail to act. Doing nothing in the face of a conviction that something is terribly wrong is irresponsible. It was Dante who wrote that the hottest places in hell are reserved for those who do nothing in a time of crisis.

Can we identify the major levers that need to be oiled and pulled to get fundamental change? Yes. Investing heavily and directly in staff development, curriculum development, and new models for assessment are the best bets. Some skills needed for the professionalization of teaching are already in place. A teacher who knows how to carry out portfolio assessment effectively, for example, already possesses the basis on which he or she can conduct action research.

Taking teaching seriously as a tool for reform means helping teachers become reflective students of their own teaching. The same portfolios and action research that are used to assess students can also prompt educators to take notice of their own understandings and act on them. Change happens when people change. Getting change started means giving teachers time, training, and resources to contribute to the ongoing pedagogical discussion (Larner, Halpern, & Harkavy, 1993). School restructuring means empowering not only teachers but also parents and students to play a major role in determining the nature of schooling, in holding schools accountable for getting results, and in orienting teachers and students toward serious, sustained engagement in academic learning.

Yet teachers remain central to the process, for they are the ones who will provide the bright tiles in the social and educational mosaic of our civic and instructional future. However, teachers *should not have to be miracle workers;* students should not come to school in desperate shape. The educational sector cannot make serious changes without parallel societal changes. The schools can influence the direction of social change, but they cannot drive it forward on their own. Transforming basic cultural institutions and belief systems is much harder than changing the structure of the schools or the technology of instructional delivery systems. Today, as schools are increasingly pushed to attend to the mind *and* the body—the soul and the spirit—it is more important than ever for society to attend to the 90 percent factor, the time students spend outside the classroom.

The public has an enormous number of unrealistic, and contradictory, expectations for the schools. Everyone seems to have a subject to be added to core curriculum goals. Are there any more requests? Yes. We want schools to discipline our children; support and encourage their independence; and help them deal with difficulties with nutrition, health, sexuality, death, morality, interpersonal relationships, and the maturation process. We want schools to provide a community for students; teach students how to participate in sports, dance, art, music, and woodworking; and be a focus for community life for adults. We want a decent place to send our children so adults can work (or play) without worrying about them, a place that provides psychological, vocational, and social counseling. We want schools to help millions of functionally illiterate adult Americans. Of course, most of these things are good. But adding one regulation and requirement on top of another limits the time that is given to key content areas and prevents the public schools from competing on a level playing field with unregulated private schools. Public indifference to our educational system and a lack of political and financial support (beyond symbolism) will defeat teachers' efforts to do even the most basic elements of their job.

Education can, of course, contribute to the solution of important problems in this country. But even at its best, it can only be a dance around the edges until coordinated societal steps are taken to meet students' social, health, and developmental needs. It was de Tocqueville (1969) who observed that "America is great because America is good. If it ever stops being good, it will stop being great." If we really want everyone educated to the extent of her or his ability, it will take the whole array of social service and health care professionals working alongside educators to bridge the gap between what the schools were designed to do and today's reality.

Teachers and Educational Reform

It is now clear that the duration and depth of educational neglect has been enormous and that conditions for U.S. children have been deteriorating for nearly twenty years (California Department of Education, 1992b). Of course, any profession experimenting and testing new approaches will find that some new methods need extensive modification to work—and some may fail outright. That is all part of advancing any field: two steps forward, one back, and (one hopes) two steps forward again. Educational risk taking does, however, require support and the recognition that well-intentioned failures can provide crucial information for school reform. It would be a tragedy if, a decade from now, we looked back on today's debate about educational reform and found that our country had had neither the will nor the wallet to do a better job of preparing students for the world that awaits them. There is more at stake here than the public may be aware of. If the U.S. educational system fails, we should fear for the soul of our democracy. To recognize the fact and the promise of public education is to keep faith with human potential.

Expecting research or leadership professionals who are entirely separate from our teaching professionals to find solutions may not be the best way to get at the deep pedagogical understandings needed to support change. Professionals such as teachers do not blossom when they spend their careers enfolded in the logic of others. In democratic institutions, power allows itself to be balanced by power—as in the checks and balances system of our own government. Asking teachers to go down paths that "authorities" have prepared for them is not good enough. Teachers themselves are in the best position to do many of the main things we would expect both researchers and leaders to do: identify the key issues, question, probe, attain clarity, authentically assess, and *do* something in an ambiguous world. That is one of the premises guiding this book's presentation of instructional methods that allow teachers to do just these things while also building students' body of knowledge. This focus on the individual teacher's ability to assess both students' learning and her or his own teaching effectiveness might seem to contradict the trend toward national standards in assessment. However, standards do not have to mean standardization. Standards do not have to mean loss of local control or unfair comparisons between wealthy and poor school districts.

Generating the energy to change today's school culture and act on new practices is an art. It will have a lot to do with understanding human nature, establishing a readiness for change, and developing an intellectual understanding of new practices (Ledell & Arnspager, 1993). The most effective innovations are turning out to be usually research based and classroom friendly. Change is, after all, a personal process. It can be supported with a team approach that recognizes the power of generating ideas from the people most directly involved. School reform without teachers is a contradiction in terms. If their voices are left out of the ongoing discussions about the nature, development, and assessment of human learning then we will miss a real opportunity.

Future Learning Communities

A conception of school as a place where students learn necessary requirements for economic and social advancement is only part of what is needed. For students to become productive citizens in a democracy, schools must also have a commitment to moral excellence that nourishes student imagination and idealism. The business world has a direct interest in preparing workers who can read, write, and compute. But the country needs more than that. *School is not just a place to learn basic skills and study ideas.* It is also a place to examine the possible impact of those ideas on society. Today's learning must become a construction of meaning, not just a rote learning of meaning. And it must be based in new organizational patterns. If the pony express (the school organization of today) can ride only so fast, then at some point, you have to move up to the telegraph (or, today, to electronic mail). As teachers become more autonomous professionally, they will have greater freedom to invent diverse ways to help students succeed in this more demanding school. As the teaching profession sheds demeaning rituals and petty indignities, teachers will be able to pay more attention to what is important—*helping students to learn.* They will be able to build on the dynamic of self-actualization and look at both what stimulates learning *and* what constrains it.

The best teachers do not try to be like surgeons, performing on others; instead, they try to help children become active learners who can "operate" on themselves. Their approach stems from the view that education at its best is personal, purposeful, and intrinsically motivated. Learning is a social process of actively constructing meaning from experience with life, books, electronic media, and a community of peers. It "involves an active reconstruction of the knowledge or skill that is presented, on the basis of the learner's existing internal model of the world. The process is therefore interactional in nature, both within the learner and between the learner and the teacher, and calls for negotiation of meaning, not its unidirectional transmission" (Wells, 1986, p. 107).

A major task for the late 1990s will be the creation of classrooms that recognize students and teachers as thinkers, doers, investigators, and cooperative problem solvers. Future lessons will include meaning-centered explorations where learning how to think and to work with others will be just as important as any set curriculum. And, as the research literature and technological base develop, directions in teaching will continue to change, making it increasingly difficult to keep teacher practice in contact with new developments. Therefore, teachers must be inspired to be lifelong learners and responsible participants in social change.

In the future, students will spend more time working together on projects. Classrooms will be arranged for cooperative learning with clustered desks and plenty of resource materials. Teachers will guide explorations and spend less time lecturing to entire classrooms of children. As children form active learning teams and communicate more freely, they will teach one another, and they will learn to extend their discoveries to the real world. For example, once a student learns individual responsibility in a small group, that idea can be extended, helping the student to understand the nature of social responsibility.

Reaching for the Challenge

As educators, we will find it greatly to our advantage to develop the power of foresight. We need to experience the rebirth of the spirit that motivated Renaissance scholars to begin to accept that the world was complex and to study it in all its complexities. It is this tough-minded, energetic, and striving spirit that will help us effectively address the problems of our schools and grasp the opportunities for educational change that the twenty-first century promises to bring.

References

Abi-Nader, J. (1993). Meeting the needs of multicultural classrooms: Family values and the motivation of minority students. In M. J. O'Hair & S. Odell (Eds.), *Diversity and teaching: Teacher Education Yearbook I.* Orlando, FL: Harcourt Brace Jovanovich.

Abraham, S. Y., & Campbell, C. (1984). *Peer teachers as mirrors and monitors.* Detroit, MI: Wayne State University Press.

Adams, D. (1983, Spring). Does what you read influence how you write? *The Leaflet* (Journal of the New England Association of Teachers of English).

Adams, D., & Hamm, M. (1987). *Electronic learning.* Springfield, IL: Charles C. Thomas.

Adams, M. J. (1990). *Beginning to read: Thinking and learning about print.* Cambridge, MA: MIT Press.

Albert, L. (1990). *Cooperative discipline.* Circle Pines, MN: American Guidance Service.

Alexander, L. (1991). *America 2000: An education strategy.* Washington, DC: United States Department of Education. (ERIC document reproduction service No. ED 059 113)

American Association for the Advancement of Science. (1990). *Science for all Americans* (Project 2061). Washington, DC: Author.

American Council on Education. (1992). *National Issues Forum in the classroom: 1990–91.* Dayton, OH: National Issues Forum.

Anderson, D. R. (1983). In J. Bryant & D. R. Anderson (Eds.), *Children's understanding of television: Research on attention and comprehension.* San Diego, CA: Academic Press.

Anderson, L., & Burns, R. (1989). *Research in classrooms: The study of teachers, teaching, and instruction.* Oxford, UK: Pergamon.

Anderson, R., Hiebert, E., Scott, J., & Wilkinson, I. (1985). *Becoming a nation of readers: Report on the commission on reading.* Washington, DC: National Institute of Education.

Andrasick, K. D. (1990). *Opening texts: Using writing to teach literature.* Portsmouth, NH: Heinemann Educational Books.

Applebee, A. (1991). Literature: Whose heritage? In E. Hiebert (Ed.), *Literacy for a new society: Perspectives, practices, and policies.* New York: Teachers College Press.

Applebee, A., Langer, J., Mullis, I., & Jenkins, L. (1990). *The writing report card.* Princeton, NJ: Educational Testing Service.

Arendt, H. (1958). *The human condition.* Chicago: University of Chicago Press.

Arnheim, R. (1990). *Notes on art education.* Los Angeles: J. Paul Getty Center for Education in the Arts.

Aronowitz, S. (1990). *Science as power: Discourse and ideology in modern society.* Minneapolis, MN: University of Minnesota Press.

Babad, E. (1990). Measuring and changing teacher's differential behavior as perceived by students and teachers. *Journal of Educational Psychology, 82*(4).

Bagdikian, B. H. (1987). *The media monopoly.* Boston: Beacon Press.

Bamberger, J. (1991). *The mind behind the musical ear.* Cambridge, MA: Harvard University Press.

Bandura, A. (1986). *Social foundations of thought and action: A cognitive theory.* Englewood Cliffs, NJ: Prentice Hall.

Baron, J. (1988). *Thinking and deciding.* New York: Cambridge University Press.

Barr, R., Kamil, M L., Mosenthal, P. B., & Pearson, P. D. (Eds.). (1993). *Handbook of reading research* (Vol. 2, pp. 630–640). White Plains, NY: Longman.

Bassarear, T., & Davidson, N. (1992). The use of small group learning situations in mathematics instruction as a tool to develop thinking. In N. Davidson & T. Worsham, *Enhancing thinking through cooperative learning.* New York: Teachers College Press.

Beane, K. (1990). *Affect in the curriculum: Toward democracy, dignity, and diversity.* New York: Teachers College Press.

Berman, L., Hultgam, F., Lee, D., Rivkin, M., & Roderick, J. (1991). *Toward a curriculum for being.* Albany, NY: State University of New York Press.

Bianculli, D. (1992). *Taking television seriously.* New York: Continuum.

Boomer, G. (1992). *Negotiating the curriculum.* Busingstake, UK: Falmer Press.

Bossert, S. T. (1989). Cooperative activities in the classroom. In E. Z. Rothkopf (Ed.), *Review of research in education.* Washington, DC: American Education Research Association.

Bowers, C. A., & Finders, D. J. (1990). *Responsive teaching: An ecological approach to patterns, language, culture, and thought.* New York: Teachers College Press.

Boyer, E. L. (1990). Civic responsibility for responsible citizens. *Educational Leadership, 48*(3), 5–7.

Boyer, E. L. (1993). *Ready to learn: A mandate for the nation.* Princeton, NJ: Carnegie Foundation for the Advancement of Teaching.

Brophy, J., & Good, T. (1986). Teacher behavior and student achievement. In M. C. Wittrock (Ed.), *Research on teaching.* New York: St. Martin's Press.

Brown, A. L. (1988). *Metacognitive skills and reading: Handbook of reading research.* White Plains, NY: Longman.

Bruner, J. (1966). *Toward a theory of instruction*. New York: W.W. Norton.

Bruner, J., & Haste, H. (1987). *Making sense: The child's construction of the world*. New York: Methuen.

Bryant, J., & Anderson, D. R. (Eds.). (1983). *Children's understanding of television: Research on attention and comprehension*. San Diego, CA: Academic Press.

Burns, M. (1977). *The good time math event book*. Sunnyvale, CA: Creative Publications.

Burns, M. (1991). *Math by all means*. New York: Math Solution Publications, Cuisinaire Company.

Burns, P., Roe, B., & Ross, E. (1988). *Teaching reading in today's elementary schools*. Boston: Houghton Mifflin.

Burton, C. B. (1987). Problems in children's peer relationships: A broadening perspective. In C. G. Katz (Ed.), *Current topics in early childhood education* (Vol. 7). Norwood, NJ: Ablex.

California Department of Education (1992a). *Mathematics framework for California public schools*. Sacramento, CA: Author.

California Department of Education. (1992b). Saving the dream. In California Department of Education, *Fourth annual report card: Children now*. Sacramento, CA: Author.

California Department of Education Elementary Grades Task Force. (1992). *It's elementary*. Sacramento, CA: California Department of Education, Bureau of Publications.

Calkins, L. (1991). *Living between the lines*. Portsmouth, NH: Heinemann Educational Books.

Carey, N., Mittman, B., & Darling-Hammond, L. (1989). *Recruiting mathematics and science teachers through nontraditional programs: A survey*. Santa Monica, CA: Rand Corporation.

Carnegie Forum on Education and the Economy, Task Force on Teaching as a Profession. (1986). *A nation prepared: Teachers for the twenty-first century*. New York: Author.

Carnegie Foundation for the Advancement of Teaching. (1988). *The condition of teaching: A state-by-state analysis*. Princeton, NJ: Princeton University Press.

Champagne, A., & Klopfer, L. (1988). Research in science education: The cognitive perspective. In *Research within reach: Science education*.

Chickering, A. (1977). *Experience and learning*. New Rochelle, NY: Change Magazine Press.

Children's Defense Fund. (1991). *The state of America's children*. Washington, DC: Author.

Clarke, A. C. (1992). *How the world was one: Beyond the global village*. New York: Bantam Books.

Clarke, J., Wideman, R., & Eadie, S. (1990). *Together we learn*. Toronto: Prentice Hall.

Clement, J. (1982). Students' preconceptions in introductory mechanics. *American Journal of Physics, 50*, 66–71.

Clement, J. (1983). A conceptual model discussed by Galileo and used intuitively by physics students. In D. Gentner & A. L. Stevens (Eds.), *Mental models*. Hillsdale, NJ: Erlbaum.

Cochran-Smith, M., Kahn, J., & Paris, C. L. (1988). When word processors come into the classroom. In J. L. Hoot & S. B. Silvern (Eds.), *Writing with computers in the early grades*. New York: Teachers College Press.

Cohen, E. (1984). The desegregated school. In N. Miller & M. Brewer (Eds.), *Groups in contact: The psychology of desegregation*. San Diego, CA: Academic Press.

Coles, R. (1993). *Moral dimensions of learning*. Paper presented at the Association for Supervision and Curriculum Development (ASCD) Conference, Washington, DC.

The College Board. (1985). *Academic preparation in the arts: Teaching for transition from high school to college*. New York.

Conley, M. (1987). *Grouping within reach*. Newark, DE: International Reading Association.

Connelly, M. F., & Clandinin, D. J. (1988). *Teachers as curriculum planners: Narratives of experience*. New York: Teachers College Press.

Corrin, S., & Corrin, S. (1982). *Once upon a rhyme: 101 poems for young children*. London: Faber & Faber.

Costa, A. L. (Ed.). (1991). *Developing minds: A resource book for teaching thinking*. Alexandria, VA: Association of Supervision and Curriculum Development.

Cruikshank, D., & Sheffield, L. (1992). *Teaching and learning elementary and middle school mathematics*. Columbus, OH: Merrill.

Dalton, J. (1991). *Adventures in thinking: Creative thinking and cooperative talk in small groups*. South Melbourne, Vic., Australia: Thomas Nelson Australia.

Damon, W. (Ed.). (1988). *Child development today and tomorrow*. San Francisco: Jossey-Bass.

Davidson, N. (Ed.). (1990). *Cooperative learning in mathematics: A handbook for teachers*. Reading, MA: Addison-Wesley.

Davidson, N., & Worsham, T. (1992). *Enhancing thinking through cooperative learning*. New York: Teachers College Press.

DeAvila, E., Cohen, E. G., & Intill, J. (1981). *Multi-cultural improvement of cognitive ability*. Executive summary to the California Department of Education (no. 9372).

Dede, C. J. (1985). Assessing the potential of educational information utilities. *Library Hi Tech, 3*(4), 115–119.

Denman, G. (1989). *When you've made it your own . . . Teaching poetry to young people*. Portsmouth, NH: Heinemann Educational Books.

De Paola, T. (1989). *The art lesson*. New York: Putnam Publishing Group.

Dewey, J. (1958). *Art as experience*. New York: Capricorn Books.

Dickinson, E. (1924). *Complete Poems* (Notable American Authors). Irvine, CA: Reprint Services.

Dissanayake, E. (1992). *Homo Aestheticus*. New York: Free Press.

Dorr, A. (1986). *Television and children*. London: Sage.

Doyle, W. (1981, November/December). Research on classroom contexts. *Journal of Teacher Education, 32*, 52.

Dublin, M. (1991). *Futurehype: The tyranny of prophecy*. New York: Dutton.

Duckworth, E. (1987). *"The having of wonderful ideas" & other essays on teaching and learning*. New York: Teachers College Press.

Dyson, A. H. (1989). *The multiple worlds of child writers: A study of friends learning to write*. New York: Teachers College Press.

Eisner, E. (1990). *The enlightened eye*. New York: Macmillan.

Elmore, R., and Associates. (1990). *Restructuring schools: The Next Generation of Educational Reform*. San Francisco, CA: Jossey-Bass.

Emerson, R. W. (1990). Self reliance. In Joel Porte (Ed.), *Ralph Waldo Emerson: Essays and lectures*. New York: Library of America.

Ennis, R. (1987). A taxonomy of critical thinking dispositions and abilities. In J. Boyokoff Baron & R. Sternberg (Eds.), *Teaching thinking skills: Theory and practice*. New York: W.H. Freeman.

Etzioni, A. (1993). *The spirit of community: Rights, responsibilities, and the communitarian agenda*. New York: Crown/Random House.

Farr, R. (1990). Trends, setting directions for language arts portfolios. *Educational Leadership, 48*(3), 103.

Fergusson, F. (1961). *Aristotle's Poetics*. New York: Macmillan.

Finch, F. (1991). *Educational performance assessment*. Chicago: Riverside.

Finn, C. E., Jr. (1992). *We must take charge: Our schools and our future*. New York: Free Press.

Forman, G., & Pufall, P. (Eds.). (1988). *Constructivism in the computer age*. Hillsdale, NJ: Erlbaum.

Forsyth, P., & Tallerico, M. (Ed.). (1993). *City schools: Leading the way*. Newbury Park, CA: Corwin Press.

Fowler, C. (1992). *Understanding how the arts contribute to excellent education* (A study prepared for the National Education Association).

Fraser, J. T. (1990). *Of time, passion, and knowledge*. Princeton, NJ: Princeton University Press.

Fuhrman, S. H. (Ed.). (1993). *Designing coherent education policy: Improving the system*. San Francisco, CA: Jossey-Bass.

Gardner, H. (1987). Developing the spectrum of human intelligences. *Harvard Educational Review, 57*, 187–193.

Gardner, H. (1990). *To open minds*. New York: Basic Books.

Gardner, H. (1991). *The unschooled mind*. New York: Basic Books.

Gay, G. (1989). Ethnic minorities and educational quality. In J. A. Banks & C. A. Banks (Eds.), *Multicultural education: Issues and perspectives*. Needham Heights, MA: Allyn & Bacon.

Gere, A. R. (1985). *Roots in the sawdust: Writing to learn across the disciplines*. Portsmouth, NH: Heinemann Educational Books.

Getty Center for Education in the Arts. (1990). *Discipline based art education*. Austin, TX: Author.

Getty Center for Education in the Arts. (1989). *Education in art: Future building*. Austin, TX: Author.

Getty Center for Education in the Arts. (1990). *Inheriting the theory: New voices and multiple perspectives on DBAE*. Austin, TX: Author.

Gill, K. (Ed.). (1993). *Process and portfolios in writing instruction*. Urbana, IL: National Council of Teachers of English.

Glickman, C. D. (1993). *Renewing America's schools: A guide for school-based action*. San Francisco, CA: Jossey-Bass.

Good, T. L., & Brophy, J. E. (1994). *Looking into classrooms* (6th ed.). New York: HarperCollins College Publishing.

Goodlad, J. I. (1983). *A place called school: Prospects for the future*. New York: McGraw-Hill.

Goodman, K. S., Goodman, Y. M., & Hood, W. J. (1989). *The whole language evaluation book*. Portsmouth, NH: Heinemann Educational Books.

Graves, D. (1983). *Writing: Teachers and children at work*. Portsmouth, NH: Heinemann Educational Books.

Graves, D., & Sunstein, B. (Eds). (1992). *Portfolio diversity in action*. Portsmouth, NH: Heinemann Educational Books.

Growing up complete: The imperative for music education. (1991, March). (Report of the National Commission on Music Education by the Music Educators National Conference). Reston, VA: Music Educators National Conference.

Grzhonko, L. (1993). *Jeff and Magic Molecule Land* (unpublished book). Discussion taken from class at San Francisco State University, April 13, 1993. (Write to author at 717 Sixth Ave., #4, San Francisco, CA 94118.)

Guilder, G. (1992). *Life after television*. New York: W.W. Norton.

Gutmann, A. (1987). *Democratic education*. Princeton, NJ: Princeton University Press.

Haberman, M. (1993). In M. J. O'Hair & S. Odell (Eds.), *Diversity and teaching: Teacher Education Yearbook I*. Orlando, FL: Harcourt Brace Jovanovich.

Hamburg, D. A. (1992). *Today's children: Creating a future for a generation in crisis*. New York: Times Books/Random House.

Hamm, M., & Adams, D. (1992). *The collaborative dimensions of learning*. Norwood, NJ: Ablex.

Hand, B., & Treagust, D. (1991). Student achievement and science development: Using a constructive framework. *School Science and Mathematics*, 91(4), 172–176.

Hansen, J. (1987). *When writers read*. Portsmouth, NH: Heinemann Educational Books.

Harasim, L. (Ed.).(1990). *Online education: Perspectives on a new environment*. New York: Praeger.

Harman, G. (1986). *Change in view: Principles of reasoning*. Cambridge, MA: MIT Press.

Hassard, J. (1990). *Science experiences: Cooperative learning in science*. Reading, MA: Addison-Wesley.

Havel, V. (1992). *Summer meditations*. New York: Knopf.

Hawkins, H. P., & Pingree, S. (1981). What children do with television: Implications for communication research. In B. Dervin and M. Voight (Eds.), *Progress in communication sciences* (Vol. 3). Norwood, NJ: Ablex.

Hayden, C. (1992). *Ventures into cultures: A resource book of multicultural materials and programs*. Chicago: American Library Association.

Hazen, R. (1991, February 25). My turn: Why my kids hate science. *Newsweek*.

Heath, S. B., & McLaughlin, M. W. (Eds.). (1993). *Identity and inner-city youth: Beyond ethnicity and gender*. New York: Teachers College Press.

Heath, S. B., & Margolies, J. (1991). *Children of promise*. Berkeley, CA: Center for the Study of Writing and Literacy.

Hechinger, F. M. (1992). *Fateful choices: Healthy youth for the 21st century*. New York: Hill & Wang.

Heilbrun, C. (1989). *Writing a woman's life*. New York: W.W. Norton.

Hendricksen, B., & Morgan, T. (Eds.). (1990). *Reorientations: Critical theories and pedagogies*. Champaign, IL: University of Illinois Press.

Hodgkinson, H. (1989). *The same client: The demographics of education and service delivery systems*. Washington, DC: Institute of Education.

Hopkins, L. B. (Ed.). (1987). *Dinosaurs: Poems*. San Diego, CA: Harcourt Brace Jovanovich.

Hughes, L. (1990). *Collected Poems of Langston Hughes*. New York: Knopf.

International Institute for Management Development. (1992). *Fourth annual report*. Geneva, Switzerland: World Economic Forum.

Johnson, D. W., & Johnson, R. (1975). *Learning together and alone*. Englewood Cliffs, NJ: Prentice Hall.

Johnson, D. W., & Johnson, R. (1982). *Joining together: Group therapy and group skills*. Englewood Cliffs, NJ: Prentice Hall.

Johnson, D. W., & Johnson, R. (1989). *Cooperation and competition: Theory and research*. Edina, MN: Interaction Book Company.

Johnson, D. W., Johnson, R., Holubec, E. J., & Roy, P. (1984). *Circles of learning: Cooperation in the classroom*. Alexandria, VA: Association for Supervision and Curriculum Development.

Johnson, D. W., Maruyama, G., Johnson, R., Nelson, D., & Skon, L. (1981). Effects of cooperative, competitive, and individualistic goal structures on achievement: A meta analysis. *Psychological Bulletin, 89*, 47–62.

Johnson, J. E., Christie, J. F., & Yawkey, T. (1987). *Play and early childhood development*. Glenview, IL: Scott Foresman.

Johnson, K. (1987). *Doing words: Using the creative power of children's personal images to teach reading and writing*. Boston: Houghton Mifflin.

Johnson, P. H. (1989, April). Teachers as evaluation experts: A cognitive basis. *The Reading Teacher, 7*, 44–48.

Johnson, S. M. (1990). *Teachers at work: Achieving success in our schools*. New York: Basic Books.

Kagan, D. (1986). Cooperative learning and sociocultural diversity: Implications for practice. In *Beyond language: Social and cultural factors in schooling language minority students* (pp. 98–110). Los Angeles: Evaluation, Dissemination and Assessment Center, California State University.

Kagan, D., & Tippins, D. (1993). Classroom cases as gauges of professional growth. In M. J. O'Hair & S. Odell (Eds.), *Diversity and teaching: Teacher Education Yearbook I*. Orlando, FL: Harcourt Brace Jovanovich.

Kagan, J., & Lamb, S. (1987). *The emergence of morality in young children*. Chicago: University of Chicago Press.

Kagan, S. (1990). *Cooperative learning: Resources for teachers*. San Juan Capistrano, CA: Resources for Teachers.

Kiesler, S., Siegel, J., & McGuire, T. W. (1984). Social psychological aspects of computer-mediated communication. *American Psychologist, 39*, 1123–1134.

King, J. P. (1993). *The art of mathematics*. New York: Ballantine Books.

Kitcher, P. (1993). *Science without legend, objectivity without illusions*. New York: Oxford University Press.

Kooser, T. (1980). *Sure signs: New and selected poems*. Pittsburgh, PA: University of Pittsburgh Press.

Kozol, J. (1991). *Savage inequalities: Children in America's schools*. New York: Crown.

Krosnick, J., & Alwin, D. (1989). Aging and susceptibility to attitude change. *Journal of Personality and Social Psychology, 57*, 416–425.

Lampert, M. (1990). When the problem is not the question and the solution is not the answer: Mathematical knowing and teaching. *American Educational Research Journal, 27*(1), 29–63.

Langbort, C., & Thompson, V. (1985). *Building success in math*. Belmont, CA: Wadsworth.

Larner, M., Halpern, R., & Harkavy, O. (1993). *Fair start for children: Lessons learned from seven demonstration projects*. New Haven, CT: Yale University Press.

Ledell, M., & Arnspager, A. (1993). *How to deal with community criticism of school change*. Alexandria, VA: Association for Supervision and Curriculum Development.

Leitzel, J.R.C. (Ed.). (1991). *A call for change: Recommendations for the mathematical preparation of teachers of mathematics*. Washington, DC: Mathematical Association of America.

Levine, M., & Trachtman, R. (Eds.). (1988). *American business and the public school: Case studies of corporate involvement in public education*. New York: Teachers College Press.

McCloskey, M. (1983). Naive theories of motion. In D. Genter & A. L. Stevens (Eds.), *Mental models*. Hillsdale, NJ: Erlbaum.

McKibben, B. (1992). *The age of missing information*. New York: Random House.

McLeod, J. M., Fitzpatrick, M. A., Glynn, C. J., & Fallis, S. F. (1982). *Television and behavior: Ten years of scientific progress* (Vol. 2, Department of Health and Human Services). Washington, DC: U.S. Government Printing Office.

Maeroff, G. (1988). *The empowerment of teachers*. New York: Teachers College Press.

Marcel, A., & Carpenter, P. (1987). *The psychology of reading and language comprehension*. Needham Heights, MA: Allyn & Bacon.

Marzano, R., Brandt, R., Hughes, C., Jones, B., Presseisen, B,, Rankin, S., & Suhor, C. (1988). *Dimensions of thinking: A framework for curriculum and instruction*. Alexandria, VA: Association for Supervision and Curriculum Development.

Mathematical Sciences Education Board and the National Research Council. (1990). *Reshaping school mathematics: A philosophy and framework for curriculum*. Washington, D.C.: National Academy Press.

Medawar, P. (1987). *Plato's Republic*. Oxford, UK: Oxford University Press.

Mehan, H. (1989). Microcomputers in classrooms: Educational technology or social practice? *Anthropology and Education Quarterly, 20*(1), 4–22.

Melville, H. (1963). Bartleby the scrivener. In P. Rahv (Ed.), *Eight great American short novels*. New York: Berkeley. (Original work published 1856)

Mercer, C. D., & Mercer, A. R. (1985). *Teaching students with learning problems*. Columbus, OH: Merrill.

Meyer, C., & Sallee, T. (1983). *Make it simpler: A practical guide to problem solving in mathematics*. Reading, MA: Addison-Wesley.

Michaelis, J. U. (1992). *Social studies for children: A guide to basic instruction* (10th ed.). Needham Heights, MA: Allyn & Bacon.

Millay, E. St. V. (1981). *Collected Poems*. New York: HarperCollins.

Miller, B. C., & Drake, S. (1990). *Holistic learning: A teacher's guide to integrated studies*. Toronto: OSICE Press.

Mitchell, R. (1989). Portfolio newsletter of *Arts PROPEL*. Cambridge, MA: Harvard University Press.

Muggeridge, M. (1989). *Chronicles of wasted time*. New York: Chapman Press.

Mumme, J. (1990). *Portfolio assessment in mathematics*. Santa Barbara, CA: California Mathematics Project, University of California, Santa Barbara.

Murray, D. (1990). *Shoptalk: Learning to write with writers*. Portsmouth, NH: Heinemann Educational Books.

Nagy, W. E. (1988). *Teaching vocabulary to improve reading comprehension*. Urbana, IL: National Council of Teachers of English.

National Art Education Associates. (1992). *Elementary art programs: A guide for administrators*. Reston, VA: National Art Education Association.

National Assessment of Educational Progress. (1983). *The third national mathematics assessment: Results, trends, and issues*. Denver: Education Commission of the States.

National Assessment of Educational Progress. (1992). *1990 Science report card*. Cambridge, MA: National Academy of Education.

National Council for the Social Studies. (1991). *Civitas*. Washington, DC: Author.

National Council of Teachers of Mathematics Commission on Standards of School Mathematics. (1989). *Curriculum and evaluation standards for school mathematics*. Reston, VA: National Council of Teachers of Mathematics.

National Council of Teachers of Mathematics. (1991). *Professional standards for teaching mathematics*. Reston, VA: Author.

National Research Council Board on Mathematical Sciences/Mathematical Sciences Education Board. (1989). *Everybody counts: A report to the nation on the future of mathematics education*. Washington, DC: National Academy Press.

Natriello, G., McDill, E., & Pallas A. (1990). *Schooling disadvantaged children: Racing against catastrophe*. New York: Teachers College Press.

Nell, V. (1989). *Lost in a book*. New Haven, CT: Yale University Press.

Nesbitt, J. (1986). *International directory of recreation-oriented assistance*. Venice, CA: Lifeboat Press.

Newmann, F. (1990). Qualities of thoughtful social studies classes: An empirical profile. *Journal of Curriculum Studies, 22*, 253–275.

Newmann, F. (Ed.). (1992). *Student engagement and achievement in American secondary schools*. New York: Teachers College Press.

Noddings, N. (1984). *Caring: A feminine approach to ethics and moral education*. Berkeley: University of California Press.

Noddings, N. (1989). The education of moral people. In N. Brabeck (Ed.), *Who cares?* New York: Praeger.

Office of Technology Assessment, U.S. Congress. (1988). *Power on! New tools for teaching and learning.* Washington, DC: U.S. Government Printing Office.

Papert, S. (1993). *The children's machine: Rethinking school in the age of the computer.* New York: Basic Books/HarperCollins.

Papert, S. (1990). Introduction. In I. Harel (Ed.), *Constructionist learning.* Cambridge, MA: Media Laboratory, Massachusetts Institute of Technology.

Pasch, S., Pasch, M., Johnson, S. I., Synder, E. S., Awilda, H., & Mooradian, P. (1993). Reflections of urban education: A tale of three cities. In M. J. O'Hair & S. Odell (Eds.), *Diversity and teaching: Teacher Education Yearbook I.* Orlando, FL: Harcourt Brace Jovanovich.

Paul, R., Binker, K., Jensen, K., & Kreklau, H. (1989). *Critical thinking handbook.* Rohnert Park, CA: Sonoma State University.

Paulos, J. A. (1988). *Innumeracy: Mathematical illiteracy and its consequences.* New York: Hill & Wang.

Paulos, J. A. (1991). *Beyond Numeracy.* New York: Knopf.

Paz, O. (1986). *On poets and others* (M. Schmidt, Trans.). New York: Seaver Books.

Perfetti, C. (1985). *Reading ability.* New York: Oxford University Press.

Perkins, D. N., & Simmons, R. (1988). Patterns of misunderstanding: An integrative model of misconceptions in science, mathematics, and programming. *Review of Educational Research, 58*(3), 303–326.

Peterson, P. L. (1988). Teachers' and students' cognitional knowledge for classroom teaching and learning. *Educational Researcher, 17*(5), 5–14.

Piaget, J. (1962). *The language and thought of the child* (M. Warden, Trans.). New York: Humanities Press. (Original work published 1923)

Power, B. M., & Hubbard, R. (Eds.). (1991). *Literacy in process: The Heinemann reader.* Portsmouth, NH: Heinemann Educational Books.

Pressley, M., et al. (1987). *What is good strategy use and why is it hard to teach?* Paper presented at the meeting of the American Educational Research Association, Washington, DC.

Prothrow-Stith, D. (1991). *Deadly consequences.* New York: HarperCollins.

Provenzo, E. F. (1991). *Video kids: Making sense of Nintendo.* Cambridge, MA: Harvard University Press, 1991.

Read, H. (1992). *The Meaning of Art.* New York: Faber & Faber.

Renninger, K., Hidi, S., & Krapp, A. (Eds.). (1992). *The role of interest in learning and development.* Hillsdale, NJ: Erlbaum.

Resnick, L. B. (1987). *Education and learning to think.* Washington, DC: National Academy Press.

Resnick, L. B., & Klopfer, L. (1989). *Toward the thinking curriculum: Current cognitive research*. Alexandria, VA: Association of Supervision and Curriculum Development.

Reys, R. E., Suydam, M. N., & Lindquist, M. M. (1989). *Helping children learn mathematics*. Englewood Cliffs, NJ: Prentice Hall.

Richardson, R., & Skinner, E. (1990). *Achieving access and quality*. New York: Macmillan.

Riel, M. (1989). The impact of computers in classrooms. *Journal of Research on Computing in Education, 22,* 180–190.

Rogoff, B. (1990). *Apprentices in thinking: Children's guided participation in culture*. New York: Oxford University Press.

Rouse, J. (1988). *Knowledge and power: Toward a political philosophy of science*. Ithaca, NY: Cornell University Press.

Routman, R. (1991). *Invitations: Changing as teachers and learners K–12*. Portsmouth, NH: Heinemann Educational Books.

Rylant, C. (1988). *All I see*. New York: Orchard Books.

Salomon, G. (1979). *Interaction of media, cognition, and learning: An exploration of how symbolic forms cultivate mental skills and affect knowledge acquisition*. San Francisco, CA: Jossey-Bass.

Saunders, W. (1992). The constructivist perspective: Implications and teaching strategies for science. *School Science and Mathematics, 92*(3), 136–138.

Schneps, M. (1988). *A private universe* [Film]. Santa Monica, CA: Pyramid Film and Video.

Schoenfeld, A. (1982). Measures of problem-solving performance and of problem-solving interactions. *Journal for Research in Mathematics Education, 13,* 31–49.

Schoenfeld, A. (1985). *Mathematical problem solving*. San Diego, CA: Academic Press.

Schrag, F. (1988). *Thinking in school and society*. New York: Routledge.

Schubert, W., & Willis, G. (1991). *Understanding curricula and teaching through the arts*. Albany, NY: State University of New York Press.

Scott, K. (1993). *Monster: The Autobiography of an L.A. Gang Member, Sanyika Shakur, a.k.a. Kody Scott*. New York: Atlantic Monthly Press.

Sears, J., & Marshall, J. D. (1990). *Teaching and thinking about curriculum*. New York: Teachers College Press.

Segal, J. W., Chipman, S. F., & Glaser, R. (Eds). (1985). *Thinking and learning skills*. Hillsdale, NJ: Erlbaum.

Sharan, S. (1990). *Cooperative learning: Theory and research*. Westport, CT: Bergin & Garvey/Praeger.

Sharon, S. (1980). Cooperative learning in small groups: Recent methods and effects on achievement, attitudes and ethnic relations. *Review of Educational Research, 50,* 241–271.

Shulman, J., & Colbert, J. (Eds.).(1987). *The mentor teacher casebook*. ERIC Clearinghouse on Educational Management. (ERIC document reproduction service No. ED 291 153)

Shulman, L. (1986). Paradigms and research programs in the study of teaching: A contemporary perspective. In M. Witrock (Ed.), *Handbook of research on teaching* (pp. 3–36). New York: Macmillan.

Siegler, R. S. (1985). *Children's thinking*. Englewood Cliffs, NJ: Prentice Hall.

Silver, E. (1979). Student perceptions of relatedness around mathematical verbal problems. *Journal for Research in Mathematics Education, 10*, 195–210.

Skemp, R. (1978). Relational understanding and instrumental understanding. *Arithmetic Teacher, 26*(3), 9–15.

Slavin, R. (1983). *Cooperative learning*. White Plains, NY: Longman.

Slavin, R. (1989). *School and classroom organization*. Hillsdale, NJ: Erlbaum.

Slavin, R. (1990). *Cooperative learning: Theory, research, and practice*. Englewood Cliffs, NJ: Prentice Hall.

Slavin, R., Sharan, S., Kagan, S., Hertz-Lazarowitz, R., Webb, C., and Schmuck, R. (Eds.). (1985). *Learning to cooperate, cooperating to learn*. New York: Plenum.

Smith, F. (1985). *Reading without nonsense*. New York: Teachers College Press.

Snauwaert, D. T. (1993). *Democracy, education, and governance: A developmental conception*. Albany, NY: State University of New York Press.

Solomon, C. (1986). *Computer environments for children: A reflection on theories of learning and education*. Cambridge, MA: MIT Press.

Stahl, S., & Miller, P. (1989). Whole language and language experiencing approaches for beginning reading: A qualitative approach. *Review of Educational Research, 59*(1), 87–116.

Stark, J. S., & Metz, L. A. (Eds.). (1988). *Improving teaching and learning through research* (New Directions for Institutional Research, No. 57). San Francisco, CA: Jossey-Bass.

Stenmark, J. K. (1989). *Assessment alternatives in mathematics: An overview of assessment techniques that promote learning* (Prepared by the EQUALS staff and the Assessment Committee of the California Mathematics Council Campaign for Mathematics). For information, contact EQUALS, Lawrence Hall of Science, University of California, Berkeley, CA 94720.

Sternberg, R., & Frensch, P. (1992). *Complex problem solving: Principles and mechanisms*. Hillsdale, NJ: Erlbaum.

Sternberg, R., & Wagner, R. (1986). *Practical intelligence: Nature and origins of competence in the everyday world*. New York: Cambridge University Press.

Stotsky, S. (1989). *Holistic scoring of school-based writing*. (ERIC document reproduction service No. ED 196 011)

Swartz, S., & Pollishuke, M. (1991). *Creating the child-centered classroom*. Katonah, NY: Richard Owens.

Tebbs, T. (1991). Unpublished paper dealing with art, collaboration, and gifted education.

Tinker, B. (1991). Thinking about science. *CEEB*.

Tobin, K., & Fraser, B. (1989). Case studies of exemplary science and mathematics teaching. *School Science and Mathematics, 89*(4), 17–24.

Tocqueville, A. de. (1969). *Democracy in America* (G. Lawrence, Trans.). New York: Doubleday.

Trafton, P. R. (Ed.). (1989). *New directions for elementary school mathematics*. Reston, VA: National Council of Teachers of Mathematics.

Tripp, D., & Hodge, B. (1986). *Children and television*. Stanford, CA: Stanford University Press.

U.S. Department of Health and Human Services. (1982). Publication No. ADM82–1186. Washington, DC: U.S. Government Printing Office.

Van de Walle, J. (1990). *Elementary school mathematics: Teaching developmentally*. White Plains, NY: Longman.

Viadero, D. (1993). *Draft standards for arts education: Knowledge, performance, and discipline-based learners*. Washington D.C.: U.S. Department of Education/National Endowment for the Arts/National Endowment for the Humanities National Panel for the Development of Standards for Art Education.

Weintraub, S. (Ed.). (1988). *Summary of investigations relating to reading*. Newark, DE: International Reading Association.

Wells, G. (1986). *The Meaning Makers*. Portsmouth, NH: Heinemann Educational Books.

Werner, E., & Smith, R. (1992). *Overcoming the odds*. Ithaca, NY: Cornell University Press.

White, R., & Gunstone, R. (1992). *Probing understanding*. Bristol, PA: Falmer Press.

Whitehead, A. N. (1933). *Adventures of Ideas*. London: Collier Macmillan.

Wiggins, G. (1987, Winter). Creating a thought-provoking curriculum. *American Educator*.

Wiggins, G. (1989, September). A True test: Toward more equitable assessment. *Phi Delta Kappan*.

Wilson, J. Q. (1993). *The moral sense*. New York: Macmillan.

Wlodkowski, R. J., & Jaynes, J. H. (1990). *Eager to learn: Helping children become motivated and love learning*. San Francisco, CA: Jossey-Bass.

Wolf, S. A., & Heath, S. B. (1992). *The braid of literature: Children's world of reading*. Cambridge, MA: Harvard University Press.

Name Index

Subject Index

A

Action research, 127–131

America 2000, 223

American Association for the Advancement of Science (AAAS), 227

Argumentative thinking skills, 29–31

Arts education, 259–298; and aesthetic creativity, 295–298; collaborative and interdisciplinary activities in, 262, 268–277; computer software for, 95–96; discipline-based, 259–260, 281–283; and metacognitive awareness, 25; and multicultural diversity, 261–262, 287–289; in national curriculum reform, 260–262; and students' personal experiences, 289–290; teachers' choice of art form, 283–286; teachers' roles and responsibilities in, 264, 298–300; thematic approach in, 276–281; vital role of, 263–267

Assessment: authentic, 114; classroom observation, 127–129; curriculum investigation, 124; ethnographic research, 130; holistic scoring, 126–127; interviews, 129–130; national standards for, 325; open-ended questions, 125–126, 128; performance, 127–131; portfolio, 115–123; of students' thinking skills, 31–34; of teachers, 71–73

Assessment questioning, 129–130

Authentic assessment, 114

C

Civic education. *See* Social studies

Classroom observation, as assessment technique, 127–129

Collaborative learning. *See* Cooperative learning

Communitarian movement, 317–318

Communities, and cognitive apprenticeships, 35–36

Communities of learners, schools as, 2–3, 326–327

Competition, in traditional learning, 42

Computer(s), 90–101; hardware, 92–93; software, 93–101; software evaluation, 100–101. *See also* Electronic learning devices

Concept circles, 237, 238

Conceptual teaching, 246

Constructivist approach to teaching, 27, 236–237

Conversation, and cooperative learning, 43–45

Cooperative construction, 241–243

Cooperative learning, 41–73; in arts education, 268–271; assessment of, 71–73; and classroom management, 55–57; conflict resolution and problem solving in, 62–65; conversation in, 43–45; group accountability in, 57–65; group structure in, 52–55; group support system in, 60–62; individual accountability in, 57–65; versus individualized learning, 41–43; interracial and cultural diversity in, 46–48; in language arts, 138–139, 170; metacognitive awareness in, 31; organizational strategies, 49–52; and peer coaching, 65; positive and unifying effects of, 45–48; problem-solving activities in, 62–64, 68–71; in science and mathematics, 238–246; in social studies, 310–315